# Study Guide

to accompany

Edwards ▪ Wattenberg ▪ Lineberry

## Government in America:

## People, Politics, and Policy,

*Tenth Edition*

Charles S. Matzke

*Indiana University Purdue University Indianapolis*

*and*

*Community College of Indiana*

Longman

New York  Boston  San Francisco
London  Toronto  Sydney  Tokyo  Singapore  Madrid
Mexico City  Munich  Paris  Cape Town  Hong Kong  Montreal

*Study Guide* to accompany Edwards/Wattenberg/Lineberry, *Government in America: People, Politics, and Policy,* *10e*

Copyright ©2002 Pearson Education, Inc.

ISBN: 0-321-09397-6

1 2 3 4 5 6 7 8 9 10-ML-08 011 01 00

# TABLE OF CONTENTS

# Chapter 1

## INTRODUCTION

### CHAPTER OUTLINE

I.      Introduction (pp. 2-6)

II.     Government (pp. 6-8)
   A.   The institutions that make authoritative decisions that apply to all of society are collectively known as **government.**
   B.   All governments have certain functions in common
      1.   Governments maintain national defense.
      2.   Governments provide public services called **public goods.**
      3.   Governments preserve order.
      4.   Governments socialize the young.
      5.   Governments collect taxes.

III.    Politics (pp. 8-10)
   A    **Politics** determine whom we select as our governmental leaders and what policies they pursue.
   B.   The ways in which people get involved in politics make up their **political participation**.
   C.   **Single-issue groups** are so concerned with one matter that their members will cast their votes on the basis of that issue only.

IV.     The Policymaking System (pp. 10-13)
   A.   People Shape Policy
      1.   The **policymaking system** is the process by which policy comes into being and evolves over time. (See Figure 1.3.)
      2.   Political parties, elections, interest groups, and the media are key **linkage institutions** that transmit the preferences of Americans to the policymakers in government.
      3.   The **policy agenda** consists of the issues that attract the serious attention of public officials and other people actively involved in politics at a given time.
      4.   A **political issue** arises when people disagree about a problem or about a public policy choice made to combat a problem.
      5.   Policymakers work within the three **policymaking institutions** (the Congress, the presidency, and the courts as established by the U.S. Constitution).

B. Policies Impact People
    1. Every decision that government makes—a law it passes, a budget it establishes, and even a decision not to act on an issue—is **public policy**. (See Table 1.2.)
    2. Policy impacts are the effects that a policy has on people and on society's problems.

V. Democracy (pp. 13-19)
    A. Defining Democracy. **Democracy** is a means of selecting policymakers and of organizing government so that policy reflects citizen's preferences.
    B. Traditional Democratic Theory
        1. Equality in voting
        2. Effective participation
        3. Enlightened understanding
        4. Citizen control of the agenda
        5. Inclusion
        6. Democracies must practice **majority rule** and preserve **minority rights.**
        7. The relationship between the few leaders and the many followers is one of **representation.**
    C. Three Contemporary Theories of American Democracy
        1. **Pluralist theory** states that groups with shared interests influence public policy by pressing their concerns through organized efforts.
        2. **Elite and class theory** contends that societies are divided along class lines, and that an upper-class elite pulls the strings of government.
        3. **Hyperpluralism** contends that many groups are so strong that government is unable to act.
    D. Challenges to Democracy
        1. Increased Technical Expertise
        2. Limited Participation in Government
        3. Escalating Campaign Costs
        4. Diverse Political Interests (**policy gridlock**)
    E. Preview Questions About Democracy

VI. The Scope of Government in America (pp. 20-23)
    A. How Active Is American Government?
    B. A Comparative Perspective on the Scope of Government
    C. American Individualism. **Individualism** in American political thought and practice is the belief that people can and should get ahead on their own.
    D. Preview Questions About the Scope of Government

VII. Summary (p. 23)

## LEARNING OBJECTIVES

*After studying Chapter 1, you should be able to:*

1. Describe what government is and what governments do.

2. Understand that politics is the struggle over "who gets what, when, and how."

3. Identify the important features of the policymaking system and explain how public policies are the choices that government makes—and declines to make—in response to political issues.

4. Understand the nature of democratic government and traditional democratic theory, and the key questions concerning democracy.

5. Distinguish between the three contemporary theories of American democracy and politics (pluralist, elite and class, and hyperpluralist) and identify some of their strengths and weaknesses.

6. Understand the nature of the scope of government in America and the key questions concerning the scope of government.

*The following exercises will help you meet these objectives:*

Objective 1. Describe what government is and what governments do.

1. Define the term "government."

2. What are the two fundamental questions about governing that serve as themes throughout the textbook?

   1.

   2.

3.    List the six ways in which all governments are similar.

     1.

     2.

     3.

     4.

     5.

     6.


Objective 2. Understand that politics is the struggle over "who gets what, when, and how."

1.    Define the term "politics."



2.    Give examples of the "who," "what," "when," and "how" of politics.




Objective 3. Identify the important features of the policy system and explain how public policies are the choices that government makes, and declines to make, in response to political issues.

1.    Draw a diagram of how a policy system works.

2.     List the four key linkage institutions in a democratic society.

     1.

     2.

     3.

     4.


3.     Define the term "policy agenda."


4.     How does a government's policy agenda change?


5.     List the four major policymaking institutions in the United States.

     1.

     2.

     3.

     4.


6.     Define the term "policy impacts."


Objective 4. Understand the nature of democratic government, traditional democratic theory, and the key questions concerning democracy.

    1.     Define the term "democracy" as used in this text.

2.      List the five cornerstones of an ideal democracy.

     1.

     2.

     3.

     4.

     5.

3.      Explain what is meant by majority rule and minority rights.

Objective 5. Distinguish between the three contemporary theories of American democracy and politics (pluralist, elite and class, and hyperpluralist) and identify some of their strengths and weaknesses.

1.      Complete the following table comparing pluralist, elite and class, and hyperpluralist theories according to who holds the power and how policy is made.

| Theory | Who Holds Power | How Policy is Made |
|---|---|---|
| Pluralist | | |
| Elite and Class | | |
| Hyperpluralist | | |

2.    List the major challenges facing American democracy.

    1.

    2.

    3.

    4.


Objective 6. Understand the nature of the scope of government in America and the key questions concerning the scope of government.

1.    Make a list of items that illustrate the scope of American government.




2.    How does the scope of American government compare to the scope of government in other countries?



3.    How has American individualism affected the scope of government?




**KEY TERMS**

*Identify and Describe:*

government

public goods

politics

political participation

single-issue groups

policymaking system

linkage institutions

policy agenda

political issue

policymaking institutions

public policy

democracy

majority rule

minority rights

representation

pluralist theory

elite and class theory

hyperpluralism

policy gridlock

gross domestic product

individualism

*Compare and Contrast:*

government and politics

policy agenda and public policy

policymaking system and linkage institutions


policymaking system and political issue


democracy and traditional democratic theory


majority rule and minority rights


democracy and representation


pluralist theory, elite and class theory, and hyperpluralism


*Name That Term:*

1. Something in which any member of society can share without diminishing the supply to any other member of society.

   _____

2. It consists of subjects and problems getting the attention of government officials and their associates.

   _____

3. This is a choice that government makes in response to an issue on its agenda.

   _____

4.  This arises when people disagree about a problem or about public policy choices made to combat a problem.

    _____

5.  Political parties, elections, and interest groups are the main ones in the United States.

    _____

6.  The effects a policy has on people and on society's problems.

    _____

7.  The most fundamental aspect of democratic theory.

    _____

8.  According to this theory of American government, many groups are so strong and numerous that government is unable to act.

    _____

9.  This problem is magnified when voters choose a president from one party and congressional majorities from the other party.

    _____

10. The total value of all goods and services produced annually by the United States.

    _____

11. One of the primary reasons for the comparatively small scope of American government.

    _____

## USING YOUR UNDERSTANDING

1. Identify and discuss, in your own words, the important features of the policymaking system. Take a problem (such as AIDS, racial discrimination, or crime) and describe how it might be dealt with in this system, from how it becomes a political issue to the policies that could be made in response to it and their impact on people. Discuss different ways in which the problem could be dealt with based on beliefs about the appropriate role of government. State your own view as well.

2. Collect some current examples of politics and policymaking that illustrate, support, or refute aspects of the three theories of American democracy. Use newspapers or newsmagazines in your search. Briefly describe what you discover. Based on your understanding of the three theories and the evidence you have collected, make an initial judgment of the applicability of each theory to political and policy realities in America. As you continue to learn about American politics and policymaking, see how your perceptions change.

## REVIEW QUESTIONS

*Check ☑ the correct answer:*

1. The age group with the lowest voter turnout rate is
   ☐ a.   25 years old or younger.
   ☐ b.   26 to 40 years old.
   ☐ c.   41 to 64 years old.
   ☐ d.   65 years old or older.

2. The institutions that make authoritative decisions that apply to all of society are collectively known as
   ☐ a.   the political system.
   ☐ b.   government.
   ☐ c.   linkage institutions.
   ☐ d.   public goods.

3. Which of the following is NOT a general characteristic of public goods?
   ☐ a.   governments usually must provide them
   ☐ b.   most businesses provide them for a profit
   ☐ c.   individuals have little incentive to provide them
   ☐ d.   every member of society can use one

4. Which of the following is NOT an example of a public good?
   - ☐ a. welfare benefits
   - ☐ b. parks
   - ☐ c. national defense
   - ☐ d. clean air policies

5. All governments
   - ☐ a. provide services.
   - ☐ b. have written constitutions.
   - ☐ c. have a president.
   - ☐ d. have a legislature.

6. One of the basic functions of government is to socialize young citizens into the political system through schooling.
   - ☐ True
   - ☐ False

7. Harold Lasswell's definition of politics is
   - ☐ a. "who gets what, when, and how."
   - ☐ b. "what gets done, then and now."
   - ☐ c. the authoritative allocation of the GNP.
   - ☐ d. voting in a duly constituted election.

8. The media usually focuses on the
   - ☐ a. "who" of politics.
   - ☐ b. "what" of politics.
   - ☐ c. "when" of politics.
   - ☐ d. "how" of politics.

9. America has one of the highest voter turnout rates in the world.
   - ☐ True
   - ☐ False

10. Single-issue groups
   - ☐ a. aid effective policymaking.
   - ☐ b. are concerned with a wide range of problems.
   - ☐ c. have very little influence on voters or politicians.
   - ☐ d. have little taste for compromise.

11. Political issues get government's attention through linkage institutions.
   - ☐ True
   - ☐ False

12. One type of linkage institution is
- □ a. an interest group.
- □ b. a bureaucracy.
- □ c. a government.
- □ d. a legislature.

13. Which of the following is NOT an example of a linkage institution?
- □ a. the National Rifle Association
- □ b. the Democratic party
- □ c. a referendum
- □ d. the Social Security Administration

14. A policy agenda is
- □ a. ignored by public officials.
- □ b. an electoral ballot.
- □ c. a list of problems to which serious attention is paid.
- □ d. a public opinion poll.

15. A government's policy agenda changes infrequently.
- □ True
- □ False

16. Which of the following policymaking institutions was NOT established by the Constitution?
- □ a. Congress
- □ b. the bureaucracy
- □ c. the presidency
- □ d. the courts

17. Public policy
- □ a. consists of laws passed by Congress.
- □ b. is what government chooses not to do.
- □ c. involves making decisions.
- □ d. all of the above.

18. Public policies include
- □ a. congressional statutes.
- □ b. court decisions.
- □ c. budgetary choices.
- □ d. all of the above.

19. The last part of the policy system concerns
☐ a. implementation.
☐ b. the policy agenda.
☐ c. policy impacts.
☐ d. elections.

20. According to *The Communist Manifesto,* the specter haunting Europe was (bonus)
☐ a. democracy.
☐ b. military dictatorship.
☐ c. communism.
☐ d. freedom.

21. The writers of the U.S. Constitution
☐ a. cherished the idea of democracy.
☐ b. favored government by the people.
☐ c. rejected democratic ideals.
☐ d. had no fondness for democracy.

22. Who said, the people "should have as little to do as may be with the government"? (bonus)
☐ a. Abraham Lincoln
☐ b. Elbridge Gerry
☐ c. Roger Sherman
☐ d. Alexis de Tocqueville

23. The basic principles of traditional democratic theory include all of the following EXCEPT
☐ a. equality in voting.
☐ b. effective participation.
☐ c. government control of information.
☐ d. inclusion.

24. In democratic theory, the principle of minority rights accompanies the principle of
☐ a. majority rule.
☐ b. representation.
☐ c. pluralism.
☐ d. equality.

25. The closer the correspondence between representatives and their electoral majority, the closer the approximation to democracy.
☐ True
☐ False

26. Pluralists argue that
☐ a. there are only a few influential groups that shape American policymaking.

☐ b. the American political system is a competition among many groups.
☐ c. the public interest rarely prevails.
☐ d. many access points diminish group influence.

27. Critics of the pluralist theory contend that it
☐ a. misses the larger question of who owns the pie by concentrating on who gets a piece of the pie.
☐ b. is overly pessimistic.
☐ c. places too much emphasis on class differences.
☐ d. fails to explain bargains and compromises.

28. Elite and class theory holds that
☐ a. power is dispersed among many institutions.
☐ b. wealth is irrelevant to political power.
☐ c. American society is divided along class lines.
☐ d. elites influence policymakers but are distinct from them.

29. According to the theory of hyperpluralism, government has become more effective with time.
☐ True
☐ False

30. The idea of powerful groups and weak government is most closely associated with
☐ a. democratic theory.
☐ b. elite and class theory.
☐ c. pluralism.
☐ d. hyperpluralism.

31. Hyperpluralism can lead to
☐ a. multi-issue groups and politics.
☐ b. muddled and inconsistent policy.
☐ c. more effective and efficient government.
☐ d. centralized power and authority.

32. Democratic theory requires citizens to become experts on most everything.
☐ True
☐ False

33. Winning a congressional seat these days requires a campaign war chest of at least
☐ a. $100,000.
☐ b. $250,000.
☐ c. $500,000.
☐ d. $1,000,000.

34. Political Action Committees usually care only about how members of Congress vote on issues that particularly affect them.
☐ True
☐ False

35. A common consequence of the situation in which different parties control the president and Congress is
☐ a. policy compromise.
☐ b. pluralism.
☐ c. policy gridlock.
☐ d. individualism.

36. The percentage of the gross domestic product currently spent by our government is about
☐ a. one-tenth.
☐ b. one-half.
☐ c. one-third.
☐ d. one-fourth.

37. Which of the following statements about the scope of our national government is TRUE?
☐ a. It spends more than $2 trillion annually.
☐ b. It employs five million people.
☐ c. It owns one-third of the land in the United States.
☐ d. all of the above.

38. The percentage of the federal budget devoted to national defense is about
☐ a. one-tenth.
☐ b. one-sixth.
☐ c. one-fourth.
☐ d. one-third.

39. Compared to most Western democracies, the United States
☐ a. has more involvement by government in the everyday lives of its citizens.
☐ b. has a greater tax burden.
☐ c. has more regulation and government ownership of utilities.
☐ d. devotes a smaller percentage of its resources to government.

40. Most advanced industrial democracies have a system of national insurance that provides most health care.
☐ True
☐ False

41. One of the primary reasons for the limited scope of government in the United States is the prominence of
☐ a. group activities.
☐ b. wealthy elites.
☐ c. individualism.
☐ d. compromise.

## ESSAY QUESTIONS

1. Define government and identify the functions that governments perform. What is the role of politics in government?

2. What are the principal choices that governments face when confronting policy problems? Illustrate your answer with an example of a policy that poses tough choices. Explain how government makes policy even when it chooses to do nothing.

3. What are the principle components of the policymaking system? Explain how a political issue travels through the policymaking system by using an example.

4. What is the definition of democracy? What are the basic principles of traditional democratic theory? What problems might emerge when the theory is put into practice?

5. Compare, contrast, and critically evaluate the three theories of American democracy: pluralist theory, elite and class theory, and hyperpluralism.

6. Summarize some of the major challenges facing American democracy today. Briefly state your opinion as to how serious these challenges are and how they might be met.

7. In what ways might it be said that American government is "big"? How does the scope of the American government compare to other Western democracies?

# Chapter 2

## THE CONSTITUTION

### CHAPTER OUTLINE

I. The Origins of the Constitution (pp. 28-33)
   - A. The Road to Revolution
   - B. Declaring Independence, the **Declaration of Independence**
   - C. The English Heritage: The Power of Ideas
     1. **Natural rights** are the rights inherent in human beings, not dependent on governments.
     2. **Consent of the governed** means the people must agree on who their rulers will be.
     3. **Limited government** means there must be clear restrictions on what rulers may do.
   - D. Jefferson's Handiwork: The American Creed
   - E. Winning Independence
   - F. The "Conservative" Revolution

II. The Government That Failed: 1776-1787 (pp. 33-36)
   - A. The **Articles of Confederation**
   - B. Changes in the States
   - C. Economic Turmoil
   - D. **Shays' Rebellion**
   - E. The Aborted Annapolis Meeting

III. Making A Constitution: The Philadelphia Convention (p. 36-39)
   - A. Gentlemen in Philadelphia
   - B. Philosophy into Action
     1. Human Nature
     2. Political Conflict (**Factions** arise from sources of conflict.)
     3. Objects of Government
     4. Nature of Government

IV. The Agenda in Philadelphia (pp. 39-44)
   - A. The Equality Issues
     1. Equality and Representation of the States
        a. **New Jersey Plan** had each state equally represented in Congress.
        b. **Virginia Plan** made state representation in Congress based on population.

     c.   **Connecticut Compromise** created two houses of Congress.
    2.   Slavery, Congress could limit the future importation of slaves and the three-fifths compromise settled how slaves would be represented.
    3.   Political Equality
  B.   The Economic Issues
  C.   The Individual Rights Issues
    1.   The Constitution says little about personal freedoms.
    2.   Article I prohibits suspension of the **writ of habeas corpus.**

V.   The Madisonian Model (pp. 44-48)
  A.   Thwarting Tyranny of the Majority
    1.   Limiting Majority Control
    2.   Separating Power (Under **separation of powers**, the three branches of government are relatively independent of each other and share powers.)
    3.   Creating Checks and Balances (Under **checks and balances**, each branch of government requires the consent of the others for many of its actions.)
    4.   Establishing a Federal System
  B.   The Constitutional Republic. A **republic** is a system based on the consent of the governed in which representatives of the public exercise power.
  C.   The End of the Beginning

VI.   Ratifying the Constitution (pp. 49-52)
  A.   Federalists and Anti-Federalists
    1.   **Federalists** supported the Constitution and **Anti-Federalists** opposed it.
    2.   **The Federalist Papers** were a series of articles supporting the Constitution.
    3.   The **Bill of Rights** is the first ten amendments to the Constitution that restrain the national government from limiting personal freedoms.
  B.   Ratification

IIIII.  Constitutional Change (pp. 52-58)
  A.   The Formal Amending Process consists of two stages, proposal and ratification.
  B.   The Informal Process of Constitutional Change
    1.   Judicial Interpretation. In *Marbury v. Madison* (1803), the Supreme Court claimed the power of **judicial review**, giving courts the right to decide the constitutionality of government actions.
    2.   Changing Political Practice includes political parties and the Electoral College.
    3.   Technology
    4.   Increasing Demands on Policymakers
  C.   The Importance of Flexibility

IVIII.  Understanding the Constitution (pp. 58-60)
  A.   The Constitution and Democracy

B.    The Constitution and the Scope of Government

IX.    Summary (pp. 60-61)


## LEARNING OBJECTIVES

*After studying Chapter 2, you should be able to:*

1.    Discuss the importance of the English philosophical heritage, the colonial experience, the Articles of Confederation, and the character of the founding fathers in shaping the agenda of the Constitution writers.

2.    Identify the important principles and issues debated at the Constitutional Convention and describe how they were resolved.

3.    Explain the Madisonian model of limiting majority control, separating powers, creating checks and balances, and establishing a federal system.

4.    Understand the conflict between the Federalists and Anti-Federalists over the ratification of the Constitution.

5.    Describe the formal and informal processes by which the Constitution is changed in response to new items on the policy agenda.

6.    Evaluate the Constitution in terms of democracy and its impact on policymaking.


*The following exercises will help you meet these objectives:*

Objective 1.  Discuss the importance of the English philosophical heritage, the colonial experience, the Articles of Confederation, and the character of the founding fathers in shaping the agenda of the Constitution writers.

1.    Make a list of the major grievances of the colonists under British rule.

2. What are the major components of John Locke's political philosophy and how did they influence Thomas Jefferson's writings?

3. Draw a schematic diagram of the American government under the Articles of Confederation.

4. Make a list of the reasons why the Articles of Confederation failed.

5. Briefly describe the general philosophical views of the founding fathers on the following issues:

Human Nature:

Political Conflict:

Objects of Government:

Nature of Government:

Objective 2.  Identify the important principles and issues debated at the Constitutional Convention and describe how they were resolved.

1.    What were the three major equality issues at the Constitutional Convention and how were they resolved?

       1.

       2.

       3.

2.    What were the major economic problems addressed at the Constitutional Convention and how were they resolved?

3.    Why did the founding fathers believe it was not necessary to address individual rights issues specifically in the Constitution?

Objective 3. Explain the Madisonian model of limiting majority control, separating powers, and creating checks and balances.

1.    Draw a schematic diagram of the Madisonian model of government.

2.    Define the term "constitutional republic."

Objective 4.  Understand the conflict between the Federalists and Anti-Federalists over the ratification of the Constitution.

1.    Complete the following table summarizing the major differences between the Federalists and the Anti-Federalists on the issues of civil liberties, power of the states, and the economy.

| Issues | Federalists | Anti-Federalists |
|---|---|---|
| Civil Liberties | | |
| Power of the States | | |
| Economy | | |

2.    Why did the Anti-Federalists believe the new Constitution was a class-based document?

Objective 5.  Describe the formal and informal processes by which the Constitution is changed in response to new items on the policy agenda.

1.    What is meant by the "unwritten constitution"?

2.    Describe the different ways in which a formal constitutional amendment might be adopted.

3.    The text examines four ways the Constitution changes informally. List these ways, define them, and give an example for each.

   1.



   2.



   3.



   4.




Objective 6.  Evaluate the Constitution in terms of democracy and its impact on policymaking.

   1.    List and explain the five Constitutional amendments that expanded the right to vote.

      1.

      2.

      3.

      4.

      5.



   2.    In what ways does the Constitution expand and diminish the scope of government?

**KEY TERMS**

*Identify and Describe:*

Constitution

Declaration of Independence

natural rights

consent of the governed

limited government

Articles of Confederation

Shays' Rebellion

U.S. Constitution

factions

New Jersey Plan

Virginia Plan

Connecticut Compromise

writ of habeas corpus

separation of powers

checks and balances

republic

Federalists

Anti-Federalists

Federalist Papers

Bill of Rights

*Marbury v. Madison*

judicial review

*Compare and Contrast:*

natural rights and consent of the governed

Constitution, Articles of Confederation, and U.S. Constitution

New Jersey Plan, Virginia Plan, and Connecticut Compromise

separation of powers and checks and balances

limited government and republic

Federalists and Anti-Federalists

*Marbury v. Madison* and judicial review

*Name That Term:*

1. The first constitution of the United States.

   _____

2. A view that contrasts sharply with the divine right of kings.

   _____

3. A series of armed attacks on courthouses in 1787 to protest farm foreclosures.

   _____

4.    Today these would be called interest groups or parties.

      _____

5.    This enables persons detained by authorities to secure an immediate inquiry into the causes of their detention.

      _____

6.    This is a system of government based on the consent of the governed in which representatives of the public exercise power.

      _____

7.    A series of articles published under the name "Publius."

      _____

8.    The first ten amendments to the Constitution.

      _____

9.    Not found in the Constitution, this power was given to the courts in the case of *Marbury v. Madison*.

      _____

## USING YOUR UNDERSTANDING

1.    Try your hand at sketching out a new Constitution for the contemporary United States. Be sure to indicate key governmental institutions and their functions. Also, include a Bill of Rights in your constitution. Keep in mind today's high-tech politics and the current policy agenda. Briefly discuss how the twentieth-century constitution you envision is similar to or different from the eighteenth-century Constitution of the Founders. Evaluate how well the Founders did in terms of these similarities or differences.

2.    Locate the written constitution of your state or that of another modern democratic system, such as France, Germany, or Japan. In reading the document or parts of it, look for similarities or differences with the American Constitution. Take note of the governmental institutions it creates, the functions they perform, and whether or not something comparable to the Bill of Rights is included. Describe briefly what you have found. Use this exercise to write a term paper comparing different types of constitutions and their effectiveness.

## REVIEW QUESTIONS

*Check ☑ the correct answer:*

1. Which of the following statements is FALSE?
   - ☐ a. A constitution is a nation's basic law.
   - ☐ b. A constitution is an unwritten accumulation of traditions and precedents.
   - ☐ c. A constitution allocates power within government.
   - ☐ d. A constitution sets neutral rules of the game of politics.

2. During the colonial period, the British King and Parliament
   - ☐ a. were involved in nearly every aspect of colonial life.
   - ☐ b. confined themselves to governing America's foreign policy and trade.
   - ☐ c. allowed the colonists a limited number of representatives in Parliament.
   - ☐ d. put strict limits on American freedom.

3. The motion for declaring the United States as free and independent was made by (bonus)
   - ☐ a. Thomas Jefferson.
   - ☐ b. Benjamin Franklin.
   - ☐ c. Richard Henry Lee.
   - ☐ d. John Adams.

4. Which of the following concepts is inconsistent with the political philosophy associated with John Locke?
   - ☐ a. natural rights
   - ☐ b. the divine right of kings
   - ☐ c. limited government
   - ☐ d. the sanctity of property

5. John Locke held that people should revolt when
   - ☐ a. injustices become deeply felt.
   - ☐ b. transient issues emerge.
   - ☐ c. government no longer has their consent.
   - ☐ d. both a. and c.

6. Which of the following Lockean concepts of government does not have a direct parallel in Thomas Jefferson's draft of the Declaration of Independence?
   - ☐ a. natural rights
   - ☐ b. limited government
   - ☐ c. the sanctity of property
   - ☐ d. the right to revolt

7. The revolutionary thought found in the American colonies was based entirely on the political philosophy of John Locke.
   ☐ True
   ☐ False

8. Our first constitution was the Articles of Confederation.
   ☐ True
   ☐ False

9. Most governmental authority in the early American experience rested with
   ☐ a. state legislatures.
   ☐ b. local townships.
   ☐ c. the Continental Congress.
   ☐ d. voluntary alliances.

10. The Articles of Confederation established the
    ☐ a. presidency.
    ☐ b. Senate and the House of Representatives.
    ☐ c. Supreme Court.
    ☐ d. Continental Congress.

11. The Continental Congress did not have the power to
    ☐ a. tax.
    ☐ b. issue securities.
    ☐ c. maintain a military.
    ☐ d. print money.

12. Which of the following did NOT occur under the Articles of Confederation?
    ☐ a. Shays' Rebellion
    ☐ b. a power shift in the states away from the elite
    ☐ c. an aborted meeting at Annapolis
    ☐ d. sweeping policies favoring creditors over debtors

13. Shays' Rebellion was
    ☐ a. a battle in the Revolutionary War.
    ☐ b. an attack on courthouses to prevent foreclosure proceedings.
    ☐ c. a constitutional debate.
    ☐ d. a colonial newspaper.

14. Which of the following does NOT, in general, describe the "Gentlemen in Philadelphia"?
☐ a. college educated
☐ b. wealthy
☐ c. Western
☐ d. successful

15. James Madison believed that factions would check themselves.
☐ True
☐ False

16. The philosophy of the Founders was based in part on
☐ a. the faith that self-restraint was part of human nature.
☐ b. a belief that political conflict is unrelated to the distribution of wealth in society.
☐ c. a view that the principal object of government is the preservation of property.
☐ d. the idea that the separation of power is not needed in balanced government.

17. Which of the following was NOT one of the key equality issues debated at the Constitutional Convention?
☐ a. representation of the states in Congress
☐ b. equal opportunity for women
☐ c. slavery
☐ d. political equality

18. Representation of the states in Congress was settled at the Constitutional Convention with the
☐ a. Connecticut Compromise.
☐ b. three-fifths compromise.
☐ c. New Jersey Plan.
☐ d. Virginia Plan.

19. Regarding the issue of slavery, the delegates to the Constitutional Convention agreed
☐ a. to abolish slavery.
☐ b. not to count slaves in determining representation in Congress.
☐ c. to sanction slavery officially.
☐ d. to limit future importing of slaves.

20. Delegates to the Constitutional Convention left it up to the states to decide who could vote in national elections.
☐ True
☐ False

21. One of the major economic issues that the writers of the Constitution felt they needed to address was
☐ a.  tariffs erected by the states.
☐ b.  virtually worthless paper money forced on creditors in some states.
☐ c.  the inability of the Continental Congress to raise needed money.
☐ d.  all of the above.

22. Which of the following statements is TRUE?
☐ a.  The writers of the Constitution believed that the national economy was in good shape.
☐ b.  Economic issues were nonexistent at the writing of the Constitution.
☐ c.  The power of Congress to make economic policy is carefully spelled out in the Constitution.
☐ d.  The Constitution writers were men of little wealth.

23. The original Constitution says very little about personal freedoms.
☐ True
☐ False

24. A writ of habeas corpus
☐ a.  enables persons detained by authorities to secure an immediate inquiry into the causes of their detention.
☐ b.  allows for the punishment of people without a judicial trial.
☐ c.  allows for people to be punished or have their penalties increased for acts that were not illegal or not punishable when committed.
☐ d.  narrowly defines and outlines strict rules of evidence for conviction of treason.

25. The principle of separation of powers resulted from the fact that the Constitution writers feared the possibility of a tyranny of the majority.
☐ True
☐ False

26. The Madisonian model of government is based on the idea that
☐ a.  as much of government as possible should be beyond the direct control of a majority.
☐ b.  the power of government's different institutions should be separated.
☐ c.  a system of checks and balances is needed in government.
☐ d.  all of the above.

27. In the Madisonian model of government, majority rule is accomplished by the election of the
☐ a.   Senate.
☐ b.   House of Representatives.
☐ c.   president.
☐ d.   Supreme Court.

28. The president's veto power is an example of
☐ a.   checks and balances.
☐ b.   majority rule.
☐ c.   presidential supremacy.
☐ d.   judicial review.

29. The Madisonian system
☐ a.   created a form of direct democracy.
☐ b.   had a liberal bias toward change.
☐ c.   created a republic based on the consent of the governed.
☐ d.   made change virtually impossible.

30. The final version of the Constitution was read aloud at a public meeting in Philadelphia.
☐ True
☐ False

31. Immediately after the Constitution was signed, the delegates to the convention (bonus)
☐ a.   returned to their rooms.
☐ b.   adjourned to a tavern.
☐ c.   attended religious services.
☐ d.   composed the national anthem.

32. The Federalist Papers were published under the name
☐ a.   Philadelphiensis.
☐ b.   Monteczuma.
☐ c.   Aggrippa.
☐ d.   Publius.

33. The Anti-Federalists were an unpatriotic and un-American group.
☐ True
☐ False

34.    Which of the following was NOT an Anti-Federalist argument against the ratification of the Constitution?
☐ a.    a charge that it was a class-based document
☐ b.    a claim that it would weaken the power of the states
☐ c.    a claim that the Bill of Rights was unnecessary
☐ d.    a charge that it would benefit creditors

35.    The Constitution was ratified by
☐ a.    state conventions.
☐ b.    a general election.
☐ c.    state legislatures.
☐ d.    a referendum.

36.    The unwritten constitution
☐ a.    is a body of tradition, practice, and procedure.
☐ b.    is represented by the Bill of Rights.
☐ c.    does not affect the spirit of the Constitution.
☐ d.    does not encompass political parties.

37.    An amendment to the Constitution can be ratified either by the legislature of three-fourths of the states or by special conventions called in three-fourths of the states.
☐ True
☐ False

38.    Taken as a whole, the amendments to the Constitution make it
☐ a.    more democratic.
☐ b.    elite- and class-oriented.
☐ c.    less egalitarian.
☐ d.    more focused on economic issues.

39.    The Equal Rights Amendment failed in part because of the system of checks and balances.
☐ True
☐ False

40.    The Constitution does not formally provide for
☐ a.    the two-party system.
☐ b.    the role of television in politics.
☐ c.    binding members of the electoral college to the preference of voters.
☐ d.    all of the above.

41.     The case of *Marbury v. Madison*
        ☐ a.   firmly established the power of judicial review.
        ☐ b.   forced the delivery of court commissions.
        ☐ c.   gave Congress the right to review the judiciary.
        ☐ d.   diminished the power of the Supreme Court.

42.     The writers of the Constitution
        ☐ a.   favored the formation of a two-party system.
        ☐ b.   intended there to be no popular vote for the president.
        ☐ c.   required presidential electors to pledge in advance to vote for the candidate
               that won their state's popular vote.
        ☐ d.   established the electoral college as a rubber stamp for the popular vote.

43.     The roles of political parties and members of the Electoral College are examples
        of constitutional change through political practice.
        ☐ True
        ☐ False

44.     Which of the following statements regarding the U.S. Constitution is FALSE?
        ☐ a.   The U.S. Constitution is a very flexible document.
        ☐ b.   The U.S. Constitution is the oldest functioning constitution.
        ☐ c.   The U.S. Constitution is very long compared to other constitutions.
        ☐ d.   The only court provided for by the U.S. Constitution is the Supreme Court.

45.     The Constitution is in many ways an undemocratic, even anti-democratic,
        document.
        ☐ True
        ☐ False

46.     Which of the following statements regarding the Constitution is FALSE?
        ☐ a.   One of the central themes of American history has been the gradual
               democratization of the Constitution.
        ☐ b.   The original Constitution was characterized by numerous restrictions on
               direct voter participation.
        ☐ c.   The original Constitution offers numerous guidelines on voter eligibility.
        ☐ d.   Five of the seventeen constitutional amendments passed since the Bill of
               Rights have focused on the expansion of the electorate.

47. During the early years of the civil rights movement, African Americans had the most luck getting their interests on the political agenda through the
□ a. Congress.
□ b. president.
□ c. Supreme Court.
□ d. state legislatures.

48. The separation of powers and the system of checks and balances promote
□ a. the politics of bargaining.
□ b. compromise.
□ c. playing one institution against another.
□ d. all of the above.

## ESSAY QUESTIONS

1. What are the historical origins of the American national government? What is the English heritage? How was the Declaration of Independence shaped by the philosophy of John Locke?

2. What philosophical views did the delegates to the Constitutional Convention share? How did they influence the nature of the Constitution?

3. How did the colonial experience shape the policy agenda at the Constitutional Convention? What issues comprised the agenda and how were they resolved?

4. What is the Madisonian model of government? How is it reflected in the structure of American government? What issues or problems does it raise?

5. Explain the process by which the Constitution was ratified. What were the major arguments raised against its ratification? How were some of these issues resolved?

6. What are the formal and informal processes by which the Constitution is changed? Include a discussion of the formal amendment process and the unwritten constitution in your answer.

7. In what ways was the original Constitution both democratic and undemocratic? How has the Constitution become democratized throughout American history?

# Chapter 3

## FEDERALISM

## CHAPTER OUTLINE

I.     Defining Federalism (pp. 66-70)
    A.    What Is Federalism?
        1.    **Federalism** is a way of organizing a nation so that two or more levels of government have formal authority over the same area and people.
        2.    **Unitary governments** place all power in the central government.
        3.    Confederations place all or most power in the hands of the components while the national government is weak.
        4.    **Intergovernmental relations** refers to the entire set of interactions among national, state, and local governments.
    B.    Why Is Federalism So Important?
        1.    Federalism decentralizes politics in America.
        2.    Federalism decentralizes policies in America.

II.     The Constitutional Basis of Federalism  (pp. 70-76)
    A.    The Division of Power
        1.    The **supremacy clause** establishes the Constitution, laws of the national government, and treaties as the supreme law of the land.
        2.    The **Tenth Amendment** states that "powers not delegated to the United States by the Constitution, nor prohibited by it to the states, are reserved to the states respectively, or to the people."
    B.    Establishing National Supremacy
        1.    Implied Powers. ***McCulloch v. Maryland,*** established the principle of **implied powers**, powers that go beyond the **enumerated powers** of the Constitution, on the basis of the **elastic clause.**
        2.    Commerce Power. ***Gibbons v. Ogden*** defined commerce very broadly.
        3.    The Civil War
        4.    The Struggle for Racial Equality
    C.    States' Obligations to Each Other
        1.    **Full Faith and Credit**
        2.    **Extradition**
        3.    **Privileges and Immunities**

III.     Intergovernmental Relations Today (pp. 77-84)
    A.    From Dual to Cooperative Federalism

1.      In **dual federalism** the states and the national government each remain supreme within their own spheres.

2.      In **cooperative federalism** powers and policy assignments are shared between states and the national government.

     a.     Shared costs

     b.     Federal guidelines

     c.     Shared administration

  B.     **Fiscal Federalism** is the pattern of spending, taxing, and providing grants in the federal system.

     1.     The Grant System: Distributing the Federal Pie

       a.     **Categorical grants** are the main source of federal aid to state and local governments.

         (1)     **Project grants** are awarded on the basis of competitive applications.

         (2)     **Formula grants** are distributed according to a formula.

       b.     **Block grants** are given more or less automatically to states or communities that have discretion in deciding how to spend the money.

     2.     The Scramble for Federal Dollars

     3.     The Mandate Blues

IV.    Understanding Federalism (pp. 84-89)

  A.     Federalism and Democracy

     1.     Advantages for Democracy

     2.     Disadvantages for Democracy

  B.     Federalism and the Scope of the National Government

V.     Summary (pp. 90-91)


## LEARNING OBJECTIVES

*After studying Chapter 3, you should be able to:*

1.     Define federalism and explain why it is important to American government and politics.

2.     Describe how the Constitution divides power between the national and state governments and understand why the supremacy of the national government is the central principle of American federalism.

3.     Explain the nature of the states' obligations to each other.

4. Explain how federalism in the United States has shifted from dual federalism to cooperative federalism.

5. Describe the nature of fiscal federalism and how states and cities compete for federal grants and aid.

6. Explain the relationship between federalism and democracy, and how federalism contributes to and detracts from democracy.

7. Understand how federalism has contributed to the scope of the national government.

*The following exercises will help you meet these objectives:*

Objective 1. Define federalism and explain why it is important to American government and politics.

1. Define the three ways of organizing a nation that were discussed in the text.

1.

2.

3.

2. In what ways does federalism decentralize politics and policies?

Objective 2. Describe how the Constitution divides power between the national and state governments and understand why the supremacy of the national government is the central principle of American federalism.

1. List the three items that are considered the supreme law of the land.

1.

2.


3.


2. What is the significance of the Tenth Amendment?


3. Explain the difference between enumerated powers and implied powers.


Objective 3. Explain the nature of the states' obligations to each other.

1. Describe the three general obligations that each state has to every other state under the Constitution.

    1.


    2.


    3.


Objective 4. Explain how federalism in the United States has shifted from dual federalism to cooperative federalism.

1. How is dual federalism analogous to a layer cake and cooperative federalism analogous to a marble cake?


2. Explain the three general standard operating procedures of cooperative federalism.

    1.

2.

3.

Objective 5. Describe the nature of fiscal federalism and how states and cities compete for federal grants and aid.

    1.      What is meant by "cross-over sanctions" and "cross-cutting requirements"?

           Cross-over Sanctions:

           Cross-cutting Sanctions:

    2.      Explain the two types of categorical grants.

           1.

           2.

    3.      What is the difference between block grants and revenue sharing?

    4.      For what reasons might a state or locality not want to receive federal aid?

Objective 6. Explain the relationship between federalism and democracy, and how federalism contributes to and detracts from democracy.

    1.      List four advantages of federalism for democracy.

           1.

2.

3.

4.

2.     List four disadvantages of federalism for democracy.

     1.

     2.

     3.

     4.

Objective 7. Understand how federalism has contributed to the scope of the national government.

     1.     How did industrialization increase the role of the national government?

     2.     Why don't the states handle more issues?

**KEY TERMS**

*Identify and Describe:*

federalism

unitary governments

intergovernmental relations

supremacy clause

Tenth Amendment

*McCulloch v. Maryland*

enumerated powers

implied powers

elastic clause

*Gibbons v. Ogden*

full faith and credit

extradition

privileges and immunities

dual federalism

cooperative federalism

fiscal federalism

categorical grants

project grants

formula grants

block grants

*Compare and Contrast:*

federalism and unitary government

intergovernmental relations and fiscal federalism

supremacy clause and Tenth Amendment

enumerated powers and implied powers

*McCulloch v. Maryland* and *Gibbons v. Ogden*

full faith and credit, extradition, and privileges and immunities

dual federalism and cooperative federalism

categorical grants and block grants

project grants and formula grants

*Name That Term:*

1.  In this type of system, the national government can redraw the boundaries of local governments or change their form.

    _____

2.  The supremacy of the national government over the states was established by this court case.

    _____

3.  Examples of this include the power of Congress to coin money, regulate its value, and impose taxes.

    _____

4.  In this case, the Supreme Court broadly defined commerce to include virtually every form of commercial activity.

    _____

5.     When a state returns a person charged with a crime in another state to that state for trial or imprisonment, they are practicing this constitutional requirement.

_____

6.     This type of federalism has been likened to a "marble cake."

_____

7.     These grants are awarded on the basis of competitive applications.

_____

8.     This was a response to state and local governmental unhappiness with cumbersome and tedious categorical grants.

_____


## USING YOUR UNDERSTANDING

1.     Try to identify all of the governments that have authority and policymaking responsibilities in your area, from the federal and state governments to the various types of local government. At the same time, identify the types of public policies for which they are responsible. Briefly discuss your impressions of the federal system from your own vantage point. Indicate whether or not you found what you expected, based on your understanding of the American federal system.

2.     Contact your local Chamber of Commerce and find out what strategies your community is pursuing in order to compete with other communities, including its efforts to win federal aid. You may even be able to find some brochures that "sell" your community to prospective residents and industries. Describe what you found in terms of how well you think your community is doing in the economic growth game. Try devising some marketing strategies for your community based on its location and other advantages.

## REVIEW QUESTIONS

*Check ☑ the correct answer:*

1. In federalism, governmental power and authority is
   - ☐ a. concentrated with the federal government.
   - ☐ b. concentrated with local governments.
   - ☐ c. shared between governments.
   - ☐ d. nonexistent.

2. The majority of the world's governments are federal systems.
   - ☐ True
   - ☐ False

3. An example of a unitary government is
   - ☐ a. the United States.
   - ☐ b. Canada.
   - ☐ c. Mexico.
   - ☐ d. France.

4. The American states are unitary with respect to their local governments.
   - ☐ True
   - ☐ False

5. When it comes to presidential campaigns, the candidates can basically ignore the states.
   - ☐ True
   - ☐ False

6. The federal system in America decentralizes
   - ☐ a. politics.
   - ☐ b. government.
   - ☐ c. policies.
   - ☐ d. all of the above.

7. In the U.S., the federal government is responsible for most social, family, and moral public policies.
   - ☐ True
   - ☐ False

8. Sometimes social issues become national issues when groups try to use the power of the national government to influence the states.
   - ☐ True
   - ☐ False

9.     Which of the following statements regarding the states is FALSE?
- ☐ a.   The states constitute a national laboratory to develop and test public policies.
- ☐ b.   Almost every policy the national government has adopted had its beginnings in the states.
- ☐ c.   The states rarely produce policy innovations.
- ☐ d.   The states often share the results of new policy ideas with other states and the national government.

10.     The term federalism is found repeatedly in the Constitution.
- ☐ True
- ☐ False

11.     Which of the following statements about the Constitution is FALSE?
- ☐ a.   It forbids Congress to divide up individual states.
- ☐ b.   It makes the federal government responsible for elections.
- ☐ c.   It is unamendable as to the equal representation of the states in the Senate.
- ☐ d.   It requires the national government to protect states against violence and invasion.

12.     According to the supremacy clause, the supreme law of the land consists of all of the following EXCEPT
- ☐ a.   the Constitution.
- ☐ b.   laws of the national government.
- ☐ c.   treaties.
- ☐ d.   state laws.

13.     The Constitution grants the national government exclusive power to
- ☐ a.   coin money.
- ☐ b.   tax.
- ☐ c.   establish courts.
- ☐ d.   charter banks

14.     The Constitution specifically denies to states the power to
- ☐ a.   make and enforce laws.
- ☐ b.   conduct elections.
- ☐ c.   establish local governments.
- ☐ d.   tax imports and exports.

15.　The Tenth Amendment provides for
☐ a.　universal suffrage.
☐ b.　civil liberties.
☐ c.　the delegation of power to the states and the people.
☐ d.　the abolition of slavery.

16.　The question of how national and state powers are related was largely settled by
☐ a.　the civil rights movement.
☐ b.　the case of *McCulloch v. Maryland.*
☐ c.　the Civil War.
☐ d.　all of the above.

17.　In 1791, the newly created national bank was regarded favorably by
☐ a.　state legislatures.
☐ b.　farmers.
☐ c.　Federalists.
☐ d.　Thomas Jefferson.

18.　One of the country's ablest lawyers, who argued the case for Maryland before the Supreme Court in *McCulloch v. Maryland,* was (bonus)
☐ a.　Daniel Webster.
☐ b.　Luther Martin.
☐ c.　Thomas Jefferson.
☐ d.　John Hancock.

19.　In *McCulloch v. Maryland,* the Supreme Court stated that as long as the national government behaves in accordance with the Constitution, its policies take precedence over state policies.
☐ True
☐ False

20.　*McCulloch v. Maryland* established the two constitutional principles of
☐ a.　equality and freedom.
☐ b.　national supremacy and implied powers.
☐ c.　checks and balances.
☐ d.　federalism and intergovernmental relations.

21.　The implied powers of Congress
☐ a.　mean that Congress has powers that go beyond those enumerated in the Constitution.
☐ b.　mean that Congress can make laws that are unconstitutional.
☐ c.　include its powers to coin money and impose taxes.
☐ d.　were listed in the Tenth Amendment.

22. New Deal and civil rights legislation illustrate the powers of the national government as derived through its constitutional requirement to regulate
☐ a. foreign policy.
☐ b. interstate commerce.
☐ c. the military
☐ d. elections.

23. Conflict over federalism was at the center of the
☐ a.   Civil War.
☐ b.   Revolutionary War.
☐ c.   War of 1812.
☐ d.   World War I.

24. The battle for racial equality
☐ a.   has been fought exclusively at the state level.
☐ b.   was resolved by the thirteenth, fifteenth, and nineteenth amendments.
☐ c.   ended with the end of the Civil War.
☐ d.   demonstrates national supremacy in the federal system.

25. The constitutional requirement that states must return a person charged with a crime in another state to that state for trial or imprisonment is called
☐ a.   full faith and credit.
☐ b.   extradition.
☐ c.   privileges and immunities.
☐ d.   dual federalism.

26. The goal of the principle of privileges and immunities is to
☐ a.   make the public acts, records, and civil proceedings of each state legal and binding in all states.
☐ b.   allow for a person charged with a crime in another state to be returned to that state for trial or imprisonment.
☐ c.   prohibit states from discriminating against citizens of other states.
☐ d.   require the national government to give each state an equivalent share of federal grant money.

27. The Supreme Court has clearly identified which privileges a state must make available to all Americans, and which privileges can be limited to its own citizens.
☐ True
☐ False

28. In dual federalism the
   - a. states are supreme over all policies.
   - b. national government is supreme over all policies.
   - c. powers and policy responsibilities of the government layers are distinct.
   - d. administration of programs is shared by governmental units.

29. Cooperative federalism has been likened to a (bonus)
   - a. layer cake.
   - b. marble cake.
   - c. upside-down cake.
   - d. fruit cake.

30. Education is a policy area that most exemplifies
   - a. dual federalism.
   - b. cooperative federalism.
   - c. federal supremacy.
   - d. state supremacy.

31. Which of the following is NOT a standard operating procedure of cooperative federalism?
   - a. exclusive control by state agencies
   - b. shared costs
   - c. federal guidelines
   - d. shared administration

32. The pattern of spending, taxing, and providing grants in the federal system is
   - a. cooperative federalism.
   - b. fiscal federalism.
   - c. extradition.
   - d. categorical federalism.

33. The federal aid system gives the national government very little control over the states.
   - True
   - False

34. Categorical grants
   - a. account for the largest share of federal aid to states and cities.
   - b. are given more or less automatically.
   - c. are designed to support broad programs.
   - d. have very few strings attached.

35. Using federal dollars in one program to influence state and local policy in another is called
   □ a.  cross-cutting requirements.
   □ b.  cross-over sanctions.
   □ c.  grantsmanship.
   □ d.  fiscal federalism.

36. Categorical grants include all of the following EXCEPT
   □ a.  project grants.
   □ b.  grants with strings attached.
   □ c.  block grants.
   □ d.  formula grants.

37. A type of grant awarded on the basis of competitive applications is the
   □ a.  project grant.
   □ b.  formula grant.
   □ c.  block grant.
   □ d.  fiscal grant.

38. The federal aid programs that allow states discretion in deciding how to spend the money are
   □ a.  categorical grants.
   □ b.  block grants.
   □ c.  project grants.
   □ d.  formula grants.

39. The National League of Cities, the United States Conference of Mayors, and the Council of State Governments are governmental interest groups.
   □ True
   □ False

40. A general rule of federalism is that, the more money at stake, the more people will argue about its distribution.
   □ True
   □ False

41. States and localities are always eager to receive increased aid from the federal government.
   □ True
   □ False

42. The Clean Air Act of 1970 is an example of
  ☐ a. the federal courts creating unfunded mandates for the states.
  ☐ b. the federal government unintentionally creating financial obligations for the states.
  ☐ c. a congressional law creating financial obligations for the states but providing no funds to meet these obligations.
  ☐ d. the federal government attaching conditions to federal grants-in-aid.

43. Federalism contributes to democracy by
  ☐ a. creating more opportunities for participation in democracy.
  ☐ b. increasing the opportunities for government to be responsive to demands for policies.
  ☐ c. ensuring that each state can establish a power base to promote its interests.
  ☐ d. all of the above.

44. Federalism tends to increase the amount of decision making and conflict at the national level.
  ☐ True
  ☐ False

45. Which of the following statements is FALSE?
  ☐ a. States differ in the resources they can devote to services like public education.
  ☐ b. Diversity in policy tends to encourage states to provide services that would otherwise not be available, such as generous welfare benefits.
  ☐ c. Local interests may be able to thwart national majority support of certain policies.
  ☐ d. The number of governments in the United States make it difficult to know which governments are doing what.

46. Voter turnout in local elections is often
  ☐ a. more than for presidential elections.
  ☐ b. over fifty percent.
  ☐ c. less than twenty percent.
  ☐ d. the same as for presidential elections.

47. A major consequence of the United States changing from an agricultural to an industrial nation was
  ☐ a. an increase in the role of state governments.
  ☐ b. a decrease in cooperative federalism.
  ☐ c. an increase in demands on the national government for new policies.
  ☐ d. a decrease in the number of federal grants.

48. Labor unions tend to channel their demands for public policies through state governments rather than through the national government.
☐ True
☐ False

49. The proportion of our GDP spent by state and local governments
☐ a. has grown less rapidly than the national government's share.
☐ b. has declined since 1929.
☐ c. is twice as much as the national government's share.
☐ d. is about the same as the national government's share.

## ESSAY QUESTIONS

1. Define federalism. How is federalism different from unitary governments and confederations? Why is federalism important to understanding American government?

2. What does the Constitution have to say about national versus state power? How was the supremacy of the national government established in the American federal system?

3. Explain the obligations that states have to each other. Give examples to illustrate your answer.

4. Why does cooperative federalism, as compared to dual federalism, best describe the American federal system today? Why is fiscal federalism important to intergovernmental relations?

5. Compare and contrast the different types of federal aid and grants given to states and cities. What is the nature of the competition for federal grants? Under what conditions might states not want to receive federal aid?

6. What are the advantages and disadvantages of federalism for democracy? Give examples to illustrate your answer.

7. How and why has federalism contributed to the growth of the national government?

8. Evaluate federalism as a way of organizing government in America. Could the American system have been a unitary system?

# Chapter 4

## CIVIL LIBERTIES AND PUBLIC POLICY

### CHAPTER OUTLINE

I.  Introduction (pp. 94-96)
    A.  **Civil liberties** are individual legal and constitutional protections against the government.
    B.  Americans' civil liberties are set down in the **Bill of Rights**, the first ten amendments to the Constitution.

II. The Bill of Rights - Then and Now (pp. 96-98)
    A.  The **First Amendment** is the source of Americans' freedom of religion, speech, press, and assembly.
    B.  The Bill of Rights and the States
        1.  *Barron v. Baltimore*. The Bill of Rights restrained only the national government.
        2.  *Gitlow v. New York* relied on the **Fourteenth Amendment** to rule that a state government must respect some First Amendment rights.
        3.  Through the **incorporation doctrine**, the Supreme Court applied to the states rights enumerated in the Bill of Rights.

III. Freedom of Religion (pp. 98-103)
    A.  The **Establishment Clause**: "Congress shall make no law respecting an establishment of religion."(*Lemon v. Kurtzman, Engel v. Vitale*, and *School District of Abington Township, PA v. Schempp*)
    B.  The **Free Exercise Clause** prohibits the abridgment of the citizens' freedom to worship, or not to worship, as they please.

IV. Freedom of Expression (pp. 103-117)
    A.  **Prior Restraint**, or governmental actions that prevent material from being published (censorship), has been consistently struck down by the Supreme Court (*Near v. Minnesota*).
    B.  Free Speech and Public Order, the right to protest has been protected to varying extent depending on the political climate. (*Schenck v. United States*)
    C.  Free Press and Fair Trials
        1.  Press coverage may interfere with a fair trial.

2.     Reporters do not always like to open their files to the courts; shield laws may protect reporters from revealing their sources. (***Zurcher v. Stanford Daily***)

  D.   Obscenity has not been regarded as a fully constitutionally protected area of free speech and press, but remains controversial. (***Roth v. United States*** and ***Miller v. California***)

  E.   **Libel** and Slander, the Supreme Court has held, ***New York Times v. Sullivan,*** that statements about public figures are libelous only if made with malice and reckless disregard for the truth.

  F.   **Symbolic Speech** is an action that does not consist of speaking or writing but that expresses an opinion. (**Texas v. Johnson**)

  G.   **Commercial Speech** is restricted far more extensively than other expressions of opinion.

  H.   Regulation of the Public Airwaves, the Federal Communications Commission regulates the content, nature, and very existence of radio and television broadcasting. (***Miami Herald Publishing Co. v. Tornillo*** and ***Red Lion Broadcasting Co. v. Federal Communication Commission***)

  I.   Freedom of Assembly
    1.   Right to Assemble, to gather together in order to make a statement.
    2.   Right to Associate, to associate with people who share a common interest, including an interest in political change. (***NAACP v. Alabama***)

V.   Defendants' Rights (pp. 117-126)
  A.   Interpreting Defendants' Rights
  B.   Searches and Seizures
    1.   Before making an arrest, police need **probable cause** to believe that someone is guilty of a crime.
    2.   The Fourth Amendment forbids **unreasonable searches and seizures.**
    3.   The Constitution requires that probable cause exists before issuing a **search warrant.**
    4.   The **exclusionary rule** prevents illegally seized evidence from being introduced in the courtroom. (***Mapp v. Ohio***)

  C.   **Self-incrimination,** the **Fifth Amendment** forbids self-incrimination and ***Miranda v. Arizona*** set guidelines for police questioning.

  D.   The Right to Counsel, the **Sixth Amendment** ensures the right to counsel and ***Gideon v. Wainwright*** extended this right to those who can not afford counsel.

  E.   Trial by Jury, most cases are settled through **plea bargaining.**

  F.   **Cruel and Unusual Punishment**
    1.   The **Eighth Amendment** forbids cruel and unusual punishment.
    2.   Almost all of the constitutional debate over cruel and unusual punishment has centered on the death penalty (***Gregg v. Georgia*** and ***McClesky v. Kemp***).

## LEARNING OBJECTIVES

*After studying Chapter 4, you should be able to:*

1. Understand the constitutional basis of civil liberties and the Supreme Court's role in defining them.

2. Discuss the religious liberties guaranteed in the First Amendment.

3. Explain the nature of and the issues involving freedom of expression in America.

4. Identify the rights of individuals accused of crimes.

5. Evaluate and discuss the issue of the right to privacy.

6. Understand the impact of civil liberties on democracy and the scope of government.

*The following exercises will help you meet these objectives:*

Objective 1. Understand the constitutional basis of civil liberties and the Supreme Court's role in defining them.

    1.       Define the term "civil liberties."

    2.       What was the most important difference between the Supreme Court's decision in *Barron v. Baltimore* and *Gitlow v. New York*?

    3.       Explain the importance of the Fourteenth Amendment.

    4.       What is the incorporation doctrine?

Objective 2. Discuss the religious liberties guaranteed in the First Amendment.

    1.       List four Supreme Court cases concerning the establishment clause and comment on their significance.

        1.

        2.

        3.

        4.

    2.       Compare and contrast the Supreme Court case of *Employment Division v. Smith* (1990) with the Religious Freedom Restoration Act of 1993.

Objective 3. Explain the nature of and the issues involving freedom of expression in America.

1.    Define the term "prior restraint."

2.    List and explain the significance of four Supreme Court cases concerning free speech and public order.

      1.

      2.

      3.

      4.

3.    What is a shield law?

4.    How did the Supreme Court define obscenity in the case of *Miller v. California*?

5.    How are the standards for winning libel lawsuits different for public figures and private individuals?

6.    Define the term "symbolic speech."

7.    Who regulates commercial speech?

8.    What is the function of the Federal Communications Commission (FCC)?

9.    Explain the two facets of the freedom of assembly.

1.

2.

Objective 4. Identify the rights of individuals accused of crimes.

1.      Draw a diagram of the criminal justice system as a series of funnels.

2.      How are the following terms interrelated: probable cause, unreasonable searches and seizures, search warrant, and exclusionary rule?

3.      What are the three guidelines for police questioning of suspects as set forth in *Miranda v. Arizona* (1966)?

      1.

      2.

      3.

4.      What is the significance of the Supreme Court case of *Gideon v. Wainwright* (1963)?

5.      What are the pros and cons of plea bargaining?

6.      List and explain the importance of three Supreme Court cases concerning the death penalty.

1.

2.

3.

Objective 5. Evaluate and discuss the issue of the right to privacy.

1.      List and explain the importance of four Supreme Court cases concerning abortion.

1.

2.

3.

4.

2.      What is the significance of the "Baby Doe" cases?

Objective 6. Understand the impact of civil liberties on democracy and the scope of government.

1.      In your opinion are the rights guaranteed in the Fourth, Fifth, Sixth, Seventh, and Eighth Amendments more beneficial to criminals or society at large?

2. In what ways do civil liberties limit the scope of government and in what ways do they expand the scope of government?

## KEY TERMS AND CASES

*Identify and Describe: Key Terms*

civil liberties

Bill of Rights

First Amendment

Fourteenth Amendment

incorporation doctrine

establishment clause

free exercise clause

prior restraint

libel

symbolic speech

commercial speech

probable cause

unreasonable searches and seizures

search warrant

exclusionary rule

Fifth Amendment

self-incrimination

Sixth Amendment

plea bargaining

Eighth Amendment


cruel and unusual punishment


right of privacy


*Identify and Describe:  Key Cases*

*Barron v. Baltimore* (1833)


*Gitlow v. New York* (1925)


*Lemon v. Kurtzman* (1971


*Engel v. Vitale* (1962)


*School District of Abington Township, Pennsylvania v. Schempp* (1963)


*Near v. Minnesota* (1931)


*Schenk v. United States* (1919)

*Zurcher v. Stanford Daily* (1976)

*Roth v. United States* (1957)

*Miller v. California* (1973)

*New York Times v. Sullivan* (1964)

*Texas v. Johnson* (1989)

*Miami Herald Publishing Co. v. Tornillo* (1974)

*Red Lion Broadcasting Co. v. Federal Communications Commission* (1969)

*NAACP v. Alabama* (1958)

*Mapp v. Ohio* (1961)

*Miranda v. Arizona* (1966)

*Gideon v. Wainright* (1963)

*Gregg v. Georgia* (1976)

*McCleskey v. Kemp* (1987)

*Roe v. Wade* (1973)

*Planned Parenthood v. Casey* (1992)

*Compare and Contrast:*

civil liberties and Bill of Rights

First Amendment and Fourteenth Amendment

*Barron v. Baltimore* and *Gitlow v. New York*

*Gitlow v. New York* and Fourteenth Amendment

establishment clause and free exercise clause

*Lemon v. Kurtzman* and the establishment clause

*Engel v. Vitale* and *School District of Abington Township, Pennsylvania v. Schempp*

prior restraint and *Near v. Minnesota*

*Roth v. United States* and *Miller v. California*

libel and *New York Times v. Sullivan*

*Texas v. Johnson* and symbolic speech

*Miami Herald Publishing Company v. Tornillo* and *Red Lion Broadcasting Company v. Federal Communications Commission*

probable cause, unreasonable searches and seizures, and search warrant

unreasonable searches and seizures and *Mapp v. Ohio*

unreasonable searches and seizures and exclusionary rule

Fifth Amendment and self-incrimination

Fifth Amendment and *Miranda v. Arizona*

Sixth Amendment and *Gideon v. Wainwright*

Eighth Amendment and cruel and unusual punishment

*Gregg v. Georgia* and *McCleskey v. Kemp*

right of privacy and *Roe v. Wade*

*Name That Term:*

1.  The Supreme Court has one-by-one done this to the Bill of Rights.

    _____

2.  This part of the First Amendment forbids the government from having an official church.

    _____

3.  A government's actions that prevent material from being published in the first place.

    _____

4.  This 1973 Supreme Court case attempted to clarify the meaning of obscenity by spelling out what would and would not be obscene.

    _____

5.  The publication of knowingly false or malicious statements that damage someone's reputation.

    _____

6.       Actions that do not consist of speaking or writing, but that express an opinion.

       _____

7.       This type of speech is restricted far more extensively than expressions of opinion on religious, political, or other matters.

       _____

8.       This case established the principle of "clear and present danger."

       _____

9.       This case upheld the right to associate.

       _____

10.      The Constitution requires that no court may issue one of these unless probable cause exists to believe that a crime has occurred or is about to occur.

       _____

11.      This case extended the exclusionary rule to the states.

       _____

12.      This case set strict guidelines for police questioning of suspects.

       _____

13.      Most criminal cases are settled through this process.

       _____

14.      Undefined by the Eighth Amendment, this has been the basis of the controversy over the death penalty.

       _____

15.      This right is implied, but not directly stated, in the Bill of Rights.

       _____

## USING YOUR UNDERSTANDING

1.     Select one of the Supreme Court cases discussed in this chapter that is of interest to you. Find and read the opinions presented in the case, including any dissenting opinions, and briefly describe what you found. Identify the social values that were in conflict in the case. Based on your understanding, state whether or not you are persuaded by the arguments presented in justification of the decision.

2.     Given the nature of American society today and advances in science and technology, compile a list of those issues that you believe might comprise the new civil liberties agenda as the United States enters the twenty-first century. Identify the civil liberties and public policy areas that they represent. For each issue, make an evaluation as to how you believe the issue should be resolved on the basis of the Bill of Rights, and the ways in which civil liberties issues have been resolved in the past. Identify cases that support your view.

## REVIEW QUESTIONS

*Check ☑ the correct answer:*

1.     Civil liberties are legal and constitutional protections against
   - ☐ a.   criminals.
   - ☐ b.   government.
   - ☐ c.   foreign invasions.
   - ☐ d.   private enterprise.

2.     Civil liberties are formally set down in the
   - ☐ a.   Bill of Rights.
   - ☐ b.   preamble to the Constitution.
   - ☐ c.   Declaration of Independence.
   - ☐ d.   Articles of Confederation.

3.     Most cases concerning civil liberties are easy and straightforward.
   - ☐ True
   - ☐ False

4. Which of the following statements about civil liberties is FALSE?
   - ☐ a. The first Congress passed the Bill of Rights.
   - ☐ b. All of the original states had their own bills of rights.
   - ☐ c. The American people are entirely devoted to political rights in both theory and practice.
   - ☐ d. Our civil liberties often conflict.

5. In literal terms, the First Amendment is directed toward
   - ☐ a. the states.
   - ☐ b. Congress.
   - ☐ c. the courts.
   - ☐ d. all units of government.

6. In the case of *Barron v. Baltimore* (1833), the Supreme Court held that the Bill of Rights restrained only the national government, not the states and cities.
   - ☐ True
   - ☐ False

7. Freedom of speech was incorporated into state laws by
   - ☐ a. *Barron v. Baltimore*.
   - ☐ b. the first Congress.
   - ☐ c. *Gitlow v. New York*.
   - ☐ d. the Tenth Amendment.

8. The Bill of Rights
   - ☐ a. applies only to the national government.
   - ☐ b. immediately applied to the states after ratification of the Fourteenth Amendment.
   - ☐ c. was gradually incorporated into state laws.
   - ☐ d. has always applied to the states as well as national government.

9. According to Thomas Jefferson, the First Amendment was designed to create
   - ☐ a. a national church.
   - ☐ b. federal support for religious pursuits.
   - ☐ c. a wall of separation between church and state.
   - ☐ d. government control of churches.

10. The "wall of separation" separates
   - ☐ a. assembly and association.
   - ☐ b. government and religion.
   - ☐ c. protected and unprotected speech.
   - ☐ d. civil liberties and civil rights.

11. According to the Supreme Court, sponsored prayers in public schools are acceptable only with certain restrictions.
☐ True
☐ False

12. Which of the following statements regarding religion in the United States in recent years is FALSE?
☐ a. Religious issues and controversies have assumed much greater importance in political debate.
☐ b. Fundamentalist religious groups have shied away from political action due to recent controversies.
☐ c. Many school districts have ignored the Supreme Court's ban on school prayer.
☐ d. Conservative Republicans have pushed for a constitutional amendment permitting school prayer.

13. The Supreme Court has been very tolerant of the right of people to believe what they want and less tolerant of their right to practice what they believe.
☐ True
☐ False

14. Who said, "The most stringent protection of free speech would not protect a man in falsely shouting 'fire' in theater and causing a panic"? (bonus)
☐ a. Justice Oliver Wendell Holmes.
☐ b. Justice Hugo Black.
☐ c. Justice Thurgood Marshall.
☐ d. Justice Potter Stewart.

15. Prior restraint
☐ a. is frequently exercised by the United States government.
☐ b. was allowed in *Near v. Minnesota* (1931).
☐ c. means government prevention of publication.
☐ d. allows a newspaper to print libelous materials.

16. According to the Supreme Court in the case of *Schenck v. United States* (1919), free speech can be restricted by the government only on the basis of
☐ a. obscenity.
☐ b. community sentiment.
☐ c. symbolic protest.
☐ d. clear and present danger.

17. In the case of *Dennis v. United States* (1951), the Supreme Court permitted the government to
☐ a. exercise prior restraint over certain publications.
☐ b. jail some American Communist Party leaders.
☐ c. prohibit all forms of symbolic speech.
☐ d. use wiretaps to spy on American citizens.

18. Constitutional protections of free speech diminish once a person steps on private property.
☐ True
☐ False

19. Some states have passed shield laws that protect
☐ a. criminals from self-incrimination.
☐ b. publications from prior restraint.
☐ c. reporters' notes and information from being revealed in court.
☐ d. courts from holding trials in public.

20. In *Roth v. United States* (1957), the Supreme Court ruled that obscene material was not within the realm of constitutionally protected speech or press.
☐ True
☐ False

21. "I know it when I see it" refers to (bonus)
☐ a. obscenity.
☐ b. libel.
☐ c. crime.
☐ d. cruel and unusual punishment.

22. In *Miller v. California* (1973), defining obscenity was left up to
☐ a. private individuals.
☐ b. courts.
☐ c. Congress.
☐ d. state and local officials.

23. The newest issue in the obscenity controversy involves
☐ a. regulations aimed at keeping obscene material away from the young.
☐ b. the proliferation of pornography on the Internet.
☐ c. the proliferation of pornography in video stores.
☐ d. the use of obscene words in public places.

24. To be libelous, a statement must be knowingly false or malicious.
☐ True
☐ False

25. The Supreme Court case of *New York Times v. Sullivan* (1964)
☐ a. made it easier for public officials to win libel cases.
☐ b. held that statements about public officials are libelous only if made with malice and reckless disregard for the truth.
☐ c. held that statements about public officials are libelous if they are intended to damage severely the person's reputation.
☐ d. severely limited the ability of the press to express its opinions freely.

26. Private individuals have a lower standard to meet for winning lawsuits for libel than public figures.
☐ True
☐ False

27. The Supreme Court has dealt with questions of free speech by
☐ a. allowing the government to regulate the content of speech on the airwaves.
☐ b. distinguishing between pure and symbolic speech.
☐ c. using a "clear and present danger" test.
☐ d. all of the above.

28. In 1989, the Supreme Court ruled that the burning of an American flag was a form of constitutionally protected speech.
☐ True
☐ False

29. Which of the following has received the greatest amount of regulation by the federal government?
☐ a. symbolic speech.
☐ b. commercial speech.
☐ c. television news.
☐ d. newspapers.

30. The Federal Communications Commission regulates the content, nature, and licensing of radio, television, and newspapers.
☐ True
☐ False

31. The Supreme Court has
    ☐ a.  ruled that newspapers must provide space for political candidates to reply to newspaper criticisms.
    ☐ b.  allowed the policy of barring certain words from radio or television when children might hear them.
    ☐ c.  ruled that cable television is subject to the same regulations as commercial television.
    ☐ d.  all of the above.

32. Freedom of assembly only concerns the literal right of people to gather in one place.
    ☐ True
    ☐ False

33. The Supreme Court has ruled that spontaneous demonstrations at anytime, anywhere, and in anyway are protected by the First Amendment's freedom of assembly.
    ☐ True
    ☐ False

34. Most of the words contained in the Bill of Rights pertain to the rights of persons accused of crime.
    ☐ True
    ☐ False

35. The most infrequent event in the criminal justice system is a
    ☐ a.  crime.
    ☐ b.  arrest.
    ☐ c.  prosecution.
    ☐ d.  trial.

36. In *Mapp v. Ohio* (1961), the Supreme Court
    ☐ a.  extended the principle of unreasonable searches and seizures to the states.
    ☐ b.  established the exclusionary rule.
    ☐ c.  required probable cause to make an arrest.
    ☐ d.  protected individuals against self-incrimination.

37. The exclusionary rule prohibits a court's use of
    ☐ a.  illegally seized evidence.
    ☐ b.  cruel and unusual punishment.
    ☐ c.  search warrants.
    ☐ d.  plea-bargaining.

38. Fifth Amendment protection against self-incrimination begins with
    - [ ] a. a trial.
    - [ ] b. prosecution.
    - [ ] c. an arrest.
    - [ ] d. criminal sentencing.

39. According to the Supreme Court's decision in *Miranda v. Arizona* (1966), police suspects must be told that
    - [ ] a. they are constitutionally entitled to remain silent.
    - [ ] b. anything they say can be used against them.
    - [ ] c. they have a right to have a lawyer present during police questioning.
    - [ ] d. all of the above.

40. The Sixth Amendment's guarantee of a right to a lawyer was extended to state courts by the Supreme Court case of
    - [ ] a. *Miranda v. Arizona* (1966).
    - [ ] b. *Gideon v. Wainwright* (1963).
    - [ ] c. *Mapp v. Ohio* (1961).
    - [ ] d. *Gregg v. Georgia* (1976).

41. Most criminal cases are settled through plea bargaining.
    - [ ] True
    - [ ] False

42. Plea bargaining usually
    - [ ] a. costs the state more money.
    - [ ] b. results in fewer defendants going to prison.
    - [ ] c. results in harsher punishment for defendants.
    - [ ] d. can only be used by defendants accused of minor crimes.

43. The Constitution
    - [ ] a. does not specify the size of a jury.
    - [ ] b. sets jury size at twelve.
    - [ ] c. sets jury size according to the type of crime.
    - [ ] d. sets jury size according to the type of court.

44. The Supreme Court has ruled that the death penalty
    - [ ] a. is suitable to the most extreme of crimes.
    - [ ] b. is always unconstitutional.
    - [ ] c. can be made mandatory for certain crimes.
    - [ ] d. is the highest form of cruel and unusual punishment.

45. The Bill of Rights spells out the right of privacy in the Second Amendment.
☐ True
☐ False

46. In *Roe v. Wade* (1973), the Supreme Court
☐ a. forbade state regulation of abortion during the first trimester.
☐ b. permitted states to allow abortion in the second trimester only to protect a mother's health.
☐ c. permitted states to forbid abortions in the third trimester.
☐ d. all of the above.

47. Which of the following statements concerning recent Supreme Court decisions concerning abortion is FALSE?
☐ a. It has upheld state laws forbidding the use of state funds to pay for abortions.
☐ b. It has upheld a ban on abortion counseling in federally supported family planning programs.
☐ c. It has upheld a law requiring a married woman to tell her husband of her intent to have an abortion.
☐ d. It has upheld a law requiring a 24-hour waiting period prior to an abortion.

48. The Supreme Court has affirmed the right of parents to make medical decisions for their children.
☐ True
☐ False

49. Which of the following statements is FALSE?
☐ a. First Amendment rights are essential to a democracy.
☐ b. Ultimately, Congress decides what constitutional guarantees mean in practice.
☐ c. The courts enhance democracy by protecting liberty and equality from the excesses of majority rule.
☐ d. The Bill of Rights places strict limitations on governmental power.

## ESSAY QUESTIONS

1. What is the relationship between the national government and the states in the protection of civil liberties? How was the issue of protecting civil liberties at the state level resolved?

2.        What would a literal interpretation of the First Amendment mean for the protection of civil liberties? What factors tend to prevent such a literal interpretation? Give examples to illustrate your answer.

3.        Compare the First Amendment freedoms in terms of the restrictions placed on their application. Do you agree with these restrictions? Support your position with examples of actual or hypothetical cases.

4.        What role has religion played in American politics? How has religious freedom been interpreted in the United States?

5.        Identify the various types of speech. Categorize the different types of speech according to the extent to which they are protected by the Constitution. Give examples of court cases that have helped to establish these protections.

6.        What are the constitutional protections of persons accused of crimes, and where are they found? How has the Supreme Court interpreted and shaped these protections?

7.        What is meant by the "right to privacy"? Explain the controversies that have arisen over the right to privacy.

8.        How do civil liberties affect the nature of democracy and the scope of government in the United States?

# Chapter 5

## CIVIL RIGHTS AND PUBLIC POLICY

### CHAPTER OUTLINE

I.    Introduction (pp. 136-138)
    A.    **Civil rights** are policies that extend basic rights to groups historically subject to discrimination.
    B.    Debates on inequality in America center on racial discrimination, gender discrimination, and discrimination based on age, disability, sexual preference, and other factors.

II.   Two Centuries Of Struggle (pp. 138-141)
    A.    Conceptions of Equality
        1.    Equality of opportunity: everyone should have the same chance.
        2.    Equal results or rewards: everyone should have the same.
    B.    Early American Views of Equality
    C.    The Constitution and Inequality. The **Fourteenth Amendment** provides for **equal protection of the laws**, resulting in expansive constitutional interpretation.

III.  Race, the Constitution, and Public Policy (pp. 141-151)
    A.    The Era of Slavery
        1.    *Dred Scott v. Sandford* (1857) upheld slavery.
        2.    The Civil War and the **Thirteenth Amendment** ended slavery.
    B.    The Era of Reconstruction and Resegregation
        1.    Jim Crow laws (segregational laws) established in the South.
        2.    *Plessy v. Ferguson* justified segregation through the "equal but separate" doctrine.
    C.    The Era of Civil Rights
        1.    *Brown v. Board of Education* (1954) overturned *Plessy* and ended legal segregation.
        2.    The civil rights movement organized to end the policies and practice of segregation.
        3.    The **Civil Rights Act of 1964** made racial discrimination illegal in places of public accommodation and in employment.
    D.    Getting and Using the Right to Vote
        1.    **Suffrage** was guaranteed to African Americans by the **Fifteenth Amendment** in 1870.

2.     Southern practices to deny African American suffrage (grandfather clause, literacy tests, **poll taxes,** and the **white primary**) were gradually struck down by the Supreme Court and the **Twenty-fourth Amendment** (poll taxes).

3.     The **Voting Rights Act of 1965** prohibited any government from using voting procedures that denied a person the vote on the basis of race or color.

E.     Other Minority Groups
1.     Native Americans
2.     Hispanic Americans
3.     Asian Americans. ***Korematsu v. United States,*** 1944 upheld the internment of Japanese Americans during World War II.

IV.     Women, the Constitution, and Public Policy (pp. 151-159)
A.     The Battle for the Vote, the **Nineteenth Amendment** gave women the right to vote.
B.     The "Doldrums": 1920-1960
1.     Public policy toward women was dominated by protectionism.
2.     The **Equal Rights Amendment** was introduced in Congress in 1923.
C.     The Second Feminist Wave
1.     ***Reed v. Reed*** ruled that any "arbitrary" sex-based classification violated the Fourteenth Amendment.
2.     ***Craig v. Boren*** established a "medium scrutiny" standard.
D.     Women in the Workplace. Congressional acts and Supreme Court decisions have reduced sex discrimination in employment and business activity.
E.     Wage Discrimination and Comparable Worth. Women should receive equal pay for jobs of "**comparable worth**."
F.     Women in the Military
1.     Only men must register for the draft.
2.     Statutes and regulations prohibit women from serving in combat.
G.     Sexual Harassment. The Supreme Court has ruled that sexual harassment that is so pervasive as to create a hostile or abusive work environment is a form of sex discrimination.

V.     Newly Active Groups Under the Civil Rights Umbrella (pp. 159-163)
A.     Civil Rights and the Graying of America
B.     Are the Young a Disadvantaged Group, Too?
C.     Civil Rights and People with Disabilities, the **Americans with Disabilities Act of 1990** required employers and public facilities to make reasonable accommodations and prohibited employment discrimination against the disabled.
D.     Gay and Lesbian Rights

VI.     Affirmative Action (pp. 163-166)

A.   **Affirmative action** involves efforts to bring about increased employment, promotion, or admission for members of groups that have suffered invidious discrimination.

B.   In ***Regents of the University of California v. Bakke*** (1978), the Court ruled against the practice of setting aside a quota of spots for particular groups.

C.   The Court has been more deferential to Congress than to local government in upholding affirmative action programs.

D.   In ***Adarand Constructors v. Peña*** (1995), the Court ruled that federal programs that classify people by race are constitutional only if they are "narrowly tailored" to accomplish a "compelling governmental interest."

E.   Opponents view affirmative action as reverse discrimination.

VII.   Understanding Civil Liberties and the Constitution (pp. 167-169)

A.   Civil Rights and Democracy, equality favors majority rule that may threaten minority rights.

B.   Civil Rights and the Scope of Government, civil rights laws increase the scope and power of government.

VIII.   Summary (p. 169)

## LEARNING OBJECTIVES

*After studying Chapter 5, you should be able to:*

1.   Understand the historical and constitutional basis of the struggle for equal rights.

2.   Discuss the struggle for equality for African Americans in terms of three historical eras, the Constitution, and public policy.

3.   Explain how women have gained civil rights and what equality issues remain important for women today.

4.   Describe the new groups in the civil rights movement.

5.   Explain the controversy over the issue of affirmative action.

6.   Understand the impact of civil rights on democracy and the scope of government.

*The following exercises will help you meet these objectives:*

Objective 1. Understand the historical and constitutional basis of the struggle for equal rights.

1.       What are the three key types of inequality in America?

        1.

        2.

        3.

2.       Explain the two major conceptions of equality.

        1.

        2.

3.       What is the only mention of the idea of equality in the Constitution?

4.       What is the difference between a "reasonable" and an "arbitrary" classification?

Objective 2. Discuss the struggle for equality for African Americans in terms of three historical eras, the Constitution, and public policy.

1.       Complete the following table listing the three eras of the struggle for African American equality, the major policy focus during each era, major court cases and their importance in each era, and any acts of Congress or constitutional amendments passed during each era.

| Historical Era | Policy Focus | Court Cases | Acts/Amendments |
|---|---|---|---|
|  |  |  |  |
|  |  |  |  |
|  |  |  |  |

2.  Compare and contrast the significance of the Supreme Court cases of *Dred Scott v. Sandford* (1857), *Plessy v. Ferguson* (1896), and *Brown v. Board of Education* (1954).

3.  What is the difference between *de jure* segregation and *de facto* segregation?

4.  List the six major provisions of the Civil Rights Act of 1964.

    1.

    2.

    3.

    4.

    5.

    6.

5.       List and explain four ways in which the southern states denied African Americans the right to vote.

        1.

        2.

        3.

        4.

6.       What was the impact of the Voting Rights Act of 1965?

7.       List three other minority groups that have faced discrimination similar to that experienced by African Americans.

        1.

        2.

        3.

Objective 3. Explain how women have gained civil rights and what equality issues remain important for women today.

1.       Explain the policy of "protectionism."

2.       What was the Equal Rights Amendment?

3.       List and explain the significance of four Supreme Court cases dealing with sex-based discrimination.

        1.

2.

3.

4.

4.      How has Congress attempted to end sex discrimination in the area of employment?

5.      What is meant by "comparable worth"?

6.      In what two ways are women legally treated differently in the military?

      1.

      2.

7.      How has the Supreme Court dealt with the issue of sexual harassment?

Objective 4. Describe the new groups in the civil rights movement.

1.      In what ways are the elderly and the young discriminated against in American society?

2.      What are the main provisions of the Rehabilitation Act of 1973 and Americans with Disabilities Act of 1990?

3.  Why might gays and lesbians face the toughest battle for equality?

Objective 5. Explain the controversy over the issue of affirmative action.

1.  Define the term "affirmative action."

2.  List four cases in which the Supreme Court seems to support affirmative action and four cases in which it seems to oppose affirmative action.

| Support | Oppose |
| --- | --- |
| 1. | 1. |
| 2. | 2. |
| 3. | 3. |
| 4. | 4. |

Objective 6. Understand the impact of civil rights on democracy and the scope of government.

1.  How does equality threaten liberty?

2.  How do civil rights laws increase the scope and power of government?

## KEY TERMS AND KEY CASES

*Identify and Describe: Key Terms*

civil rights

Fourteenth Amendment

equal protection of the laws

Thirteenth Amendment

Civil Rights Act of 1964

suffrage

Fifteenth Amendment

poll taxes

white primary

Twenty-fourth Amendment

Voting Rights Act of 1965

Nineteenth Amendment

Equal Rights Amendment

comparable worth

Americans with Disabilities Act of 1990 (ADA)

affirmative action

*Identify and Describe:  Key Cases*

*Dred Scott v. Sandford* (1857)

*Plessy v. Ferguson* (1896)

*Brown v. Board of Education* (1954)

*Korematsu v. United States* (1944)

*Reed v. Reed* (1971)

*Craig v. Boren* (1976)

*Regents of the University of California v. Bakke* (1978)

*Adarand Constructors v. Peña* (1995)

*Compare and Contrast:*

Fourteenth Amendment and equal protection of the laws

*Dred Scott v. Sandford* and Thirteenth Amendment

*Plessy v. Ferguson* and *Brown v. Board of Education*

Civil Rights Act of 1964 and Voting Rights Act of 1965

suffrage and Fifteenth Amendment

poll taxes and white primary

Twenty-fourth Amendment and poll taxes

Nineteenth Amendment and Equal Rights Amendment

*Reed v. Reed* and *Craig v. Boren*


affirmative action and *Regents of the University of California v. Bakke*


affirmative action and *Adarand Constructors v. Peña*


*Name That Term:*

1.  Policies that extend basic rights to groups historically subject to discrimination.

    _____

2.  The Fourteenth Amendment forbids the state from denying this to their citizens.

    _____

3.  The Supreme Court case that justified segregation.

    _____

4.  This law made racial discrimination illegal in hotels, motels, restaurants, and other places of public accommodations.

    _____

5.  A device that permitted political parties in the heavily Democratic South to exclude blacks from primary elections.

    _____

6.  This case upheld the internment of Japanese Americans in encampments during World War II.

    _____

7.      "Equality of rights under the law shall not be denied or abridged by the United States or by any state on account of sex."

        _____

8.      This idea suggests that women should receive equal pay with men for jobs demanding similar skills.

        _____

9.      The law that requires employers and public facilities to make reasonable accommodations for disabled people.

        _____

## USING YOUR UNDERSTANDING

1.      Investigate the policy that your college or university follows with regard to the admission of minority and women students. Also find out about its employment practices, and whether or not it has an affirmative action program. Collect statistics on the percentage of minorities enrolled and employed by the school. Does your college or university offer special academic programs for minorities and women? Evaluate whether or not you believe your school is doing too much or too little in addressing equality issues. Include a recommendation as to how you believe the school's policy might be improved, describing what consequences your recommendation would have.

2.      The onslaught of the AIDS epidemic has raised new issues of equality in the United States. Examine this issue. Should AIDS victims receive the same protections as other handicapped people? How has AIDS affected the gay rights movement? Compile a list of state and local ordinances concerning homosexuals. Do most of these laws protect or discriminate against homosexuals? Also compile survey research results on public opinion towards gays and lesbians. Has the public become more or less tolerant of gays and lesbians? How has AIDS affected public attitudes? Compare the gay rights movement with the civil rights and women's movements. How are they similar and how are they different?

## REVIEW QUESTIONS

*Check ☑ the correct answer:*

1. The rallying cry for groups demanding more equality has been
   - ☐ a. civil rights.
   - ☐ b. civil liberties.
   - ☐ c. civil disobedience.
   - ☐ d. civil war.

2. Policies that extend basic rights to groups historically subject to discrimination are called
   - ☐ a. social policies.
   - ☐ b. civil liberties.
   - ☐ c. civil rights.
   - ☐ d. civil equalities.

3. Today, debates about equality typically center on each of the following key types of inequality in America EXCEPT
   - ☐ a. discrimination based on income.
   - ☐ b. racial discrimination.
   - ☐ c. gender discrimination.
   - ☐ d. discrimination based on age, disability, and other factors.

4. American society tends to emphasize
   - ☐ a. equal results.
   - ☐ b. equal rewards.
   - ☐ c. equal opportunities.
   - ☐ d. equal distributions.

5. The word "equality" does not appear in the original Constitution.
   - ☐ True
   - ☐ False

6. The idea of equality first appeared in the
   - ☐ a. original Constitution.
   - ☐ b. Bill of Rights.
   - ☐ c. Fourteenth Amendment.
   - ☐ d. Nineteenth Amendment.

7.      The five words in the Constitution that refer to equality are
        ☐ a.   "all men are created equal."
        ☐ b.   "equality and justice for all."
        ☐ c.   "equal protection of the laws."
        ☐ d.   "equal representation of the states."

8.      The Supreme Court has ruled that classifications based on gender are subject to a lower level of scrutiny than classifications based on race.
        ☐ True
        ☐ False

9.      In the case of *Dred Scott v. Sandford* (1857), the Supreme Court defended the idea of
        ☐ a.   slavery.
        ☐ b.   equality.
        ☐ c.   civil rights.
        ☐ d.   equal protection of the laws.

10.     The Thirteenth Amendment
        ☐ a.   promoted equal protection of the laws.
        ☐ b.   gave women the right to vote.
        ☐ c.   abolished slavery.
        ☐ d.   legalized segregation.

11.     During the first ten years after the Civil War many African-American men held both state and federal offices.
        ☐ True
        ☐ False

12.     In the case of *Plessy v. Ferguson* (1896), the Supreme Court upheld a Louisiana law providing for
        ☐ a.   slavery.
        ☐ b.   the civil rights movement.
        ☐ c.   equal opportunity.
        ☐ d.   segregated facilities.

13.     The case of *Brown v. Board of Education* (1954) ended the era of
        ☐ a.   slavery.
        ☐ b.   legal segregation.
        ☐ c.   civil rights.
        ☐ d.   equal opportunity.

14. School busing was used as a tool for segregation after the passage of the Civil Rights Act of 1964.
☐ True
☐ False

15. School busing was a practice upheld in the case of
☐ a.  *Dred Scott v. Sandford.*
☐ b.  *Plessy v. Ferguson.*
☐ c.  *Brown v. Board of Education.*
☐ d.  *Swann v. Charlotte-Mecklenberg County Schools.*

16. Children assigned to schools near their homes when those homes are in racially segregated neighborhoods is an example of
☐ a.  separate but equal.
☐ b.  *de jure* segregation.
☐ c.  *de facto* segregation.
☐ d.  all of the above.

17. Rosa Parks became a champion for the cause of civil rights by
☐ a.  refusing to give up a seat on the bus.
☐ b.  organizing a series of marches and sit-ins.
☐ c.  writing speeches for Martin Luther King, Jr.
☐ d.  staging acts of civil disobedience.

18. Which of the following was NOT a key strategy of the civil rights movement?
☐ a.  sit-ins
☐ b.  marches
☐ c.  quiet acceptance
☐ d.  civil disobedience

19. The 1950s and 1960s saw a marked increase in public policies to foster racial equality primarily due to
☐ a.  court decisions.
☐ b.  the civil rights movement.
☐ c.  increased African-American voting.
☐ d.  all of the above.

20. Racial discrimination in public places became illegal by the
☐ a.  Supreme Court case of *Brown v. Board of Education.*
☐ b.  Civil Rights Act of 1964.
☐ c.  Voting Rights Act of 1965.
☐ d.  Equality in Employment Act of 1991.

21. By the 1980s, few, if any, forms of racial discrimination were left to legislate against.
☐ True
☐ False

22. Suffrage is the legal right to
☐ a. free speech.
☐ b. vote.
☐ c. equal opportunities.
☐ d. suffer.

23. The Fifteenth Amendment extended suffrage to
☐ a. African Americans.
☐ b. women.
☐ c. Native Americans.
☐ d. naturalized citizens.

24. Implementation of the Fifteenth Amendment proceeded swiftly and with the total support of the states.
☐ True
☐ False

25. Southern states attempted to deny African Americans the right to vote through the use of the
☐ a. literacy test.
☐ b. poll tax.
☐ c. white primary.
☐ d. all of the above.

26. Poll taxes were declared void by the
☐ a. Thirteenth Amendment.
☐ b. Fifteenth Amendment.
☐ c. Nineteenth Amendment.
☐ d. Twenty-fourth Amendment.

27. Which of the following was NOT a consequence of the Voting Rights Act of 1965?
☐ a. the registration of many southern black voters
☐ b. the use of white primaries
☐ c. the election of more black officials
☐ d. the intervention of federal election registrars

28. Which of the following statements is FALSE?
☐ a. Native Americans comprise the oldest American minority.
☐ b. African Americans achieved citizenship before Native Americans.
☐ c. The Indian Claims Act was passed by Congress to settle disputes arising from lands taken from Indians.
☐ d. Native Americans are not protected by policy protections against discrimination.

29. Hispanic Americans will soon displace African Americans as the largest minority group in the United States.
☐ True
☐ False

30. In the case of *Korematsu v. United States* (1944), the Supreme Court upheld
☐ a. affirmative action programs for Asian Americans.
☐ b. the tribal system of government for Native Americans.
☐ c. the internment of Americans of Japanese descent.
☐ d. the enforcement of immigration policies.

31. Equality for women did not appear on the nation's political agenda until the middle of the twentieth century.
☐ True
☐ False

32. Suffrage for women was achieved with the passage of the
☐ a. Tenth Amendment.
☐ b. Fifteenth Amendment.
☐ c. Nineteenth Amendment.
☐ d. Twenty-fourth Amendment.

33. Winning the right to vote gave the women's movement great momentum in the fight for equality.
☐ True
☐ False

34. After women received the right to vote, public policy toward women was dominated by the idea of
☐ a. protectionism.
☐ b. equality.
☐ c. coverture.
☐ d. autonomy.

35. The Equal Rights Amendment was first introduced in Congress as an Amendment in 1923.
☐ True
☐ False

36. The Supreme Court ruled in *Reed v. Reed* (1971) that
☐ a. any arbitrary sex-based classification under state law violated the equal protection clause.
☐ b. people should be paid comparable wages for comparable jobs.
☐ c. women should be allowed to hold combat positions in the military.
☐ d. sexual harassment violates federal policies against sexual discrimination in the workplace.

37. The Supreme Court has voided laws that
☐ a. provide for alimony payments to women only.
☐ b. close nursing schools to men.
☐ c. set a higher age for drinking for men than for women.
☐ d. all of the above.

38. Most American mothers who have children below school age are in the labor force.
☐ True
☐ False

39. The Civil Rights and Women's Equity in Employment Act of 1991
☐ a. banned sex discrimination in employment.
☐ b. forbade sex discrimination in federally subsidized education programs.
☐ c. shifted the burden of proof in justifying hiring and promotion practices to employers.
☐ d. made it illegal for employers to exclude pregnancy and childbirth from their health-benefits plans.

40. Comparable worth is based on the idea that comparable wages should be paid to
☐ a. blacks and whites.
☐ b. men and women.
☐ c. people performing jobs requiring comparable skill.
☐ d. people holding comparable job titles.

41. The subject referred to by the head of the U.S. Civil Rights Commission in the Reagan administration as "the craziest idea since Looney Tunes" was (bonus)
☐ a. suffrage for women.
☐ b. comparable worth.
☐ c. the Equal Rights Amendment.
☐ d. affirmative action.

42. Statutes and regulations prohibit women from serving in combat.
☐ True
☐ False

43. The Supreme Court has made it very difficult to prove sexual harassment.
☐ True
☐ False

44. Age discrimination is one area that has received very little attention from the U.S. Congress.
☐ True
☐ False

45. The Americans with Disabilities Act of 1990
☐ a. strengthened previous protections against discrimination against the disabled.
☐ b. required employers and public facilities to make reasonable accommodations.
☐ c. prohibited employment discrimination against the disabled.
☐ d. all of the above.

46. The one group that probably faces the toughest battle for equality is
☐ a. the handicapped.
☐ b. the elderly.
☐ c. young people.
☐ d. gay people.

47. Members of the armed services who declare their homosexuality face discharge unless they can prove they will remain celibate.
☐ True
☐ False

48. The women's movement and the civil rights movement converged when it came to the debate over
□ a. comparable worth.
□ b. the Equal Rights Amendment.
□ c. affirmative action.
□ d. protectionism.

49. Affirmative action emphasizes equal opportunities over equal results.
□ True
□ False

50. The Supreme Court held that an admissions quota for particular groups was illegal in
□ a. *United Steelworkers of America, AFL-CIO v. Weber.*
□ b. *Fullilove v. Klutznick.*
□ c. *Regents of the University of California v. Bakke.*
□ d. *Wygart v. Jackson Board of Education.*

51. Opposition to affirmative action is especially strong when people view it as
□ a. affecting only African Americans.
□ b. a form of separate-but-equal.
□ c. reverse discrimination.
□ d. discriminating against women.

52. Which of the following statements is FALSE?
□ a. Equality is a basic principle of democracy.
□ b. The principle of equality can invite the denial of minority rights.
□ c. Civil rights laws and court decisions tell groups and individuals that there are certain things they may and may not do.
□ d. Current civil rights policies conform to the eighteenth-century idea of limited government.


**ESSAY QUESTIONS**

1. How would you define the term "equality"? What does the U.S. Constitution say about equality?

2. What have been the different eras in the struggle for racial equality? What public policy achievements were made in each era?

3.    Explain how the right to vote has been extended in the United States to include both African Americans and women. How was the struggle for suffrage among these two groups similar and different?

4.    Explain the nature of the feminist movement in the United States. What policies have resulted from the struggle for equal rights for women? Explain the controversy over the issue of comparable worth.

5.    Who are the new groups under the civil rights umbrella and what issues are they concerned about? What equality issues might arise in the near future?

6.    What is meant by affirmative action? How has the Supreme Court dealt with the issue of affirmative action?

7.    How do civil rights affect the nature of democracy and the scope of government in the United States?

# Chapter 6

## PUBLIC OPINION AND POLITICAL ACTION

**CHAPTER OUTLINE**

I.  The American People (pp. 174-180)
    A.  The study of American **public opinion** aims to understand the distribution of the population's belief about politics and policy issues.
    B.  **Demography** is the science of human populations. The Constitution requires a **census**, "an actual enumeration" of the population, every ten years.
    C.  The Immigrant Society, there have been three great waves of immigration.
    D.  The American Mosaic
        1.  A **melting pot** refers to a mixture of cultures, ideas, and peoples.
        2.  The United States will soon experience a **minority majority** where white Anglo-Saxons will no longer be a majority.
        3.  The Simpson-Mazzoli Act required employers to document the citizenship of their employees.
        4.  Americans share a common **political culture**—an overall set of values widely shared within a society.
    E.  The Regional Shift
        1.  In the last fifty years, the Sunbelt has had the greatest population growth.
        2.  **Reapportionment** occurs after every census. House seats are reallocated to the states based on population changes.
    F.  The Graying of America, citizens over 65 compose the fastest growing age group.

II. How Americans Learn About Politics: Political Socialization (pp. 180-184)
    A.  **Political socialization** is "the process through which an individual acquires his or her particular political orientations."
    B.  The Process of Political Socialization
        1.  The Family.
        2.  The Mass Media
        3.  School
    C.  Political Learning Over a Lifetime.

III. Measuring Public Opinion and Political Information (pp. 184-192)
    A.  How Polls are Conducted
        1.  A **sample** of the population is a relatively small proportion of people who are chosen as representative of the whole.

2. **Random sampling** operates on the principle that everyone should have an equal probability of being selected.
3. **Sampling error** depends on the size of the sample.
4. Most polling is done on the telephone with samples selected through **random digit dialing.**

B. The Role of Polls in American Democracy
   1. Polls help political candidates detect public preferences.
   2. Polls may make politicians followers rather than leaders.
   3. Polls can distort the election process.
   4. **Exit polls** may discourage people from voting.
   5. Polls can be manipulated by altering the wording of questions.
C. What Polls Reveal About Americans' Political Information. Americans are not well informed about politics.
D. The Decline of Trust in Government

IV. What Americans Value: Political Ideologies (pp. 192-196)
   A. A **political ideology** is a coherent set of values and beliefs about public policy.
   B. Who are the Liberals and Conservatives?
      1. More Americans consistently choose the ideological label of conservative over liberal.
      2. Liberals generally like to see the government do more.
      3. Groups with political clout tend to be more conservative than groups whose members have often been shut out from political power.
      4. Ideological differences between men and women has led to the **gender gap** where women are more likely to support Democratic candidates.
      5. The role of religion in influencing political ideology has changed greatly in recent years.
   C. Do People Think in Ideological Terms? For most people the terms liberal and conservative are not as important as they are for the political elite.
   D. Has There Been a Turn toward Conservatism?

V. How Americans Participate In Politics (pp. 196-200)
   A. **Political participation** encompasses the many activities used by citizens to influence the selection of political leaders or the policies they pursue.
   B. Conventional Participation. The majority of Americans participate only by voting in presidential elections.
   C. Protest As Participation
      1. **Protest** is designed to achieve policy change through dramatic and unconventional tactics.
      2. **Civil disobedience** is consciously breaking a law thought to be unjust.
   D. Class, Inequality, and Participation. Lower rates of political participation among minority groups are linked with lower socioeconomic status.

## LEARNING OBJECTIVES

*After studying Chapter 6, you should be able to:*

1.    Describe how demographic factors shape who we are politically.

2.    Identify the processes through which people learn about politics.

3.    Define public opinion, identify how it is measured, explain its role in shaping public policy, and discuss the nature of political information in America.

4.    Understand the concept of political ideology in American politics and government.

5.    Explain the ways in which people participate in politics and in the policymaking process, and discuss the implications of unequal political participation.

6.    Understand the relationship between the scope of government, democracy, public opinion, and political action.

*The following exercises will help you meet these objectives:*

Objective 1. Describe how demographic factors shape who we are politically.

1.    What were the three great waves of immigration to the United States?

      1.


      2.


      3.

2. What is meant by the term "minority majority"?

3. What was the goal of the Simpson-Mazzoli Act?

4. How have the following demographic changes affected political changes?

   1. Immigration

   2. Regional Shifts

   3. Aging Population

Objective 2. Identify the processes through which people learn about politics.

1. Explain the significance of each of the following as sources for political learning:

   1. Family:

   2. Mass media:

   3. Schools:

2. Name two ways in which aging affects political behavior.

   1.

   2.

Objective 3. Define public opinion, identify how it is measured, explain its role in shaping public policy, and discuss the nature of political information in America.

1.      What is the key to the accuracy of opinion polls?

2.      Explain the technique of random digit dialing.

3.      List three criticisms of public opinion polling.

     1.

     2.

     3.

4.      What is the "paradox of mass politics," according to Russell Neuman?

Objective 4. Understand the concept of political ideology in the context of American politics and government.

1.      Fill in the following table concerning political ideology.

| Ideology | General Beliefs | Typical Demographic Characteristics |
|---|---|---|
| Liberals | | |
| Conservatives | | |

2.  Fill in the following table on the classification of the ideological sophistication of American voters according to the study *The American Voter*.

| Ideological Classification | Definition | Percent |
|---|---|---|
|  |  |  |
|  |  |  |
|  |  |  |
|  |  |  |

3.  How would you explain President Ronald Reagan's popularity?

Objective 5. Explain the ways in which people participate in politics and in the policymaking process, and discuss the implications of unequal political participation.

1.  List five activities of conventional political participation, placing a star next to the most common activity.

    1.

    2.

    3.

    4.

    5.

2.      Define civil disobedience and give an example.

3.      How does minority group status affect political participation?

Objective 6. Understand the relationship between the scope of government, democracy, public opinion, and political action.

1.      What is the public's general attitude about the scope of government?

2.      Comment on how Americans' lack of political knowledge and low participation rate affects democracy.

**KEY TERMS**

*Identify and Describe:*

public opinion

demography

census

melting pot

minority majority

political culture

reapportionment

political socialization

sample

random sampling

sampling error

random-digit dialing

exit poll

political ideology

liberalism

conservatism

gender gap

political participation

protest

civil disobedience

*Compare and Contrast:*

demography and census

melting pot and minority majority

public opinion and political ideology

sample, random sampling, and sampling error

random digit dialing and exit poll

liberalism and conservatism

protest and civil disobedience

*Name that Term:*

1. The mixing of cultures, ideas, and peoples.

   _____

2. An overall set of values widely shared within a society.

   _____

3. This occurs when the 435 seats in the House of Representatives are reallocated to the states based on population changes.

   _____

4. The process through which an individual acquires his or her particular political orientations.

   _____

5. The distribution of the population's beliefs about politics and policy issues.

   _____

6. This technique is the key to the accuracy of public opinion polls.

   _____

7. This is the most criticized type of poll.

   _____

8. In American politics, this is usually characterized by the liberal-conservative dimension.

   _____

9. Ideological differences between men and women have led to this.

   _____

10.     Voting, running for office, and even violent protest are examples of this.

_____

## USING YOUR UNDERSTANDING

1.     Locate the published results of an opinion poll by Gallup, Harris, or one of the news organizations on a topic that is of interest to you. You may want to use polls that focus on the Clinton-Lewinsky scandal or the 2000 presidential election. Assess the results in terms of the demographic distributions, if any that are reflected in the results. See if males differed from females, whites from non-whites, and so on. If the results are compared with the findings of an earlier poll, see if public opinion on the topic is changing. Briefly describe what you found and what its implications are for policymaking. Alternatively, design a small questionnaire for your class dealing with questions of information, ideology, and political participation. Have the respondents to your survey provide demographic information. Summarize your findings in a table or two presenting the overall responses and those for particular demographic groups. Keep in mind that you will probably face the problems of a limited sample size and a lack of representativeness for the general population.

2.     Conduct a study on the role of unconventional political participation in the United States. Compare and contrast the different types of unconventional political participation. Identify examples of historical events in the United States that exemplify unconventional political participation. Present an analysis of these events in terms of the number of people involved, the type of activity, the target of the activity, and the short-term and long-term results of the activity. Critically evaluate the effectiveness of unconventional political participation as compared to conventional political participation.

## REVIEW QUESTIONS

*Check ☑ the correct answer:*

1.     Most Americans view cultural diversity as one of the most appealing aspects of their society.
       ☐ True
       ☐ False

2.	Demography is the
☐ a.	historical analysis of political participation.
☐ b.	study of public opinion.
☐ c.	science of human populations.
☐ d.	enumeration of a population.

3.	The enumeration of a population is called
☐ a.	an opinion poll.
☐ b.	demography.
☐ c.	a census.
☐ d.	cartography.

4.	The Constitution requires an actual enumeration of the population
☐ a.	annually.
☐ b.	every ten years.
☐ c.	every twenty-five years.
☐ d.	never.

5.	The census is basically a procedural requirement that creates very little controversy.
☐ True
☐ False

6.	The third great wave of immigration, after World War II, consisted primarily of
☐ a.	northwestern Europeans.
☐ b.	southern and eastern Europeans.
☐ c.	Africans.
☐ d.	Hispanics and Asians.

7.	The American "melting pot" refers to the mix of
☐ a.	cultures.
☐ b.	ideas.
☐ c.	people.
☐ d.	all of the above.

8.	The largest component of the minority majority in the United States today is
☐ a.	African Americans.
☐ b.	Hispanics.
☐ c.	Asians.
☐ d.	American Indians.

9.  The Hispanics in the United States tend to be concentrated in the cities.
    ☐ True
    ☐ False

10. The Simpson-Mazzoli Act
    ☐ a.  allowed employers to employ illegal immigrants.
    ☐ b.  required documentation of the citizenship of all employees.
    ☐ c.  provided for legal discrimination against minority workers.
    ☐ d.  put an end to all immigration from Mexico.

11. The most highly skilled immigrant group in American history is
    ☐ a.  African Americans.
    ☐ b.  Hispanic Americans.
    ☐ c.  Asian Americans.
    ☐ d.  Eastern European Americans.

12. Over the last fifty years, much of America's population growth has been concentrated
    ☐ a.  north of the Mason-Dixon line.
    ☐ b.  east of the Mississippi River.
    ☐ c.  in the West and South.
    ☐ d.  in the Midwest.

13. Reapportionment can lead to
    ☐ a.  an increase in the number of members of the House of Representatives.
    ☐ b.  power shifts among the states.
    ☐ c.  an increase or decrease in the number of Senators from each state.
    ☐ d.  none of the above.

14. The biggest reapportionment winner in the most recent census has been
    ☐ a.  California.
    ☐ b.  New York.
    ☐ c.  Florida.
    ☐ d.  Ohio.

15. The fastest growing age group in America is composed of citizens
    ☐ a.  over the age of 65.
    ☐ b.  under the age of 18.
    ☐ c.  between the ages of 19 and 35.
    ☐ b.  between the ages of 36 and 55.

16. By the year 2020 the Social Security system will be solvent and self-sufficient.
☐ True
☐ False

17. The process of acquiring political orientations is called political socialization.
☐ True
☐ False

18. Which of the following statements regarding political socialization is FALSE?
☐ a. Only a small portion of Americans' political learning is formal.
☐ b. Most of what Americans learn about politics is acquired from high school civic courses.
☐ c. As one becomes more socialized with age, one's political orientations grow firmer.
☐ d. Governments largely aim their socialization efforts at the young.

19. Formal learning about politics is far more important than informal learning.
☐ True
☐ False

20. Which of the following statements about political socialization and the family is FALSE?
☐ a. The influence of families is central to socialization because of time and emotional commitment.
☐ b. One can predict how the majority of young people will vote simply by knowing the political leanings of their parents.
☐ c. Family influence on socialization is mostly informal.
☐ d. The generation gap is a well-proven phenomenon.

21. According to many observers, the "new parents" are
☐ a. the mass media.
☐ b. peer groups.
☐ c. schools.
☐ d. government agencies.

22. One of the most obvious intrusions of the government into Americans' socialization is
☐ a. political parties.
☐ b. schools.
☐ c. television.
☐ d. the military.

23. As people grow older,
    - [ ] a. political party attachment declines.
    - [ ] b. political participation rises steadily.
    - [ ] c. voting declines.
    - [ ] d. political learning ends.

24. The public opinion poll was perfected by (bonus)
    - [ ] a. Abraham Lincoln.
    - [ ] b. the *Literary Digest*.
    - [ ] c. George Gallup.
    - [ ] d. Alf Landon.

25. Which of the following statements is FALSE?
    - [ ] a. As long as a survey is large enough, representativeness is not important.
    - [ ] b. All surveys have sampling error.
    - [ ] c. A sample of about 1,500 to 2,000 people can represent faithfully the "universe" of potential voters.
    - [ ] d. Random digit dialing costs about a fifth of the cost of person-to-person interviewing.

26. The key to the accuracy of opinion polls is the
    - [ ] a. number of people interviewed.
    - [ ] b. technique of random sampling.
    - [ ] c. use of telephones for interviewing.
    - [ ] d. use of computers.

27. The *Literary Digest* poll of 1936 wrongly predicted the results of the presidential election because
    - [ ] a. they did not interview enough people.
    - [ ] b. they used exit polls to predict the election results.
    - [ ] c. most of the people they interviewed did not vote.
    - [ ] d. they did not interview a random sample of voters.

28. Most polling today is done through
    - [ ] a. random digit dialing.
    - [ ] b. door-to-door interviews.
    - [ ] c. exit polls.
    - [ ] d. mail surveys.

29. Public opinion polling is almost exclusively an American phenomenon.
    - [ ] True
    - [ ] False

30. Exit polls allow television networks to project all but very close races before the polls close.
☐ True
☐ False

31. Which of the following statements is NOT a criticism of public opinion polling?
☐ a. Public opinion polling makes politicians more concerned with following than leading.
☐ b. Polls can weaken democracy by distorting the election process.
☐ c. Polling is a fad that should not be taken seriously.
☐ d. Pollsters can often get the results they want by altering the wording of questions.

32. Thomas Jefferson believed that
☐ a. education is irrelevant to good citizenship.
☐ b. the people are "a great beast."
☐ c. a majority of people will exercise good sense.
☐ d. people lack a capacity for self-government.

33. Who said, "Your people, sir, are a great beast"? (bonus)
☐ a. Abraham Lincoln
☐ b. Thomas Jefferson
☐ c. Alexander Hamilton
☐ d. Winston Churchill

34. One thing that public opinion polls have shown is that the
☐ a. United States is becoming more conservative.
☐ b. level of public knowledge about politics is dismally low.
☐ c. American people have strong opinions about political issues.
☐ d. American people are becoming more ideologically oriented.

35. Public opinion polls have shown that the majority of Americans
☐ a. can name the chief justice of the Supreme Court.
☐ b. can explain their opinion on major political issues.
☐ c. can locate Bosnia on a map.
☐ d. recognize commercial slogans better than the names of political figures.

36. According to Russell Neuman, the paradox of mass politics is that the American political system works as well as it does given the
☐ a. discomforting lack of public knowledge about politics.
☐ b. high degree of ideologically oriented people in the United States.
☐ c. lack of opinions on major issues in American politics.
☐ d. none of the above.

37. Political ideology consists of views that are simply "gut reactions."
☐ True
☐ False

38. A liberal ideology favors
☐ a. a strong central government.
☐ b. greater reliance on the private sector.
☐ c. smaller government.
☐ d. passive government.

39. Conservatives would tend to support all of the following EXCEPT
☐ a. a strong military.
☐ b. school prayer.
☐ c. low taxes.
☐ d. affirmative action.

40. No significant difference has ever been found between the ideological orientations of men and women.
☐ True
☐ False

41. Researchers in the 1950s found that the largest share of the electorate consisted of
☐ a. no-issue-content voters.
☐ b. nature-of-the-times voters
☐ c. highly ideological voters.
☐ d. group-benefits voters.

42. When identical methods were used to update the analysis of the 1956 study *The American Voter* in 1988, researchers found
☐ a. a majority of the people identified as ideologues in 1988.
☐ b. a huge increase in the no-issue-content group in 1988.
☐ c. just six percent more ideologues in 1988 than in 1956.
☐ d. a disappearance of the nature-of-the-times voters in 1988.

43. The elections of Dwight Eisenhower in the 1950s and Ronald Reagan in the 1980s represented a public ideological shift in the conservative direction.
☐ True
☐ False

44. The electoral successes of Reagan and Bush have been attributed to
   - [ ] a. a public shift in ideology.
   - [ ] b. the lack of support for Democratic Party policies.
   - [ ] c. low voter turnout.
   - [ ] d. nature-of-the-times voters who reacted to the years of relative peace and prosperity.

45. Political participation
   - [ ] a. is aimed at influencing the selection of political leaders and the policies they pursue.
   - [ ] b. is higher in the U.S. than anywhere in the world.
   - [ ] c. consists exclusively of voting and campaigning.
   - [ ] d. excludes unconventional political actions such as protest.

46. When it comes to political participation, the common denominator among political activists is
   - [ ] a. campaigning.
   - [ ] b. protesting.
   - [ ] c. voting.
   - [ ] d. contacting.

47. Protest is a form of political participation that loses its effectiveness because the media are unwilling to cover unusual activities.
   - [ ] True
   - [ ] False

48. The conscious decision to break a law believed to be immoral and suffer the consequences is called
   - [ ] a. protest.
   - [ ] b. civil disobedience.
   - [ ] c. political participation.
   - [ ] d. activation.

49. Nearly every study of participation in America has concluded that citizens of higher social and economic status participate more in politics.
   - [ ] True
   - [ ] False

50.     Income and education being equal, African Americans and Hispanics participate in politics
  ☐ a.    the same as whites.
  ☐ b.    more than whites.
  ☐ c.    less than whites.
  ☐ d.    none of the time.

51.     For most of the population, questions about the scope of government
  ☐ a.    elicit no or little opinion.
  ☐ b.    guide their ideological leanings.
  ☐ c.    are consistent with their policy choices.
  ☐ d.    produce strong emotional responses.

52.     Even if people only vote according to the nature of the times with no knowledge of the issues, they are holding presidents accountable for their actions.
  ☐ True
  ☐ False

## ESSAY QUESTIONS

1.      What is demography, and why is it important to understanding political changes? What demographic changes have occurred in the United States and what are their political and public policy consequences?

2.      What is political socialization? What is the difference between formal and informal learning? Which do you think is most important and why? Give examples to support your answer.

3.      Explain how public opinion is measured. What scientific techniques are used to measure public opinion? What are the arguments against public opinion polling?

4.      Contrast the views of Thomas Jefferson and Alexander Hamilton on the political sophistication of the American electorate. Be sure to include a discussion of political information and ideology in your answer. Based on the available evidence, defend one view over the other.

5.      To what extent is ideology important in the United States? Explain the main differences between liberals and conservatives. What are the public's attitudes on the scope of government?

6.     What are some of the ways in which people participate in politics? Compare conventional and unconventional participation. How do they affect policy in different ways?

7.     Why is participation in America unequal? What are the political and policy implications of unequal participation?

# Chapter 7

## THE MASS MEDIA AND THE POLITICAL AGENDA

### CHAPTER OUTLINE

I. Introduction (pp. 206-208)
   A. **High-tech politics** is a politics in which technology increasingly shapes the behavior of citizens and policymakers, as well as the political agenda itself.
   B. The **mass media** consist of television, radio, newspapers, magazines, and other means of popular communication that reach, and profoundly influence, not only the elites but also the masses.

II. The Mass Media Today (pp. 208-210)
   A. A **media event** is staged primarily for the purpose of being covered.
   B. Image making is critical to campaigning and day-to-day governing.

III. The Development of the Media Politics (pp. 211-216)
   A. Introduction
      1. Franklin D. Roosevelt practically invented media politics, holding two **press conferences** (presidential meetings with reporters) a week.
      2. The Vietnam War and the Watergate scandal soured the press on government.
      3. **Investigative journalism** is the use of detective-like reporting methods to unearth scandals.
   B. The **Print Media**
      1. Newspapers grew from the "penny press," through the era of yellow journalism, consolidating into **chains,** and becoming part of today's massive media conglomerates.
      2. The political content of leading magazines is slim.
   C. The **Broadcast Media**
      1. During World War II, radio went into the news business in earnest.
      2. Since the 1960s, television has had a profound impact on politics.
   D. **Narrowcasting**: Cable TV and the Internet
      Information about politics on cable and the Internet is presented in a way that appeals to a rather narrow and specific audience rather than to the general public.

IV. Reporting the News (pp. 216-223)
   A. News is what is timely and different.

B. Finding News
   1. Most news organizations assign reporters to **beats,** specific locations where news frequently happens.
   2. **Trial balloons** consist of information leaked to discover the political reaction.
C. Presenting the News, as technology has enabled the media to pass along information with greater speed, news coverage has become less complete and **sound bites** are more common.
D. Bias in the News
   1. News reporting is not systematically biased toward a particular ideology or party.
   2. Television is biased toward stories that generate good pictures. The **talking head** is considered boring.

V. The News and Public Opinion (pp. 223-225)
   A. Although studies show that the media do not affect how people vote, they do affect what they think about and the priorities they attach to problems.
   B. People's opinions shift with the tone of news coverage.

VI. The Media's Agenda-Setting Function (pp. 225-227)
   A. The **policy agenda** is "the list of subjects or problems to which government officials, and people outside of government closely associated with those officials, are paying some serious attention at any given time."
   B. **Policy entrepreneurs** are people who invest their political "capital" in an issue.
   C. The media can be used by the poor and downtrodden as well as the elite.

VII. Understanding the Mass Media (pp. 227-229)
   A. The Media and the Scope of Government
   B. Individualism and the Media
   C. Democracy and the Media

VIII. Summary (pp. 229-231)


**LEARNING OBJECTIVES**

*After studying Chapter 7, you should be able to:*

1. Describe the characteristics of the mass media today.

2. Explain the difference between the print media and the broadcast media from a historical perspective.

3.        Understand how news is found and reported by the media.

4.        Describe how the news media affect public opinion.

5.        Discuss what is meant by the concepts of policy agenda and policy entrepreneur and the media's importance to them.

6.        Understand how the media affect the scope of government and the democratic process.

*The following exercises will help you meet these objectives:*

Objective 1. Describe the characteristics of the mass media today.

    1.        Explain the purpose of a media event.

    2.        List the seven principles of news management as practiced in the Reagan White House.

        1.

        2.

        3.

        4.

        5.

        6.

        7.

Objective 2. Explain the difference between the print media and the broadcast media from a historical perspective.

    1.        Explain two media techniques used most effectively by President Franklin Roosevelt.

1.

2.

2.       What is meant by investigative journalism?

3.       Explain the significance of the era of the "penny press," the era of "yellow journalism," and the era of "chains" as they relate to the print media.

Era of Penny Press:

Era of Yellow Journalism:

Era of Chains:

4.       Explain three ways in which television affected the political career of Richard Nixon.

1.

2.

3.

5.       What effect did television have on the war in Vietnam?

6.        What impact has cable TV and the Internet had on news reporting?

Objective 3. Understand how news is found and reported by the media.

1.        Where does most news come from?

2.        What is meant by a "sound bite" and what does it tell us about news coverage?

3.        Explain how the news media tend to be biased.

Objective 4. Describe how the news media affect public opinion.

1.        In the experiments by Shanto Iyengar and Donald Kinder, what effect did manipulating T.V. stories have on viewers?

2.        According to a study by Page, Shapiro, and Dempsey, who has the strongest impact on public opinion changes?

Objective 5. Discuss what is meant by the concepts of policy agenda and policy entrepreneur, and the media's importance to them.

1.        Define the term "policy agenda."

2.        List five items in the policy entrepreneurs' "arsenal of weapons."

        1.

        2.

3.

4.

5.


Objective 6. Understand how the media affect the scope of government and the democratic process.

    1.       How does the media act as a "watchdog"?


    2.       What is the difference between the "information society" and the "informed society"?


## KEY TERMS

*Identify and Describe:*

high-tech politics


mass media


media event


press conferences


investigative journalism

print media

broadcast media

chains

narrowcasting

beats

trial balloons

sound bites

talking head

policy agenda

policy entrepreneurs

*Compare and Contrast:*

high-tech politics and mass media


media event and press conferences


print media and broadcast media


sound bites and talking head


policy agenda and policy entrepreneur


*Name That Term:*

1.     It reaches the elite as well as the masses.

       _____

2.     These are staged primarily for the purpose of being covered.

       _____

3.     This tends to pit reporters against political leaders.

       _____

4.     These control newspapers with most of the nation's circulation.

       _____

5.     The primary mission of cable and Internet news.

       _____

6.  Specific locations from where news frequently emanates.

    _____

7.  Information leaked to see what the political reaction would be.

    _____


## USING YOUR UNDERSTANDING

1.  Choose one of the three major networks, CBS, NBC, or ABC, and watch the evening news every day for a week. While watching, write down the topic of each news story, the amount of time spent on the story, and an assessment of the story's content and the issues it raises. Read a daily newspaper (preferably the *New York Times* or another major paper) for the same days. Compare the television and newspaper coverage of the same news stories. Analyze the differences between these media in terms of how the stories were presented, depth of coverage, and issue orientation. Evaluate how the print media and the broadcast media might differ in their influence on public opinion.

2.  Based on your understanding of the role of the media in the agenda-building process, critique a news item or article that concerns a policy issue. Your critique should begin by asking how well the item identified the policy issue, the policy entrepreneurs, and people in government concerned about the issue. Assess the news item as both a source of information and a source of influence on your perceptions of politics, government, and policy. Consider how policymakers might use the news item as well. Put yourself in the position of the reporter and consider how the story might have been improved. In light of your critique, discuss your impressions of the media as unofficial but important sources of influence on public opinion and the policy agenda.


## REVIEW QUESTIONS

*Check ☑ the correct answer:*

1.  The American political system has entered a new period of high-tech politics.
    ☐ True
    ☐ False

2. Television, radio, newspapers, and other means of popular communication are called
   - ☐ a. chains.
   - ☐ b. high-tech politics.
   - ☐ c. mass media.
   - ☐ d. public relations.

3. The influence of the mass media is limited to the elites in the United States.
   - ☐ True
   - ☐ False

4. Media events are spontaneous circumstances that get the media's attention.
   - ☐ True
   - ☐ False

5. A president who was particularly successful in playing to the media was
   - ☐ a. George Bush.
   - ☐ b. Ronald Reagan.
   - ☐ c. Richard Nixon.
   - ☐ d. Jimmy Carter.

6. News management in the Reagan White House operated on each of the following principles EXCEPT
   - ☐ a. staying on the offensive.
   - ☐ b. controlling the flow of information.
   - ☐ c. speaking in one voice.
   - ☐ d. spontaneity.

7. Today, for a president to ignore the power of image and the media would be perilous.
   - ☐ True
   - ☐ False

8. Who said, "The President of the United States will not stand and be questioned like a chicken thief by men whose names he does not even know"? (bonus)
   - ☐ a. Herbert Hoover
   - ☐ b. Franklin D. Roosevelt
   - ☐ c. Lyndon Johnson
   - ☐ d. Richard Nixon

9.  The president who held numerous press conferences and practically created media politics was
    - ☐ a.  Herbert Hoover.
    - ☐ b.  Franklin Roosevelt.
    - ☐ c.  John F. Kennedy.
    - ☐ d.  Ronald Reagan.

10. Prior to the 1960s, the relationship between politicians and the press was one of skepticism and distrust.
    - ☐ True
    - ☐ False

11. The press soured on government as a result of the events of the
    - ☐ a.  Vietnam War.
    - ☐ b.  Watergate scandal.
    - ☐ c.  Korean War.
    - ☐ d.  Both a and b.

12. The early expansion of print media was made possible by
    - ☐ a.  cheap paper.
    - ☐ b.  the wire service.
    - ☐ c.  rapid printing technology.
    - ☐ d.  all of the above.

13. Joseph Pulitzer and William Randolph Hearst were
    - ☐ a.  inventors of the printing press.
    - ☐ b.  strong opponents of yellow journalism.
    - ☐ c.  turn-of-the-century newspaper magnates.
    - ☐ d.  presidential candidates.

14. Who said, "The essence of American journalism is vulgarity divested of truth"? (bonus)
    - ☐ a.  Joseph Pulitzer
    - ☐ b.  Horace Greeley
    - ☐ c.  William Randolph Hearst
    - ☐ d.  Winston Churchill

15. Newspaper chains
    - ☐ a.  are organizations loosely linked by the wire services.
    - ☐ b.  are controlled by conglomerates that often control broadcast media as well.
    - ☐ c.  began to disappear with the advent of television.
    - ☐ d.  are local papers owned by fearless local editors.

16. Gradually, the broadcast media have replaced the print media as our principal source of news and information.
    ☐ True
    ☐ False

17. The political career of Richard Nixon was made and unmade by television.
    ☐ True
    ☐ False

18. Richard Nixon's experiences during the 1960 presidential campaign illustrate the
    ☐ a.  power of television in American politics.
    ☐ b.  insignificance of presidential debates.
    ☐ c.  greater importance of print media.
    ☐ d.  friendly relationship between the media and political candidates.

19. Using the broadcast media, Lyndon Johnson was successful in persuading the public that America was winning the war in Vietnam.
    ☐ True
    ☐ False

20. Which of the following statements is TRUE?
    ☐ a.  Newspapers are the main source of news for Americans.
    ☐ b.  Most of the news originates from correspondents.
    ☐ c.  In-depth analyses of policy issues are common in the media.
    ☐ d.  People think television reports are more believable than newspaper stories.

21. News on cable TV and the Internet
    ☐ a.  is not available to most people
    ☐ b.  appeals to a rather narrow and specific audience.
    ☐ c.  does not go into much depth.
    ☐ d.  is widely used by most Americans.

22. The bottom line that shapes how journalists define news, where they get news, and how they present news is
    ☐ a.  objectivity.
    ☐ b.  truth.
    ☐ c.  profits.
    ☐ d.  comprehensiveness.

23. The news media avoid odd events in favor of reporting only objective conditions.
    ☐ True
    ☐ False

24. Most news organizations assign their best reporters to particular beats.
☐ True
☐ False

25. Trial balloons are used by politicians to
☐ a.   put issues on the policy agenda.
☐ b.   see their constituents.
☐ c.   test political reactions.
☐ d.   take public polls.

26. If you had to pick a single word to describe news coverage by the print and broadcast media, it would be
☐ a.   comprehensive.
☐ b.   biased.
☐ c.   misleading.
☐ d.   superficial.

27. Which of the following statements is FALSE?
☐ a.   Television analysis of news events rarely lasts more than a minute.
☐ b.   In-depth attention to the issues is given only during presidential campaigns.
☐ c.   Newspapers rarely reprint the entire text of important political speeches.
☐ d.   Snappy soundbites of fifteen seconds or less are more common than full speeches on television.

28. Studies on bias in the news have found that the news media tend to
☐ a.   favor the Democratic Party.
☐ b.   be politically conservative.
☐ c.   be politically neutral.
☐ d.   favor the Republican Party.

29. Which of the following statements is FALSE?
☐ a.   Most reporters strongly believe in journalistic objectivity.
☐ b.   Most news stories are presented in a "point/counterpoint" format.
☐ c.   The news media do not want to lose their audience by appearing biased.
☐ d.   Most studies have shown that the media are systematically biased toward a liberal ideology.

30. The news media tend to do all of the following EXCEPT
☐ a.   mirror reality.
☐ b.   show more bad news than good news.
☐ c.   focus on stories that generate good pictures.
☐ d.   overemphasize dramatic events.

31. A "talking head" is a media term referring to a shot of a person's face talking directly to the camera.
☐ True
☐ False

32. To which of the following news stories did Americans pay closest attention?
☐ a. Arrest of O.J. Simpson.
☐ b. Los Angeles riots.
☐ c. Passage of the 1994 Crime Bill.
☐ d. Congressional debate over NAFTA.

33. Studies have shown that the news media
☐ a. have only a marginal effect on public opinion.
☐ b. directly affect how people vote.
☐ c. affect what Americans think about.
☐ d. can conceal problems that actually exist.

34. By increasing public attention to specific problems, television news can influence the criteria by which the public evaluates political leaders.
☐ True
☐ False

35. Research indicates that public opinions remain constant even when news coverage changes.
☐ True
☐ False

36. Of all the influences the news media have on opinion change, the strongest impact is from
☐ a. field reporters.
☐ b. news commentators.
☐ c. radio announcers.
☐ d. anchors.

37. Issues on the policy agenda are always defined by government officials, but not by people outside of government.
☐ True
☐ False

38. Which of the following characteristics is NOT common among policy entrepreneurs?
   - ☐ a.  commitment to a single policy issue
   - ☐ b.  investment of personal political capital
   - ☐ c.  avoidance of the media
   - ☐ d.  concern about government's priorities

39. Which of the following people would NOT qualify to be a policy entrepreneur?
   - ☐ a.  an elected official
   - ☐ b.  an interest group leader
   - ☐ c.  an academic researcher
   - ☐ d.  none of the above

40. The media act as key linkage institutions between the people and the policymakers, having a profound impact on the policy agenda.
   - ☐ True
   - ☐ False

41. The watchdog function of the media
   - ☐ a.  contributes to the growth of government.
   - ☐ b.  can be characterized as reformist.
   - ☐ c.  has a liberal political orientation.
   - ☐ d.  is no longer a central concern of the media.

42. When the media focus on injustice in society, they inevitably help keep government small.
   - ☐ True
   - ☐ False

43. The American institutional agenda has changed dramatically because television finds it easier to focus on groups than on individuals.
   - ☐ True
   - ☐ False

44. Which of the following statements is TRUE?
   - ☐ a.  The media are at their best when reporting stories about complex, high-tech issues.
   - ☐ b.  The amount of information available through the news media has decreased.
   - ☐ c.  The rise of the information society has brought about a rise in the informed society.
   - ☐ d.  The media do a better job of covering the "horse race" aspects of politics than they do covering substantive issues.

45.     The news media's defense for being superficial is to say that this is what the
        people want.
        ☐ True
        ☐ False


## ESSAY QUESTIONS

1.      Using examples from presidential politics, explain why image and the use of the
        media are so important in the American political system.

2.      Explain the historical development of the print and broadcast media in the United
        States. Use examples to illustrate your answer.

3.      How does television define what is newsworthy? Explain where television finds
        its news stories and how they are presented to the American public.

4.      Describe how the media shape public opinion. What are the consequences of the
        media's influence on public opinion?

5.      What is the policy agenda? Who are the policy entrepreneurs and how do they
        utilize the media to get their issues on the policy agenda?

6.      Explain how the news media affect the scope of government and American
        individualism. How have they helped and hindered the growth of democracy in
        the United States?

# Chapter 8

## POLITICAL PARTIES

## CHAPTER OUTLINE

I.  The Meaning of Party (pp. 236-240)
    A.  Introduction
        1.  **Party competition** is the battle between Democrats and Republicans for the control of public offices.
        2.  A **political party** is a "team of men and women seeking to control the governing apparatus by gaining office in a duly constituted election."
        3.  Political parties are viewed as "three-headed political giants."
            a.  The *party-in-the-electorate*
            b.  The *party as an organization*
            c.  The *party-in-government*
    B.  Tasks of the Parties, parties act as **linkage institutions**, translating inputs from the public into outputs from the policymakers.
        1.  Parties pick candidates.
        2.  Parties run campaigns.
        3.  Parties give cues to voters (**party image**).
        4.  Parties articulate policies.
        5.  Parties coordinate policymaking.
    C.  Parties, Voters, and Policy:  The Downs Model
        1.  **Rational-choice theory** "seeks to explain political processes and outcomes as consequences of purposive behavior."
        2.  The wise party selects policies that are widely favored.

II. The Party In The Electorate (pp. 240-241)
    A.  Party images help shape people's **party identification,** the self-proclaimed preference for one party or the other.
    B.  **Ticket-splitting,** voting with one party for one office and another for other offices, is near an all-time high.

III. The Party Organizations:  From the Grassroots to Washington (pp. 241-245)
    A.  Local Parties
        1.  Urban political parties were once dominated by **urban machines**.
        2.  **Patronage** is one of the key inducements used by party machines.
    B.  The 50 State Party Systems
        1.  American national parties are a loose aggregation of state parties.

2.    States limit who can participate in their nomination contests by using **closed primaries**, **open primaries**, or **blanket primaries**.
C.    The National Party Organizations
    1.    The supreme power within each of the parties is the **national convention**.
    2.    The **national committee** keeps the party operating between conventions.
    3.    The **national chairperson** is responsible for the day-to-day activities of the national party.

IV.    The Party In Government:  Promises and Policy (pp. 245-247)
  A.    The party in control ultimately determines who gets what, where, when, and how.
  B.    A **coalition** is a set of individuals and groups supporting a party.
  C.    Parties have done a fairly good job of translating their platform promises into public policy.

V.    Party Eras In American History (pp. 247-253)
  A.    Introduction
    1.    **Party eras** are long periods of time when one party has been the dominant majority party.
    2.    Party eras are punctuated by a **critical election.**
    3.    **Party realignment** is a rare event when the party system is transformed.
  B.    1796-1824:  The First Party System
  C.    1828-1856:  Jackson and the Democrats versus the Whigs
  D.    1860-1928:  The Two Republican Eras
    1.    1850s-1896, Republican Party as the antislavery party.
    2.    1896-1928, Republican Party as the party of the new working class and moneyed interests.
  E.    1932-1964:  The **New Deal Coalition,** following the Great Depression, a new Democratic coalition remained dominant for decades.
  F.    1968-Present:  The Era of Divided Government
    1.    **Party dealignment** means that people are moving away from both parties.
    2.    Recent dealignment has been characterized by a growing **party neutrality**.

VII.    **Third Parties:**  Their Impact on American Politics (pp. 254-256)
  A.    Parties that promote certain causes.
  B.    Splinter parties.
  C.    Parties that are an extension of a popular individual with presidential hopes.

VI.    Understanding Political Parties (pp. 256-260)
  A.    Democracy and Responsible Party Government, the **responsible party model** would make it easier to convert party promises into governmental policy.
  B.    Individualism and Gridlock
  C.    American Political Parties and the Scope of Government
  D.    Is the Party Over?

IX.   Summary (pp. 260-261)


**LEARNING OBJECTIVES**

*After studying Chapter 8, you should be able to:*

1.   Discuss the meaning and functions of a political party.

2.   Discuss the nature of the party-in-the-electorate, party organizations, and the party-in-government.

3.   Describe the party eras in American history and how parties realign and dealign.

4.   Evaluate the two-party system, its consequences, and the place of third parties in the system.

5.   Identify the challenges facing the American political parties and explain their relationship to American democracy, individualism, and the scope of government.


*The following exercises will help you meet these objectives:*

Objective 1.  Discuss the meaning and functions of a political party.

1.   Define the term "political party."


2.   Explain the three heads of the political party as a "three-headed political giant."

   1.


   2.


   3.


3.   What are the five tasks political parties should perform if they are to serve as effective linkage institutions?

1.

2.

3.

4.

5.

4.     Draw a graph or diagram depicting Anthony Downs' rational-choice model of political parties.

Objective 2. Discuss the nature of the party-in-the-electorate, party organizations, and the party-in-government.

1.     What has been the most prominent trend in party identification in recent years?

2.     What is meant by "ticket-splitting"?

3.     Draw an organizational chart of an American political party and then mark where most of the power actually exists.

4.     What is meant by a "party machine"?

5.      What is the difference between the following types of party primaries?

1.  closed primaries

2.  open primaries

3.  blanket primaries

6.      What is the function of each of the following national party organizations?

1. National Convention:

2. National Committee:

3. National Chairperson:

7.      What is the relationship between party promises and party performance?

Objective 3. Describe the party eras in American history and how parties realign and dealign.

1.      List four elections which might be considered "critical" or "realigning" and explain why.

1.

2.

3.

4.

2.      Complete the following table on party eras.

| Party Era | Major Party | Major Party Coalition | Minor Party | Minor Party Coalition | Prominent President(s) |
|-----------|-------------|-----------------------|-------------|-----------------------|------------------------|
| 1796-1824 | | | | | |
| 1828-1856 | | | | | |
| 1860-1892 | | | | | |
| 1896-1928 | | | | | |
| 1932-1964 | | | | | |

3.     List the six presidents since 1968 and complete the following table on divided government.

| President and Party Affiliation | Number Of Years With Republican Congress | Number Of Years With Democratic Congress |
|---------------------------------|------------------------------------------|------------------------------------------|
| | | |
| | | |
| | | |
| | | |
| | | |
| | | |
| | | |

4.     What is meant by "party neutrality"?

Objective 4. Evaluate the two-party system, its consequences, and the place of third parties in the system.

    1.       What are the three basic varieties of third parties?

          1.

          2.

          3.

    2.       What are two ways in which third parties can have an impact on American politics?

          1.

          2.

    3.       What is the most important consequence of two-party governance in the United States?

Objective 6. Identify the challenges facing the American political parties, and explain their relationship to American democracy, individualism, and the scope of government.

    1.       List the four conditions that advocates of the responsible party model believe the parties should meet.

          1.

          2.

          3.

          4.

    2.       What is the major consequence of the prominence of individualism within American political parties?

3.	How does the American party system affect the scope of government?


4.	What is the key problem of the American political parties today?



## KEY TERMS

*Identify and Describe:*

party competition


political party


linkage institutions


party image


rational-choice theory


party identification


ticket-splitting


party machines

patronage

closed primaries

open primaries

blanket primaries

national convention

national committee

national chairperson

coalition

party eras

critical election

party realignment

New Deal Coalition

party dealignment

party neutrality

third parties

winner-take-all system

proportional representation

coalition government

responsible party model

*Compare and Contrast:*

political party and linkage institutions

party identification and ticket-splitting

party machines and patronage

closed primaries, open primaries, and blanket primaries


national convention, national committee, and national chairperson


party eras and critical election


party realignment and party dealignment


party realignment and New Deal Coalition


party dealignment and party neutrality


winner-take-all system and proportional representation



*Name That Term:*

1. The battle between the parties for the control of public offices.

   _____

2. The perception of what the Republicans and Democrats stand for.

   _____

3. This seeks to explain political processes and outcomes as consequences of purposive behavior.

   _____

4.      Voting with one party for one office and another for other offices.

_____

5.      One of the key inducements used by political machines.

_____

6.      A set of individuals and groups who support a political party.

_____

7.      Political party eras are punctuated by these.

_____

8.      Often a consequence of proportional representation; many European governments are ruled by these.

_____

9.      Examples of these include the Free Soil party, the Jobless party, and the American Independent party.

_____

10.     Advocates of this reform believe that it would make it easier for party promises to be turned into governmental policy.

_____

## USING YOUR UNDERSTANDING

1.      Investigate the party system of another Western democratic political system that is of interest to you, such as Great Britain. Try to identify the major features of the political parties in the system in terms of the party-in-the-electorate, the party as organization, and the party-in-government. Briefly describe what you found in comparison to the two-party system in the United States. Include a discussion of whether the party system is experiencing realignment, dealignment, or another form of change.

2.	Gerald Pomper's study of party platforms covered the years 1944-1976. Follow up on this study by examining the Republican Party platforms for 1980, 1984, 1988, and 2000 and the Democratic Party platforms for 1992 and 1996. Make a list of the promises made in the Republican platforms and compare them to the accomplishments of the Reagan, George Bush, and George W. Bush administrations. Make a list of the promises of the 1992 and 1996 Democratic platform and compare them to the policy initiatives of the Clinton administration. For the party not occupying the presidency, you might compare legislative initiatives by that party in Congress with their party platform. Evaluate the degree to which the parties keep the policy promises they set forth. If possible, look at public opinion polls to see if public opinion supports platform positions on key issues. Develop an analysis of the importance of party platforms in the electoral process and in making public policy.

## REVIEW QUESTIONS

*Check ☑ the correct answer:*

1.	The framers of the U.S. Constitution approved of the formation of political parties. ☐ True
☐ False

2.	Which of the following statements regarding political parties is FALSE?
☐ a.	The main goal of political parties is to try to win elections.
☐ b.	Party teams are well disciplined and single-minded.
☐ c.	Party leaders often disagree about policy.
☐ d.	Between elections the parties seem to all but disappear.

3.	The largest component of the political party is the
☐ a.	party-in-the-electorate.
☐ b.	party as an organization.
☐ c.	party-in-government.
☐ d.	local party machine.

4. The people who keep the party running between elections and make its rules are members of the
☐ a. party-in-the-electorate.
☐ b. party as an organization.
☐ c. party-in-government.
☐ d. local party machine.

5. Which of the following is NOT one of the four key linkage institutions?
☐ a. parties
☐ b. elections
☐ c. interest groups
☐ d. policymakers

6. According to Kay Lawson, the key tasks that parties perform, or should perform, include
☐ a. articulating policies.
☐ b. picking policymakers.
☐ c. running campaigns.
☐ d. all of the above.

7. The concept of party image is most important for parties to
☐ a. pick policymakers.
☐ b. run campaigns.
☐ c. give cues to voters.
☐ d. articulate party policies.

8. According to Anthony Downs, political parties and voters are both irrational.
☐ True
☐ False

9. According to the Downsian model, the most successful political parties would be
☐ a. extremely conservative.
☐ b. liberal.
☐ c. moderate.
☐ d. slightly conservative.

10. More than half of the population currently feels that important differences exist between the parties.
☐ True
☐ False

11. Party identification
    ☐ a. requires formal membership with one of the parties.
    ☐ b. is strongest for young Americans.
    ☐ c. has declined while there has been an upsurge of people identifying as independents.
    ☐ d. can always predict voting behavior.

12. In an era of growing political independence, the group with a growing attachment to the Democratic Party has been
    ☐ a. African Americans
    ☐ b. poor whites.
    ☐ c. Jews.
    ☐ d. Southerners.

13. For white Americans,
    ☐ a. the Republican party is the only party of choice.
    ☐ b. party abandonment for a nonpartisan stance is well advanced.
    ☐ c. party identification is stronger than ever.
    ☐ d. party membership is constant over time.

14. In America, ticket-splitting is
    ☐ a. rare.
    ☐ b. illegal.
    ☐ c. near an all-time high.
    ☐ d. a sign of party renewal.

15. Power in the American political parties is highly centralized.
    ☐ True
    ☐ False

16. Urban political machines depended on
    ☐ a. specific inducements.
    ☐ b. material inducements.
    ☐ c. patronage.
    ☐ d. all of the above.

17. The national parties are actually a loose aggregation of state parties.
    ☐ True
    ☐ False

18. State party organizations are better organized and have more funds than most national interest groups in Washington.
☐ True
☐ False

19. Primaries that allow voters to decide on election day whether they want to participate in the Democratic or Republican contests are called
☐ a. closed primaries.
☐ b. open primaries.
☐ c. blanket primaries.
☐ d. political primaries

20. The supreme power within each of the parties is the
☐ a. national chairperson.
☐ b. national convention.
☐ c. local party organization.
☐ d. president.

21. The day-to-day activities of the national party are the responsibility of the
☐ a. president.
☐ b. national committee.
☐ c. national chairperson.
☐ d. national convention.

22. Which of the following presidents failed to keep his campaign promise to balance the budget? (bonus)
☐ a. Lyndon Johnson
☐ b. Richard Nixon
☐ c. Jimmy Carter
☐ d. Ronald Reagan

23. Most promises by presidential candidates are kept once they take office.
☐ True
☐ False

24. Gerald Pomper found that party platforms
☐ a. do not predict party performance.
☐ b. are ignored after elections.
☐ c. consist of promises that are kept more often than not.
☐ d. are very similar for the two major parties.

25. Most democratic nations have a
☐ a. one-party system.
☐ b. two-party system.
☐ c. multi-party system.
☐ d. regional party system.

26. During party eras, one party is the dominant majority party for long periods of time.
☐ True
☐ False

27. Party eras are punctuated by
☐ a. critical election periods.
☐ b. party reforms.
☐ c. national party conventions.
☐ d. political coalitions.

28. Party realignment occurs with great frequency in American party politics.
☐ True
☐ False

29. The coalition behind the Democratic-Republican Party included
☐ a. Federalists.
☐ b. capitalists.
☐ c. farmers.
☐ d. silver interests.

30. More than anyone else, the person who founded the modern American political party was
☐ a. Alexander Hamilton.
☐ b. Andrew Jackson.
☐ c. Martin Van Buren.
☐ d. Abraham Lincoln.

31. Which of the following was NOT a part of the Republican era from 1860 to 1928?
☐ a. the battle to outlaw slavery
☐ b. the fight to establish the gold standard
☐ c. a shifting of party coalitions
☐ d. the New Deal

32. The New Deal was a political response to the
   - [ ] a. Great Depression.
   - [ ] b. Civil War.
   - [ ] c. rise of agrarian interests.
   - [ ] d. resurgence of capitalism.

33. Which of the following groups were NOT associated with the New Deal coalition?
   - [ ] a. Catholics and Jews
   - [ ] b. urban working classes
   - [ ] c. Republicans
   - [ ] d. intellectuals

34. Lyndon Johnson's programs to help the poor, dispossessed, and minorities are known as the
   - [ ] a. New Deal.
   - [ ] b. Fair Deal.
   - [ ] c. New Frontier.
   - [ ] d. Great Society.

35. The Democratic Party was torn apart in 1968 by
   - [ ] a. Johnson's War on Poverty.
   - [ ] b. Johnson's Vietnam War policies.
   - [ ] c. economic depression.
   - [ ] d. the Watergate scandal.

36. The recent party dealignment has been characterized by a
   - [ ] a. growing party neutrality.
   - [ ] b. dramatic decline in voter participation.
   - [ ] c. decline in party organization.
   - [ ] d. growth in the strength of third parties.

37. Party loyalty today is at an all-time high.
   - [ ] True
   - [ ] False

38. Which of the following observations about the parties today is FALSE?
   - [ ] a. In recent years, the party system has dealigned rather than realigned.
   - [ ] b. Party loyalty has declined.
   - [ ] c. Party dealignment has been characterized by a growing party neutrality.
   - [ ] d. Most Americans today have extremely negative attitudes toward the parties.

39.   Throughout American history, third parties have
      □ a.   developed as offshoots of a major party.
      □ b.   promoted specific causes.
      □ c.   developed as an extension of a popular presidential aspirant.
      □ d.   all of the above.

40.   Which of the following consequences is LEAST associated with third parties in America?
      □ a.   serving as safety valves for popular discontent
      □ b.   bringing new groups into the electorate
      □ c.   consistent victories in federal offices
      □ d.   "sending a message" to Washington

41.   Consequences of the two-party system include
      □ a.   increased political conflict.
      □ b.   moderation of conflict and policy ambiguity.
      □ c.   more distinct policy choices.
      □ d.   representation of extreme ideologies.

42.   The system in which whoever gets the most votes wins the election is called the
      □ a.   winner-take-all system.
      □ b.   proportional representation system.
      □ c.   coalition system.
      □ d.   multi-party system.

43.   The founding of the world's first party system in the United States was seen as a risky adventure in the unchartered waters of democracy.
      □ True
      □ False

44.   In a system that employs proportional representation,
      □ a.   whoever gets the most votes wins the election.
      □ b.   parties are awarded legislative seats in proportion to their votes.
      □ c.   every party gets represented in the legislature.
      □ d.   there is very little difference between the political parties.

45.   According to the responsible party model, which of the following is NOT one of the functions of the parties?
      □ a.   They should present distinct, comprehensive programs.
      □ b.   They should implement their programs once in office.
      □ c.   They should create a fragmented decisional system.
      □ d.   They should accept responsibility for the performance of government.

46. The 1991 Republican nominee for Governor of Louisiana who was denounced by Republican President George Bush was (bonus)
☐ a. George Wallace.
☐ b. David Duke.
☐ c. Ross Perot.
☐ d. David Mayhew.

47. Which of the following statements is FALSE?
☐ a. American parties are too decentralized to take a single national position and then enforce it.
☐ b. Party discipline in America has resulted in members of Congress voting with their party about 90 percent of the time.
☐ c. Most candidates are self-selected, gaining their nomination by their own efforts and not the party's.
☐ d. Parties do not have control over those who run under their labels.

48. A major consequence of individualism in American party politics is
☐ a. party cooperation in Congress.
☐ b. the need for coalition building.
☐ c. gridlock in policymaking.
☐ d. the growth of third party politics.

49. The lack of disciplined and cohesive parties in America explains much of why the scope of governmental activity is less in the United States compared to other established democracies.
☐ True
☐ False

50. Which of the following is NOT one of the contemporary rivals of the political parties?
☐ a. the media
☐ b. urban machines
☐ c. interest groups
☐ d. campaign technology

## ESSAY QUESTIONS

1. What is the meaning of a political party? What functions do parties in America perform? How well do you think they perform them, especially in comparison to other linkage institutions?

2.      What is the Downsian model of party government?  What are its limitations as a normative model for the American party system?

3.      How has party identification changed over the years and what affect has it had on elections?

4.      Describe the organization of the American political parties.  How do party politics at the local, state, and national levels differ?  Which level is most important and why?

5.      How did the American two-party system evolve?  How were coalitions important to this evolution?  Include in your answer a discussion of party eras and critical elections.

6.      What are the political and policy consequences of having a two-party system?  How have third parties made a difference?

7.      What is the responsible party model and what are its consequences for democracy?

8.      In what ways have the American political parties declined?  What are the principal rivals of the political parties?  Speculate on the future of political parties in America.

# Chapter 9

## NOMINATIONS AND CAMPAIGNS

### CHAPTER OUTLINE

I.   The Nomination Game (pp. 266-277)
    A.    Introduction
        1.    A **nomination** is a party's official endorsement of a candidate for office.
        2.    **Campaign strategy** is the way in which candidates attempt to manipulate each of these elements to achieve the nomination.
    B.    Deciding to Run
    C.    Competing for delegates, the goal of the nomination game is to win the majority of delegates' support at the **national party convention.**
        1.    The Caucus Road
            a.    A **caucus** is a meeting of state party leaders.
            b.    Caucuses usually are organized like a pyramid.
        2.    The Primary Road
            a.    In **presidential primaries**, voters in a state go to the polls and vote for a candidate or delegates pledged to one.
            b.    The **McGovern-Fraser Commission** had a mandate to make Democratic Party conventions more representative.
            c.    The proliferation of presidential primaries has transformed politics.
            d.    Politicians who are awarded convention seats on the basis of their position are known as **superdelegates**.
            e.    More states have moved their primaries up in the calendar in order to capitalize on media attention. (**frontloading**)
        3.    Evaluating the Primary and Caucus System
            a.    Disproportionate attention goes to the early caucuses and primaries.
            b.    Prominent politicians find it difficult to take time out from their duties to run.
            c.    Money plays too big a role in the caucuses and primaries.
            d.    Participation in primaries and caucuses is low and unrepresentative.
            e.    The system gives too much power to the media.
    D.    The Convention Send-off
        1.    Conventions are no longer dramatic; the winner is a foregone conclusion.
        2.    Conventions orchestrate a massive send-off for the candidates.
        3.    Conventions develop the party's policy positions (**party platform**) and promote representation.

II. The Campaign Game (pp. 277-281)
  A. The High-Tech Media Campaign
    1. The technique of **direct mail** helps identify potential supporters and contributions.
    2. Candidates use their advertising budget.
    3. Candidates get free attention as newsmakers.
  B. Organizing the Campaign
    1. Line up a campaign manager.
    2. Get a fund-raiser.
    3. Get a campaign counsel.
    4. Hire media and campaign consultants.
    5. Assemble a campaign staff.
    6. Plan the logistics.
    7. Get a research staff and policy advisors.
    8. Hire a pollster.
    9. Get a good press secretary.

III. Money and Campaigning (pp. 282-288)
  A. The Maze of Campaign Finance Reforms **(Federal Election Campaign Act, 1974)**.
    1. It created the **Federal Election Commission (FEC).**
    2. It provided public financing for presidential primaries and general elections.
    3. It limited presidential campaign spending.
    4. It required disclosure.
    5. It limited contributions.
    6. 1979 amendments placed no limits on **soft money.**
  B. The Proliferation of **Political Action Committees (PACs).**
  C. Are Campaigns Too Expensive?
  D. Does Money Buy Victory?

IV. The Impact of Campaigns (pp. 288-289)
  A. Campaigns have three potential effects: reinforcement, activation, and conversion.
  B. Factors that weaken campaigns' impact on voters include: **selective perception,** party identification, and incumbency.

V. Understanding Nominations and Campaigns (pp. 289-290)
  A. Are Nominations and Campaigns Too Democratic?
  B. Do Big Campaigns Lead to an Increase in the Scope of Government?

VIII. Summary (pp. 291-292)

## LEARNING OBJECTIVES

*After studying Chapter 9, you should be able to:*

1.  Explain the nomination process and the role of the national party conventions.

2.  Discuss the role of campaign organizations and the importance of the media in campaigns.

3.  Understand the role of money in campaigns, campaign finance reform, and the impact of political action committees.

4.  Explain the impact of campaigns on the voters.

5.  Understand how campaigns affect democracy, public policy, and the scope of government.


*The following exercises will help you meet these objectives:*

Objective 1.  Explain the nomination process and the role of the national party conventions.

1.  List the three elements needed for success in the nomination game.

    1.

    2.

    3.


2.  Draw a diagram depicting the pyramid structure of the typical state party caucus.


3.  What reforms did the McGovern-Fraser Commission bring to the Democratic Party?

4.       List five criticisms of the primary and caucus system.

1.

2.

3.

4.

5.

5.       What are the primary functions of the national party conventions?

Objective 2. Discuss the role of campaign organizations and the importance of the media in campaigns.

1.       What are the two factors that determine media coverage of a campaign?

1.

2.

2.       Using a rating system of strong, medium, and weak, rate campaign advertisement and campaign news coverage in terms of their attention to candidate image, issues, and the campaign itself.

|          | Campaign Advertisements | Campaign News Coverage |
|----------|-------------------------|------------------------|
| Image    |                         |                        |
| Issues   |                         |                        |
| Campaign |                         |                        |

3.       List nine things candidates must do to effectively organize their campaigns.

        1.

        2.

        3.

        4.

        5.

        6.

        7.

        8.

        9.

Objective 3. Understand the role of money in campaigns, campaign finance reform, and the impact of political action committees.

1.       What were the main features of the Federal Election Campaign Act of 1974?

        1.

        2.

        3.

        4.

        5.

2.       Present an argument that political action committees are essential to a successful campaign.

Objective 4. Explain the impact of campaigns on the voters.

    1.       What are the three effects campaigns can have on voters?

          1.

          2.

          3.

    2.       What three factors tend to weaken campaigns' impacts on voters?

          1.

          2.

          3.

Objective 5. Understand how campaigns affect democracy, public policy, and the scope of government.

    1.       What is meant by the "permanent campaign"?

    2.       How might campaigns affect the scope of government?

**KEY TERMS**

*Identify and Describe:*

nomination

campaign strategy

national party convention

caucus

presidential primaries

McGovern-Fraser Commission

superdelegates

frontloading

party platform

direct mail

Federal Election Campaign Act

Federal Election Commission (FEC)

soft money

Political Action Committees (PACs)


selective perception


*Compare and Contrast:*

nomination and national party convention


caucus and presidential primaries


McGovern-Fraser Commission and superdelegates


Federal Election Campaign Act and Federal Election Commission



*Name That Term:*

1.      The way in which candidates attempt to manipulate resources to achieve their party's nomination.

        _____


2.      A meeting of state party leaders.

        _____


3.      Moving a state primary earlier in the calendar year to take advantage of media attention.

        _____

4.  A bipartisan body that administers the campaign finance laws.

    _____

5.  These party contributions are not presently subject to contribution limits.

    _____

6.  These organizations must register with the FEC and make meticulous reports about their expenditures.

    _____

7.  When people pay most attention to things they already agree with and interpret events according to their own predispositions.

    _____


## USING YOUR UNDERSTANDING

1.  Present an analysis of the 2000 presidential campaign in terms of what you have learned in this chapter. In particular, compare the three candidates in terms of their campaign organization, their access to and use of money, their use of the media, and their attention to the issues. Did PAC money make a difference in the campaign? Which candidate received the most PAC money? Did the media treat the candidates differently? Which candidate do you believe was able to use the media most effectively and why? How did the campaign of independent candidate Ralph Nader compare to that of Al Gore and George W. Bush who had political party organizations behind them?

2.  Find out which political action committees contribute to the member of Congress from your district and the two senators from your state. Determine what issues these PACs are most concerned with and investigate how your representative and senators voted on policies that would be relevant to the PACs' interests. Make a table or graph to illustrate your findings and use your results as the basis for a discussion of the relationship between members of Congress and political action committees.

## REVIEW QUESTIONS

*Check ☑ the correct answer:*

1.  A political party's official endorsement of a candidacy for office is called
    - ☐ a.  a campaign.
    - ☐ b.  an election.
    - ☐ c.  a platform.
    - ☐ d.  a nomination.

2.  Which of the following is NOT a key element of campaign strategy?
    - ☐ a.  momentum
    - ☐ b.  money
    - ☐ c.  mediocracy
    - ☐ d.  media attention

3.  The presidential campaign game
    - ☐ a.  lasts only a few weeks.
    - ☐ b.  is limited to two contenders.
    - ☐ c.  is not played by every politician.
    - ☐ d.  is given scant media attention.

4.  Who said that to run for president a person needs "fire in the belly"?  (bonus)
    - ☐ a.  George Romney
    - ☐ b.  Walter Mondale
    - ☐ c.  Richard Nixon
    - ☐ d.  Colin Powell

5.  The vast majority of presidential candidates since 1972 have been
    - ☐ a.  senators and governors.
    - ☐ b.  businessmen and generals.
    - ☐ c.  ministers and teachers.
    - ☐ d.  college professors and scientists.

6.  The number of roads to the national party convention is about
    - ☐ a.  2.
    - ☐ b.  50.
    - ☐ c.  100.
    - ☐ d.  2,000.

7. Delegates to the national party convention are determined by
   - ☐ a. a general election.
   - ☐ b. presidential primaries.
   - ☐ c. state party caucuses.
   - ☐ d. both b. and c.

8. Once, all state parties selected their delegates to the national party convention in caucuses.
   - ☐ True
   - ☐ False

9. Which of the following characteristics is NOT associated with today's state caucuses?
   - ☐ a. a private meeting of party elites
   - ☐ b. open meetings and wide participation
   - ☐ c. strict adherence to complex rules of representation
   - ☐ d. a pyramid selection process

10. In selecting delegates to the national party convention, most states use
    - ☐ a. party bosses.
    - ☐ b. caucuses.
    - ☐ c. debates.
    - ☐ d. presidential primaries.

11. The purpose of the McGovern-Fraser Commission was to
    - ☐ a. regenerate the Republican party organization.
    - ☐ b. conduct an investigation of the 1968 convention riots in Chicago.
    - ☐ c. draft reforms to increase the representativeness of the Democratic National Convention.
    - ☐ d. choose superdelegates from among national party leaders.

12. Superdelegates to the Democratic National Convention
    - ☐ a. consist of minority groups previously not represented.
    - ☐ b. help restore an element of peer review to the process.
    - ☐ c. were established by the McGovern-Fraser Commission.
    - ☐ d. are observers only, without a formal vote.

13. The early caucuses and primaries get very little media attention relative to those later in the campaign.
    - ☐ True
    - ☐ False

14. Congress makes the laws determining the way in which primaries are set up and the delegates are allocated.
☐ True
☐ False

15. The first presidential primary takes place in
☐ a. Delaware.
☐ b. New Hampshire.
☐ c. Maine.
☐ d. Virginia.

16. The Iowa caucus and the New Hampshire primary play a disproportionate role in
☐ a. building momentum.
☐ b. generating money.
☐ c. generating media attention.
☐ d. all of the above.

17. Running for the presidency is a full-time job.
☐ True
☐ False

18. The percentage of voters who turn out for the presidential primaries is about
☐ a. 10 percent.
☐ b. 20 percent.
☐ c. 50 percent.
☐ d. 60 percent.

19. Voters in primaries and caucuses are highly representative of the electorate at large.
☐ True
☐ False

20. Most candidates are very critical of the present primary/caucus method of choosing presidential nominees.
☐ True
☐ False

21. Each of the following is an important function of the national party convention EXCEPT to
☐ a. nominate a candidate for president.
☐ b. develop the party's policy positions.
☐ c. select members of the electoral college.
☐ d. get the campaign rolling.

22. Most delegates to the national party convention are not committed to vote for a particular candidate.
☐ True
☐ False

23. Television networks have substantially scaled back their coverage of national party conventions.
☐ True
☐ False

24. Which of the following is central to the success of a campaign?
☐ a. a campaign organization
☐ b. money
☐ c. media attention
☐ d. all of the above

25. What president said, " How does this damned thing work, anyway?" when referring to a TelePrompTer? (Bonus)
☐ a. Franklin Roosevelt
☐ b. Dwight Eisenhower
☐ c. John Kennedy
☐ d. Richard Nixon

26. Which of the following statements is FALSE?
☐ a. Advertising and news coverage are central to media attention to campaigns.
☐ b. Most television advertising has little to do with salient campaign issues.
☐ c. Candidates have less control over news coverage than advertising.
☐ d. More political news has to do with campaign details than the policy positions of candidates.

27. Newspapers and newsmagazines pay little attention to the campaign itself in favor of comprehensive coverage of the issues.
☐ True
☐ False

28. The political candidate can handle most of the tasks of a campaign without assistance.
☐ True
☐ False

29. Which of the following is NOT a part of the Federal Election Campaign Act, as amended?
   - ☐ a. partial public financing for candidates
   - ☐ b. disclosure of contributions
   - ☐ c. limits on contributions
   - ☐ d. elimination of Political Action Committees (PACs)

30. The Supreme Court case of *Buckley v. Valeo* (1976)
   - ☐ a. limited the amount individuals could contribute to their own campaigns.
   - ☐ b. extended the right of free speech to PACs.
   - ☐ c. required PACs to register with the FEC.
   - ☐ d. declared the Federal Election Campaign Act unconstitutional.

31. The formation of a Political Action Committee (PAC) makes it possible to avoid reporting expenditures to the Federal Election Commission (FEC).
   - ☐ True
   - ☐ False

32. In return for contributions, Political Action Committees (PACs) hope to gain
   - ☐ a. campaign finance reform.
   - ☐ b. access to officeholders.
   - ☐ c. bribes.
   - ☐ d. recognition for public service.

33. Which of the following statements about Political Action Committees is FALSE?
   - ☐ a. There is no data to support the contention that PACs can "buy" Congress.
   - ☐ b. Most PACs support those who agree with them in the first place.
   - ☐ c. Presidents are particularly vulnerable to PAC influence.
   - ☐ d. Candidates need PACs because high-tech campaigning is expensive.

34. American elections cost, per person, about as much as an audio CD.
   - ☐ True
   - ☐ False

35. The most important ingredient of electoral success is
   - ☐ a. having enough money to get a message across.
   - ☐ b. outspending opponents.
   - ☐ c. getting interest group endorsements.
   - ☐ d. kissing babies.

36. The LEAST frequent consequence of campaigns for voters is
☐ a. reinforcement.
☐ b. activation.
☐ c. conversion.
☐ d. both a. and b.

37. Which of the following does NOT weaken the impact of campaigns?
☐ a. selective perception
☐ b. the advantage of incumbents
☐ c. party identification
☐ d. close elections

38. Campaigns today tend to promote individualism in American politics.
☐ True
☐ False

39. To secure votes from each region and state of the country, candidates
☐ a. promise to reduce government programs and spending.
☐ b. develop a national policy platform.
☐ c. end up supporting a variety of local interests.
☐ d. avoid talking about local issues.

## ESSAY QUESTIONS

1. How is a candidate nominated for the presidency? What functions do national party conventions perform? What criticisms have been raised about the nomination process? Is it a representative process?

2. What are the elements of a successful political campaign? What impacts do campaigns have on voters? What factors tend to weaken these impacts?

3. What is the role of money in campaigns? What campaign finance reforms have been adopted? What effects have they had?

4. What are the positive and negative features of Political Action Committees? How might they affect politicians and policymaking?

5. How do campaign images and issues conflict; or do they? What is the role of the media in shaping both?

6. How do campaigns affect democracy, public policy, and the scope of government?

# Chapter 10

## ELECTIONS AND VOTING BEHAVIOR

### CHAPTER OUTLINE

I.    How American Elections Work (pp. 296-297)
    A.    Elections socialize and institutionalize political activity and provide regular access to political power, thus establishing **legitimacy**.
    B.    A **referendum** gives voters the chance to approve or disapprove some legislative act or constitutional amendment.
    C.    **Initiative petitions** enable voters to put proposed legislation on the ballot.

II.    A Tale Of Three Elections (pp. 297-302)
    A.    1800: The First Electoral Transition of Power
    B.    1896: A Bitter Fight Over Economic Interests
    C.    2000: What a Mess!

III.    Whether To Vote: A Citizen's First Choice (pp. 303-309)
    A.    Deciding Whether to Vote
        1.    The costs of voting may rationally outweigh the benefits.
        2.    People who see policy differences in the parties are more likely to vote.
        3.    People with a high sense of **political efficacy** are more likely to vote.
        4.    People with a high sense of **civic duty** are more likely to vote.
    B.    Registering to Vote
        1.    **Voter registration** procedures currently differ greatly from state to state.
        2.    The 1993 **Motor Voter Act** requires states to permit people to register at the same time they apply for driver's licenses.
    C.    Who Votes?
        1.    People with a higher education vote more regularly.
        2.    Older people vote more regularly than younger people.
        3.    African Americans and Hispanics vote less regularly.
        4.    Women vote slightly more regularly than men.
        5.    Married people are more likely to vote than nonmarried.
        6.    People who move often are less likely to vote.
        7.    Union members vote more than nonunion members.
    D.    The Political Consequences of Turnout Bias

IV.    How Americans Vote: Explaining Citizens' Decisions (pp. 309-314)
    A.    The **mandate theory of elections** suggests that the winner has a mandate to carry out promised policies.
    B.    Party Identification provides a perspective through which voters can view the political world.
    C.    Candidate Evaluations: How Americans see the Candidates
    D.    **Policy Voting** occurs when people base their choices in an election on their own issue preferences.

V.    The Last Battle: The **Electoral College** (p. 314)

VI.    Understanding Elections and Voting Behavior (pp. 314-317)
    A.    Democracy and Elections
        1.    The greater the policy differences between the candidates, the more likely voters will be able to steer government policies by their choices.
        2.    People who feel better off than before will vote for candidates who pledge to continue the status quo, those who feel worse off will vote for the opposition (**retrospective voting**).
    B.    Elections and the Scope of Government

VII.    Summary (p. 317)


## LEARNING OBJECTIVES

*After studying Chapter 10, you should be able to:*

1.    Explain the functions and unique features of American elections.

2.    Describe how American elections have evolved using the presidential elections of 1800, 1896, and 2000 as examples.

3.    Discuss the factors that affect a citizen's choice of whether to vote.

4.    Explain how Americans vote and what factors influence how they vote.

5.    Explain how the electoral college works and what biases it can introduce.

6.    Understand how elections affect democracy, public policy, and the scope of government.

*The following exercises will help you meet these objectives:*

Objective 1. Explain the functions and unique features of American elections.

1.     List the three kinds of elections found in the United States and their purpose.

     1.

     2.

     3.

2.     What is the difference between an initiative petition and a referendum?

Objective 2. Describe how American elections have evolved using the presidential elections of 1800, 1896, and 2000.

1.     Complete the following table on the elections of 1800, 1896, and 2000.

| Year | Candidates and Party | Winner | Major Issues | Campaign Style | Significance of Election |
|------|---------------------|--------|--------------|----------------|--------------------------|
| 1800 | | | | | |
| 1896 | | | | | |
| 2000 | | | | | |

2.   Briefly summarize the positions of the three candidates in the 1996 presidential election concerning economic policy.

Al Gore:

George W. Bush:

Ralph Nader:

Objective 3. Discuss the factors that affect a citizen's choice of whether to vote.

1.     List three major reasons why people might vote.

       1.

       2.

       3.

2.     What is the major provision of the 1993 Motor Voter Act?

3.     List and explain seven demographic factors that are related to voter turnout.

       1.

       2.

       3.

       4.

       5.

       6.

       7.

Objective 4. Explain how Americans vote and what factors influence how they vote.

   1.     What is meant by the "mandate theory of elections"?

   2.     How has the influence of party identification on voting changed since the 1950s?

3.  What are the three most important dimensions of candidate image?

    1.

    2.

    3.

4.  What are the three conditions necessary for true policy voting to take place?

    1.

    2.

    3.

Objective 5. Explain how the electoral college works and what biases it can introduce.

    1.  Briefly explain how the electoral college works.

    2.  What are the two reasons why the electoral college is important to presidential elections?

        1.

        2.

Objective 6. Understand how elections affect democracy, public policy, and the scope of government.

    1.  What are the two tasks that elections accomplish, according to democratic theory?

1.

2.

2.     According to the text, what is the clearest way in which elections broadly affect public policy?

3.     What does retrospective voting mean?

## KEY TERMS

*Identify and Describe:*

legitimacy

referendum

initiative petition

suffrage

political efficacy

civic duty

voter registration

Motor Voter Act

mandate theory of elections

policy voting

electoral college

retrospective voting

*Compare and Contrast:*

initiative petition and referendum

suffrage and voter registration

voter registration and Motor Voter Act

policy differences and civic duty


mandate theory of elections and policy voting


*Name That Term:*

1.   A term used to describe elections that are almost universally accepted as a fair and free method to select political leaders.

     _____

2.   This enables voters in twenty-three states to put proposed legislation on the ballot.

     _____

3.   It varies among the states and tends to dampen voter turnout.

     _____

4.   This reflects the belief that one's vote can make a difference.

     _____

5.   Politicians are more attracted to this idea than are political scientists.

     _____

6.   A unique American institution created by the Constitution.

     _____

7.   When voters essentially ask the simple question, "What have you done for me lately?"

     _____

## USING YOUR UNDERSTANDING

1. The text points out that the United States has one of the lowest voter turnout rates among all democratic nations. Examine the reasons why voter turnout is so low and outline a comprehensive plan that would increase voter turnout in the United States. What policies need to be changed to increase voter turnout? How might incentives be used to get people to vote? You might want to look at voting laws in other countries with high turnout rates to get ideas. Also include an examination of the Motor Voter Act. Speculate on how the Motor Voter Act might increase participation. What are the main criticisms of the Motor Voter Act? Comment on how your suggestions might be implemented.

2. Find out about electoral turnout in your state for the 1998 and 2000 elections. How did the participation rates for various population groups (based on race, income, region, etc.) differ? Compare your state's voting rate to the national turnout rate and to that of other states. How well does your state fare? See if you can identify some of the demographic features of your state that might help explain its rate of turnout, such as its size, urbanization, or population composition. How did participation rates differ between 1998 and 2000 and why? How might the voter registration system in your state affect turnout? Briefly describe what you found and suggest ways to improve electoral participation.

## REVIEW QUESTION

*Check ☑ the correct answer:*

1. Elections serve the purpose of
   ☐ a. socializing and institutionalizing political activity.
   ☐ b. providing regular access to political power.
   ☐ c. providing a legitimate means to replace leaders.
   ☐ d. all of the above.

2. In the United States, elections are used to
   ☐ a. select party nominees.
   ☐ b. select officeholders.
   ☐ c. make or ratify legislation.
   ☐ d. all of the above.

3. Voters in some states can put a proposed law on the ballot with
   - ☐ a. an initiative petition.
   - ☐ b. an opinion poll.
   - ☐ c. a referendum.
   - ☐ d. a three-fifths vote.

4. A referendum is used to give voters a chance to approve a proposed legislative act or constitutional amendment.
   - ☐ True
   - ☐ False

5. In the election of 1800,
   - ☐ a. candidates were nominated at national conventions.
   - ☐ b. the focus of the campaign was on the voters.
   - ☐ c. the candidate with the second highest number of electoral votes became vice-president.
   - ☐ d. media coverage was extensive.

6. In the election of 1896, the Republicans supported
   - ☐ a. low tariffs.
   - ☐ b. the gold standard.
   - ☐ c. rural farmers in debt.
   - ☐ d. unlimited coinage of silver.

7. Which candidate traveled through 26 states and logged 18,000 miles? (bonus)
   - ☐ a. William McKinley
   - ☐ b. Grover Cleveland
   - ☐ c. John Adams
   - ☐ d. William Jennings Bryan

8. Voter turnout in 1896 approached
   - ☐ a. 20 percent.
   - ☐ b. 60 percent.
   - ☐ c. 50 percent.
   - ☐ d. 80 percent.

9. The election of 2000 boiled down to who would win the state of
   - ☐ a. California.
   - ☐ b. Pennsylvania.
   - ☐ c. Florida.
   - ☐ d. New York.

10. The courts played a pivotal role in the 2000 election for the first time ever.
☐ True
☐ False

11. In 2000, Ralph Nader argued that the Republican and Democratic parties
☐ a. were both too liberal for the American people.
☐ b. were controlled by labor groups.
☐ c. focused too much on international issues.
☐ d. were dominated by corporate interests.

12. The 2000 election marked the first time since 1888 that the winner of the popular vote lost the electoral college count.
☐ True
☐ False

13. A paradox in American electoral history is that while suffrage has expanded,
☐ a. fewer Americans exercise the right to vote.
☐ b. participation in elections has increased,
☐ c. people place greater value on their right to vote.
☐ d. fewer people are eligible to vote.

14. Rational people might decide that the costs of voting outweigh the benefits.
☐ True
☐ False

15. Which of the following factors is NOT central to the decision of whether or not to vote?
☐ a. perceived policy differences between the parties
☐ b. the knowledge that most elections are extremely close
☐ c. a sense of political efficacy
☐ d. a sense of civic duty

16. The belief that ordinary people can influence the government is known as
☐ a. political efficacy.
☐ b. rational behavior.
☐ c. civic duty.
☐ d. class-based voting.

17.     The voter registration system is
        ☐ a.   implemented by federal authorities.
        ☐ b.   more restrictive in northern states.
        ☐ c.   an important factor in low voter turnout.
        ☐ d.   the same in every state.

18.     The Motor Voter Act establishes national standards for voter registration for the
        first time in the United States.
        ☐ True
        ☐ False

19.     All other things being equal, who of the following individuals is most likely to
        vote?
        ☐ a.   a single person
        ☐ b.   a married union member
        ☐ c.   a high school drop out
        ☐ d.   a southern black

20.     African Americans and other minorities with high income and education levels
        vote with greater frequency than whites with high income and education.
        ☐ True
        ☐ False

21.     Politicians and political scientists agree on the relevance of the mandate theory of
        elections.
        ☐ True
        ☐ False

22.     Which of the following factors is NOT central to the decision of how to vote?
        ☐ a.   simplified registration procedures
        ☐ b.   party identification
        ☐ c.   candidate evaluation
        ☐ d.   policy voting

23.     In the 1950s, the single best predictor of a voter's decision of how to vote was
        ☐ a.   political efficacy.
        ☐ b.   policy voting.
        ☐ c.   party identification.
        ☐ d.   candidate evaluation.

24. A study by Rosenberg and McCafferty concluded that
   - ☐ a. a candidate's appearance and image has no real effect on voters.
   - ☐ b. policy voting has become the single most important determinant of how to vote.
   - ☐ c. it is possible to manipulate a candidate's appearance in a way that affects voters' choices.
   - ☐ d. party identification has all but disappeared as a determinant of how to vote.

25. Studies have shown that the most important dimension of candidate image is
   - ☐ a. integrity.
   - ☐ b. reliability.
   - ☐ c. competence.
   - ☐ d. all of the above.

26. Which of the following conditions is NOT central to policy voting?
   - ☐ a. a voter's clear view of his or her policy preferences
   - ☐ b. a voter's knowledge of where the candidates stand
   - ☐ c. a voter's party identification
   - ☐ d. a vote for the candidate whose positions match those of the voter

27. No longer can a candidate get a party's nomination without taking stands on the major issues of the day.
   - ☐ True
   - ☐ False

28. The electoral college system was created by
   - ☐ a. political practice.
   - ☐ b. political parties.
   - ☐ c. an act of Congress.
   - ☐ d. the Constitution.

29. Which of the following statements about the electoral college is FALSE?
   - ☐ a. It is used in many countries of the world.
   - ☐ b. Each state has as many electors as it has senators and representatives.
   - ☐ c. In most states, there is a winner-take-all system.
   - ☐ d. Electoral college votes are counted when the new congressional session opens in January.

30. Electoral college votes are cast in proportion to the popular vote for each candidate.
    ☐ True
    ☐ False

31. The electoral college is important to the presidential election because it
    ☐ a. introduces a bias into the campaign and electoral process.
    ☐ b. gives an advantage to big states.
    ☐ c. may result in the election of a president who did not receive the most popular votes.
    ☐ d. all of the above.

32. The electoral college system can introduce bias in the electoral process that favors
    ☐ a. rural states.
    ☐ b. small states.
    ☐ c. big states.
    ☐ d. states without big cities.

33. It is possible for the electoral college to choose a president who did not win a majority of the popular vote.
    ☐ True
    ☐ False

34. The greater the policy differences between the candidates, the more likely voters will be able to steer government policies by their choices.
    ☐ True
    ☐ False

35. Parties and candidates
    ☐ a. are skilled in the art of ambiguity.
    ☐ b. prefer to tackle the controversial issues.
    ☐ c. use the media for comprehensive issue coverage.
    ☐ d. always provide voters with sharp choices.

36. Who said that candidates should offer "a choice, not an echo"? (bonus)
    ☐ a. Jimmy Carter
    ☐ b. Barry Goldwater
    ☐ c. Benjamin Page
    ☐ d. Ronald Reagan

37. Retrospective voting refers to voting
   - ☐ a. by absentee ballot.
   - ☐ b. for an incumbent because the perception that his or her policies have made you better off.
   - ☐ c. according to party identification.
   - ☐ d. the same way year after year.

38. Because of retrospective voting, nothing makes incumbent politicians more nervous than the state of
   - ☐ a. foreign affairs.
   - ☐ b. the environment.
   - ☐ c. the economy.
   - ☐ d. all of the above.

39. Individuals who believe they can influence the government's actions are also more likely to believe, in turn, that the government should have more power.
   - ☐ True
   - ☐ False

## ESSAY QUESTIONS

1. What are the functions of elections in American society? What are some of the electoral features that are unique to the United States?

2. How has the American electoral system evolved? How did the election of 2000 contrast with elections of the past, particularly the elections of 1800 and 1896?

3. What is the electoral paradox of more suffrage and less participation? Why would we expect people to vote more today and why do they not do so? How does the voter registration system affect the decision to vote?

4. What factors determine why people choose to vote? What groups are most likely to vote and what groups are least likely to vote? What are the implications of these differences in electoral participation?

5. Why do people vote the way they do? Which reason do you believe is most important and why?

6.       What is the electoral college and how does it work?  What biases in the electoral process does it introduce?  Should the electoral college system be preserved or abolished?

7.       How do elections affect democracy, public policy, and the scope of government?

# Chapter 11

## INTEREST GROUPS

### CHAPTER OUTLINE

I.     The Role And Reputation Of Interest Groups (pp. 322-324)
    A.     Defining Interest Groups
        1.     An **interest group** is an organization of people with similar policy goals who enter the political process to try to achieve those aims.
        2.     Interest groups are often policy specialists, whereas parties are policy generalists.
    B.     Why Interest Groups Get Bad Press

II.    Theories Of Interest Group Politics (pp. 324-328)
    A.     Pluralism and Group Theory
        1.     **Pluralist theory** argues that interest group activity brings representation to all.
        2.     The group theory of politics contains several arguments.
            a.     Groups provide a key link between people and government.
            b.     Groups compete.
            c.     No one group is likely to become too dominant.
            d.     Groups usually play by the "rules of the game."
            e.     Groups weak in one resource can use another.
    B.     Elites and the Denial of Pluralism
        1.     **Elite theory** argues that a few groups, primarily the wealthy, have most of the power.
        2.     Groups are extremely unequal in power.
        3.     Awesome power is controlled by the largest corporations.
        4.     The power of a few is fortified by a system of interlocking directorates.
        5.     Corporate elites prevail when it comes to the big decisions.
    C.     Hyperpluralism and Interest Group Liberalism
        1.     **Hyperpluralist theory** asserts that too many groups are getting too much of what they want, resulting in a government policy that is often contradictory and lacking in direction.
        2.     Interest group liberalism refers to government's excessive deference to groups.
            a.     Groups have become too powerful in the political process as government tries to aid every conceivable interest.

b.     Interest group liberalism is aggravated by numerous **subgovernments**.

c.     Trying to please every group results in contradictory and confusing policy.

III.     What Makes An Interest Group Successful? (pp. 328-332)

    A.     The Surprising Ineffectiveness of Large Groups

       1.     A **potential group** is composed of all people who might be group members because they share some common interest.

       2.     An **actual group** is composed of those in the potential group who choose to join.

       3.     A **collective good** is something of value that cannot be withheld from a potential group member.

       4.     The **free-rider problem** occurs when members of the potential group share in benefits that members of the actual group work to secure.

       5.     **Olson's law of large groups** states that the larger the group, the further it will fall short of providing an optimal amount of a collective good.

       6.     **Selective benefits** are goods that a group can restrict to those who pay their yearly dues.

    B.     Intensity

       1.     Intensity is a psychological advantage that can be enjoyed by small and large groups alike.

       2.     A **single-issue group** is a group that has a narrow interest, dislikes compromise, and single-mindedly pursues its goal.

    C.     Financial Resources

IV.     The Interest Group Explosion (p. 332)

V.     How Groups Try To Shape Policy (pp. 333-339)

    A.     Lobbying

       1.     **Lobbying** is a communication, by someone other than a citizen acting on his or her own behalf, directed to a governmental decision-maker with the hope of influencing his or her decision.

       2.     Lobbyists can help a member of Congress

          a.     They are an important source of information.

          b.     They can help politicians with political strategy.

          c.     They can help formulate campaign strategy.

          d.     They are a source of ideas and innovations.

    B.     Electioneering

       1.     **Electioneering** consists of aiding candidates financially and getting group members out to support them.

       2.     **Political Action Committees (PACs)** provide a means for groups to participate in electioneering.

C. Litigation
  1.  ***Amicus curiae* briefs** consist of written arguments submitted to the courts in support of one side of a case.
  2.  **Class action lawsuits** enables a group of similarly situated plaintiffs to combine similar grievances into a single suit.
D. Going Public

VI. Types Of Interest Groups (pp. 339-345)
  A. Economic Interests
    1.  Labor
      a.  The **union shop** requires new employees to join the union representing them.
      b.  **Right-to-work laws** outlaw union membership as a condition of employment.
    2.  Agriculture
    3.  Business
  B. Environmental Interests
  C. Equality Interests
  D. Consumers and Public Interest Lobbies
    1.  **Public interest lobbies** are organizations that seek a collective good.
    2.  The consumer movement was spurred by the efforts of Ralph Nader.

VII. Understanding Interest Groups (pp. 346-348)
  A. Interest Groups and Democracy
  B. Interest Groups and the Scope of Government

VIII. Summary (pp. 348-349)


## LEARNING OBJECTIVES

*After studying Chapter 11, you should be able to:*

1.  Define interest groups and distinguish them from political parties.

2.  Compare and contrast the pluralist, elite, and hyperpluralist theories of interest groups.

3.  Explain what makes an interest group successful and why small groups have an advantage over large groups.

4.  Identify and describe the strategies that groups use to shape public policy.

5.      Describe some of the many types of groups in the American political system.

6.      Evaluate interest groups in terms of their influence on democracy and the scope of government.

*The following exercises will help you meet these objectives:*

Objective 1.  Define interest groups and distinguish them from political parties.

1.      Provide a definition of the term "interest group."

2.      Name two factors that distinguish interest groups from political parties.

1.

2.

Objective 2.  Compare and contrast the pluralist, elite, and hyperpluralist theories of interest groups.

1.      Complete the following table on the theories of interest group politics.

| Theory | Definition | Role of Groups | Who Holds Power | Group Impact on Public Policy |
|---|---|---|---|---|
| Pluralist Theory | | | | |
| Elite Theory | | | | |
| Hyper-pluralist Theory | | | | |

2.    List five essential arguments of the group theory of politics.

1.

2.

3.

4.

5.

3.    List four major points made by the elitist view of the interest group system.

1.

2.

3.

4.

4.     List the three major points of the hyperpluralist position on group politics.

   1.

   2.

   3.

Objective 3.  Explain what makes a group successful and why small groups have an advantage over large groups.

   1.     What is the difference between a potential group and an actual group?

   2.     What is Olson's law of large groups?

   3.     Define the term single-issue group and give an example.

Objective 4.  Identify and describe the strategies that groups use to shape public policy.

1.　　　List the four general strategies used by interest groups to shape public policy.

　　　　1.

　　　　2.

　　　　3.

　　　　4.

2.　　　What are the two basic types of lobbyists?

　　　　1.

　　　　2.

3.　　　List four important ways lobbyists can help a member of Congress

　　　　1.

　　　　2.

　　　　3.

　　　　4.

4.　　　Why does PAC money go so overwhelmingly to incumbents?

5.　　　What is an *amicus curiae* brief?

Objective 5. Describe some of the many types of groups in the American political system.

    1.        What was the main purpose of the Taft-Hartley Act?

    2.        What are the two main organizations that speak for corporations and business?

           1.

           2.

    3.        What is meant by a public interest lobby?

    4.        List three items environmental groups have promoted and three items they have opposed.

           Promoted:

           1.

           2.

           3.

           Opposed:

           1.

           2.

           3.

    5.        Name two important organizations involved in promoting equality and summarize their major goals.

           1.

2.

Objective 6. Evaluate interest groups in terms of their influence on democracy and the scope of government.

    1.       Summarize the pluralist, elitist, and hyperpluralist perspectives on interest groups and democracy.

        1. Pluralist:

        2. Elitist:

        3. Hyperpluralist:

    2.       How do interest groups affect the scope of government?

**KEY TERMS**

*Identify and Describe:*

interest group

pluralist theory

elite theory

hyperpluralist theory

subgovernments

potential group

actual group

collective good

free-rider problem

Olson's law of large groups

selective benefits

single-issue group

lobbying

electioneering

Political Action Committees (PACs)

*amicus curiae* briefs

class action lawsuits

union shop

right-to-work laws

public interest lobbies

*Compare and Contrast:*

pluralist theory, elite theory, and hyperpluralist theory

hyperpluralist theory and subgovernments

potential group and actual group

collective good and free-rider problem


Olson's law of large groups and selective benefits


lobbying and electioneering


electioneering and Political Action Committees


*amicus curiae* briefs and class action lawsuits


union shop and right-to-work laws


*Name That Term:*

1. An organization of people with similar policy goals entering the political process to try to achieve those goals.

   _____

2. These are also known as iron triangles.

   _____

3. There are usually more members in this group than in the actual group.

   _____

4. When it is easier to not join a group because you will receive the benefits anyway.

_____

5. "The larger the group, the further it will fall short of providing an optimal amount of a collective good."

_____

6. People in this group tend to dislike compromise and single-mindedly pursue their goal.

_____

7. In recent years, these have provided a means for groups to participate in electioneering more than ever before.

_____

8. This enables a group of similarly situated plaintiffs to combine similar grievances into a single suit.

_____

9. These organizations seek a collective good that will not selectively benefit the membership of the organization.

_____

## USING YOUR UNDERSTANDING

1. Investigate an interest group that is of interest to you. Contact the group to see if they can provide information on the group and its policy goals. Find out how the group's actual membership compares to its potential membership. Try to identify the strategies that the group uses in trying to achieve its policy goals. Briefly describe what you found in terms of how well the group is achieving its goals and forging a link between people and policy.

2. Using newspapers or newsmagazines, collect some current examples of group involvement in the policy process. Try to find examples of various types of groups—groups in different policy arenas, public interest lobbies, and single-issue

groups. Analyze each example in terms of the policy-making area in which group activity was focused (e.g., electoral, legislative, administrative, or judicial), strategies used by the group to affect policy, and the degree to which the group was successful in achieving its policy goals. Discuss whether or not your findings support the interpretation of groups provided by pluralist theory, elite theory, and hyperpluralist theory.

## REVIEW QUESTIONS

*Check ☑ the correct answer:*

1. Participation in both elections and interest groups has declined dramatically since 1960.
   ☐ True
   ☐ False

2. Interest groups have no formal Constitutional protections.
   ☐ True
   ☐ False

3. Interest groups differ from political parties because
   ☐ a. parties use technology more effectively.
   ☐ b. groups tend to be policy specialists while parties tend to be policy generalists.
   ☐ c. the group's main arena is the electoral system.
   ☐ d. parties seek many access points in government.

4. James Madison's derogatory term "faction" would include both political parties and interest groups.
   ☐ True
   ☐ False

5. The theory that argues that just a few groups have most of the power is the
   ☐ a. pluralist theory.
   ☐ b. elite theory.
   ☐ c. group theory of politics.
   ☐ d. hyperpluralist theory.

6. The group theory of politics
   ☐ a. is a part of traditional democratic theory.
   ☐ b. supports the idea that elites run the government.
   ☐ c. sees groups as an important linkage institution.
   ☐ d. states that groups have become too powerful.

7. Which of the following is NOT an essential part of the group theory of politics?
   ☐ a. Groups are extremely unequal in power.
   ☐ b. Groups usually play by the rules of the game.
   ☐ c. Groups weak in one resource can use another.
   ☐ d. Groups compete.

8. Public opinion polls have shown that most people believe that government is pretty much run by a few big interests looking out for themselves.
   ☐ True
   ☐ False

9. Which of the following statements about the elite theory perspective on groups is FALSE?
   ☐ a. Real power is held by relatively few key groups.
   ☐ b. The power of a few is fortified by an extensive system of interlocking directorates.
   ☐ c. The real game of group politics is the one played by the corporate elites.
   ☐ d. Groups provide an effective check on elite power.

10. According to elite theorists, interest group lobbying is a problem because
    ☐ a. it is open to too many groups.
    ☐ b. it benefits the few at the expense of the many.
    ☐ c. it disperses power among a wide range of groups.
    ☐ d. legislators have become immune to group pressures.

11. Interest-group liberalism is characterized by the philosophy that all interests are almost equally legitimate and the job of government is to advance them all.
    ☐ True
    ☐ False

12. Which of the following is NOT a part of subgovernments?
    ☐ a. interest group leaders
    ☐ b. interlocking directorates
    ☐ c. administrative agencies
    ☐ d. congressional committees and subcommittees

13. The Tobacco Institute, the Department of Agriculture, and the House Tobacco Subcommittee working together to protect the interest of tobacco farmers is a classic example of
☐ a. interlocking directorates.
☐ b. the group theory of politics.
☐ c. a subgovernment.
☐ d. elite control of government.

14. The hyperpluralist position on groups is that
☐ a. groups have become too powerful in the political process.
☐ b. interest group liberalism is aggravated by numerous subgovernments.
☐ c. the result of group conflict is contradictory and confusing policy.
☐ d. all of the above.

15. The larger the group, the
☐ a. more government support it receives.
☐ b. more it behaves like a party.
☐ c. less effective it is.
☐ d. more specialized it becomes.

16. Large groups have organizational advantages over small groups.
☐ True
☐ False

17. A potential group
☐ a. is composed of people who share a common interest.
☐ b. is usually smaller than an actual group.
☐ c. is composed of only active group members.
☐ d. always consists of all consumers.

18. Collective goods
☐ a. can be packaged and sold separately.
☐ b. can be withheld from any group member.
☐ c. are available only to members of the actual group who secure them.
☐ d. are shared by members of the potential group.

19. Free-riders
☐ a. are actual group members.
☐ b. avoid collective goods.
☐ c. aggravate large groups more than small groups.
☐ d. automatically share in group benefits.

20.     Which of the following matters could NOT be explained by Mancur Olson's law of large groups?
☐ a.    the problems of public interest lobbies
☐ b.    why small groups are easier to organize
☐ c.    why large groups are less effective
☐ d.    the successes of the Consumers Union

21.     Which of the following organizations has the largest potential membership? (bonus)
☐ a.    National Association for the Advancement of Colored People
☐ b.    National Organization for Women
☐ c.    Consumers Union
☐ d.    American Medical Association

22.     Goods that a group can restrict to those who pay their yearly dues are called
☐ a.    free-rider goods.
☐ b.    selective benefits.
☐ c.    collective goods.
☐ d.    actual benefits.

23.     Which of the following is NOT true of single-issue groups?
☐ a.    They are the same as public interest lobbies.
☐ b.    They have narrow interests.
☐ c.    They dislike compromise.
☐ d.    They single-mindedly pursue their goal.

24.     One of the most emotional issues to generate single-issue groups has been that of abortion.
☐ True
☐ False

25.     Critics charge that PACs distort the governmental process in favor of the largest groups in American society.
☐ True
☐ False

26. Which of the following statements regarding the Tax Reform Act of 1986 is FALSE?
☐ a. The Tax Reform Act eliminated all but a very few loopholes.
☐ b. The Tax Reform Act is a classic example of how PACs can influence votes.
☐ c. The Chairman of the Senate Finance Committee was Congress' top PAC recipient during the tax reform struggle.
☐ d. Senator Packwood turned against lobbyists trying to get his ear on behalf of various tax loopholes.

27. Technology has facilitated the explosion in the number of interest groups in the United States.
☐ True
☐ False

28. Which of the following is NOT among the strategies used by interest groups to shape public policy?
☐ a. lobbying
☐ b. litigation
☐ c. electioneering
☐ d. avoiding publicity

29. Lobbying
☐ a. is aimed at influencing decisionmaking.
☐ b. is confined solely to the legislative branch.
☐ c. was made illegal with the Federal Regulation of Lobbying Act.
☐ d. is most effective in converting legislators.

30. Which of following is NOT one of the ways that lobbyists can help a member of Congress?
☐ a. helping to formulate campaign strategy
☐ b. writing and introducing bills
☐ c. providing important information
☐ d. providing ideas and innovations

31. Lobbyists are relatively ineffective in winning over legislators who are opposed to their goals.
☐ True
☐ False

32. Which of the following statements regarding lobbying is FALSE?
☐ a. Studies have shown that lobbyists are particularly effective as information sources.
☐ b. There is plenty of evidence to suggest that sometimes lobbying can persuade legislators to support a certain policy.
☐ c. It is hard to isolate the effects of lobbying from other influences.
☐ d. Unlike campaigning, lobbying is directed primarily toward conversion activities.

33. Which of the following is generally NOT a major part of electioneering?
☐ a. providing financial aid to candidates, frequently through PACs
☐ b. encouraging group members to campaign for a favorite candidate
☐ c. running an interest group leader as a political candidate
☐ d. activating group members to vote for a favorite candidate

34. Most PAC contributions are given to challengers rather than incumbents.
☐ True
☐ False

35. Congressional candidate Steve Sovern organized a PAC called LASTPAC in order to (bonus)
☐ a. get PAC money since no other PAC would support him.
☐ b. urge candidates to shun PAC-backing.
☐ c. unite the PACs under one political organization.
☐ d. get other candidates to support the goals of the Legal Assistance Support Team (LAST).

36. Which of the following types of groups has NOT resorted to litigation as a strategy for affecting policy?
☐ a. groups interested in equality
☐ b. groups interested in the environment
☐ c. public interest lobbies
☐ d. none of the above

37. *Amicus curiae* briefs
☐ a. enable a group of similarly situated plaintiffs to combine similar grievances into a single suit.
☐ b. consist of written arguments submitted to the courts in support of one side of a case.
☐ c. are required before an interest group can sue for enforcement of a particular piece of legislation.
☐ d. are most often used by political action committees.

38. Most interest groups are not concerned with the opinions of people outside of their membership.
☐ True
☐ False

39. Public policy in America has economic effects through
☐ a. regulations.
☐ b. tax advantages.
☐ c. subsidies and contracts.
☐ d. all of the above.

40. Right-to-work laws are generally supported by
☐ a. business groups.
☐ b. labor unions.
☐ c. public interest groups.
☐ d. all of the above.

41. The concept of the "union shop" illustrates the seriousness of the free-rider problem for labor organizations.
☐ True
☐ False

42. Unlike small businesses, the family farm has remained the backbone of American agriculture.
☐ True
☐ False

43. The influence of business groups would best illustrate
☐ a. pluralist theory.
☐ b. elite theory.
☐ c. hyperpluralist theory.
☐ d. democratic theory.

44. Which of the following statements regarding business groups is FALSE?
☐ a. Business PACs have increased more dramatically than any other category of PACs.
☐ b. The National Association of Manufacturers and the Chamber of Commerce include most corporations and businesses.
☐ c. Business interests are generally unified when it comes to promoting greater profits.
☐ d. The specific trade and product associations are far more visible than the National Association of Manufacturers and the Chamber of Commerce.

45. Which of the following issues is NOT on the hit list of environmentalist groups?
☐ a. alternative energy sources
☐ b. strip mining
☐ c. offshore oil drilling
☐ d. supersonic aircraft

46. When the two public interests of environmental protection and an ensured supply of energy clash,
☐ a. group conflict intensifies.
☐ b. compromise is achieved.
☐ c. the need for energy always wins.
☐ d. groups play a secondary role to elite interests.

47. Today, civil rights groups are particularly concerned with affirmative action programs to ensure equal educational and employment opportunities.
☐ True
☐ False

48. Most recently, the National Organization for Women has been most active in
☐ a. getting the Equal Rights Amendment ratified.
☐ b. the enactment of individual statutes on equal rights for women.
☐ c. achieving equal voting rights.
☐ d. all of the above.

49. Organizations that seek a collective good, the achievement of which will not selectively and materially benefit the membership or activists of the organization, are called
☐ a. single-issue groups.
☐ b. public interest lobbies.
☐ c. political action committees.
☐ d. pluralistic groups.

50. Which of the following would NOT be considered a public interest lobby?
☐ a. Common Cause
☐ b. the Sierra Club
☐ c. the Chamber of Commerce
☐ d. the Moral Majority

51. James Madison
   - □ a. favored a wide-open system in which many groups would be able to participate to counterbalance one another.
   - □ b. wanted the Constitution to forbid the growth of groups and factions.
   - □ c. believed American society would be best served by a relatively small number of powerful groups.
   - □ d. believed that public interest groups were dangerous because the common man was not qualified to speak for the public interest.

52. Presidents Carter and Reagan both felt that interest groups were beneficial to their administrations and helped with policy formation.
   - □ True
   - □ False

## ESSAY QUESTIONS

1. What are interest groups? How do groups differ from political parties?

2. Compare and contrast the pluralist, elite, and hyperpluralist theories of interest groups. In your opinion, which theory best describes reality and why?

3. What is the difference between a potential group and an actual group? Why is this difference important to understanding the free-rider problem? Be sure to include a discussion of collective goods in your answer.

4. Why are small groups generally more effective than large groups? Explain Olson's law of large groups.

5. How do intensity and financial resources affect interest group success? What are single-issue groups and how effective have they been in American politics?

6. What are the principal strategies that groups use to affect policymaking? Which strategy seems to be the most effective, and why? Are certain strategies better suited for different types of interest groups?

7. What impact do political action committees have on interest group behavior? Evaluate the role of political action committees.

8.	What are the different types of interest groups?  What are their primary goals, what strategies do they use, and how successful have they been?

9.	How do interest groups affect democracy and the scope of government in the United States?

# Chapter 12

## CONGRESS

## CHAPTER OUTLINE

I.    The Representatives And Senators  (pp. 354-358)
    A.    The Job
    B.    The Members

II.   Congressional Elections  (pp. 358-364)
    A.    Who Wins Elections?
        1.    **Incumbents** are individuals who already hold office.
        2.    Incumbents usually win.
    B.    The Advantages of Incumbents
        1.    Advertising
        2.    Credit Claiming
            a.    **Casework** is helping constituents as individuals.
            b.    **Pork barrel** is the mighty list of federal projects, grants, and contracts available to cities, businesses, colleges, and institutions.
        3.    Position Taking
        4.    Weak Opponents
    C.    The Role of Party Identification
    D.    Defeating Incumbents
    E.    Money In Congressional Elections
    F.    Stability and Change

III.  How Congress Is Organized To Make Policy  (pp. 364-375)
    A.    American Bicameralism
        1.    A **bicameral legislature** is a legislature divided into two houses.
        2.    The House
            a.    The House is more institutionalized and less anarchic than the Senate.
            b.    The **House Rules Committee** reviews most bills coming from a House committee before they go to the full House.
        3.    The Senate
            a.    The Senate is less disciplined and centralized than the House.
            b.    **Filibusters** allow unlimited debate in the Senate until a vote for cloture halts a filibuster.

B.    Congressional Leadership
    1.    The House
        a.    The **Speaker of the House** is the most important leadership position in the House.
        b.    The **majority leader** is responsible for scheduling bills and rounding up votes in behalf of the party.
        c.    The party **whips** carry the word to party troops and help round up votes in behalf of the party.
        d.    The **minority leader** is responsible for party cohesion among the minority party members.
    2.    The Senate
        a.    The vice president of the United States is the president of the Senate.
        b.    Power is widely dispersed in the Senate.
    3.    Congressional Leadership in Perspective
C.    The Committees and Subcommittees
    1.    Types of committees
        a.    **Standing committees** are formed to handle bills in different policy areas.
        b.    **Joint committees** exist in a few policy areas and are composed of both House and Senate members.
        c.    **Conference committees** are formed when the Senate and House pass a particular bill in different forms.
        d.    **Select committees** are appointed for a specific purpose.
    2.    The Committees at Work: Legislation and Oversight
        a.    All bills go though a committee that has considerable power over the fate of the bill.
        b.    **Legislative oversight** is the process of monitoring the bureaucracy and its administration of policy.
    3.    Getting on a Committee
    4.    Getting Ahead on the Committee: Chairs and the Seniority System
        a.    **Committee chairs** are the most important influencers of the committee agenda.
        b.    The **seniority system** is the general rule for selecting chairs, but there are exceptions.
D.    Caucuses: The Informal Organization of Congress
    1.    A **caucus** is a grouping of members of Congress who share some interest or characteristic.
    2.    The explosion of caucuses has made the representation of interests in Congress a more direct process.
E.    Congressional Staff

## LEARNING OBJECTIVES

*After studying Chapter 12, you should be able to:*

1. Describe the characteristics of our senators and representatives, and the nature of their jobs.

2. Explain what factors have the greatest influence in congressional elections.

3. Explain the structure of power and leadership in the United States Congress, and the role of committees.

4. Identify what members of Congress do and discuss the congressional process and the many influences on legislative decisionmaking.

5. Evaluate Congress in terms of American democracy, congressional reforms, and the scope of government.

*The following exercises will help you meet these objectives:*

Objective 1.  Describe the characteristics of our senators and representatives, and the nature of their jobs.

    1.       List seven perks members of Congress receive.

          1.

          2.

          3.

          4.

          5.

          6.

          7.

    2.       Describe a "typical" member of Congress in terms of the following categories.

          Sex:

          Race:

          Age:

          Religion:

          Prior Occupation:

          Wealth:

    3.       What is the difference between descriptive and substantive representation?

          Descriptive:

          Substantive:

Objective 2. Explain what factors have the greatest influence in congressional elections.

1. List and explain four advantages incumbents have over their opponents in congressional elections.

   1.

   2.

   3.

   4.

2. What is the difference between casework and pork barrel?

   Casework:

   Pork barrel:

3. List and explain three ways that an incumbent might be defeated.

   1.

   2.

   3.

4. What are the main criticisms of political action committees?

5.      List three criticisms of term limitations.

      1.

      2.

      3.


Objective 3.  Explain the structure of power and leadership in the United States Congress, and the role of committees.

1.      What are the main functions of the House Rules Committee?


2.      List four formal powers of the Speaker of the House.

      1.

      2.

      3.

      4.


3.      List the four types of congressional committees.

      1.

      2.

      3.

4.

4.      What is meant by legislative oversight?

5.      How does the seniority system work?

6.      What is the difference between the personal staff and the committee staff?

7.      List three congressional staff agencies.

        1.

        2.

        3.

Objective 4.  Identify what members of Congress do and discuss the congressional process and the many influences on legislative decisionmaking.

    1.      Draw a diagram of how a bill becomes a law.

    2.      List the ten times a president must usually win in order to hope for final passage of his or her proposed legislation.

1.

2.

3.

4.

5.

6.

7.

8.

9.

10.

3.    What is the difference between trustees, instructed delegates, and politicos?

Trustees:


Instructed Delegates:


Politicos:

4.    List three ways Congress can frustrate the activities of lobbyists.

1.


2.


3.

Objective 5. Evaluate Congress in terms of American democracy, congressional reforms, and the scope of government.

    1.    What were the main reforms passed by the Republicans when they took control of the House in 1995?

    2.    How does the organization of Congress contribute to the expanding scope of government?

## KEY TERMS

*Identify and Describe:*

incumbents

casework

pork barrel

bicameral legislature

House Rules Committee

filibuster

Speaker of the House

majority leader

whips

minority leader

standing committees

joint committees

conference committees

select committees

legislative oversight

committee chairs

seniority system

caucus

bill

*Compare and Contrast:*

casework and pork barrel

majority leader, minority leader, and whips

standing committees and select committees

joint committees and conference committees

committee chairs and seniority system

*Name That Term:*

1. They usually win congressional elections.

   _____

2. Two houses.

   _____

224

3.  Unlimited debate in the U.S. Senate.

    _____

4.  Reviews most of the bills coming from a House committee before they go to the full House.

    _____

5.  He or she exercises substantial control over which bills get assigned to which committees in the House.

    _____

6.  This monitoring process is handled mainly through congressional hearings.

    _____

7.  A grouping of members of Congress sharing some interest.

    _____

8.  A proposed law, drafted in precise, legal language.

    _____


## USING YOUR UNDERSTANDING

1.  Investigate one or more of the members of Congress from your state or congressional district. Find out about their membership on congressional committees and their leadership positions. Also find out whether or not one of your members might be called a policy entrepreneur, because much of his or her political capital is invested in a particular cause or issue. See how well your representatives are doing in the media, whether or not they have achieved a reputation for servicing their constituency and representing it adequately in Washington. Do your representatives tend to act as trustees, delegates, or politicos on particular issues? Profile your representatives or Senators in terms of how well they seem to be performing their many duties.

2.  Study the legislative history of a particular law in a particular policy area. Trace the law from its original sources to its enactment. Try to find out when and

where the bill originated, where its support came from (the president, interest groups, etc.), how it was altered by congressional committees, who voted for it, and whether or not the president actually signed it into law. Assess how long the process took from beginning to end and how much the law changed during the process. How did the final product compare with the original intent? Evaluate the legislative process in terms of this particular law and your perspective on how the system works.

## REVIEW QUESTIONS

*Check ☑ the correct answer:*

1.    In recent years, Congress has been the true center of power in Washington.
   ☐ True
   ☐ False

2.    The foremost attraction to a congressperson's job is
   ☐ a.   power.
   ☐ b.   money.
   ☐ c.   easy work.
   ☐ d.   leisure time.

3.    Members of Congress use their virtually unlimited franking privileges to
   ☐ a.   pay staff salaries.
   ☐ b.   travel to their home state.
   ☐ c.   communicate with constituents.
   ☐ d.   get research services from the Library of Congress.

4.    Who of the following would NOT be allowed to take a seat in the Senate?
   ☐ a.   someone who was a citizen for ten years
   ☐ b.   someone who had been a resident of their state for only one year
   ☐ c.   a twenty-eight year old
   ☐ d.   none of the above

5.    Which of the following statements concerning members of Congress is FALSE?
   ☐ a.   The dominant occupation of members of Congress is law.
   ☐ b.   There is only one African American in the Senate.
   ☐ c.   Proportionately, women are well represented in Congress today.
   ☐ d.   Most members of Congress share the beliefs and attitudes of a large proportion of their constituents.

6. Most members of Congress are better at substantive representation than descriptive representation.
   ☐ True
   ☐ False

7. The single most important advantage when running for Congress is being
   ☐ a.   photogenic.
   ☐ b.   an incumbent.
   ☐ c.   better funded than the opponent.
   ☐ d.   a challenger.

8. Which of the following is NOT a reason for greater competition for senatorial seats in Congress?
   ☐ a.   Senators have less personal contact with their constituents.
   ☐ b.   Senators have more visibility and media coverage.
   ☐ c.   An entire state is usually less diverse than a single congressional district.
   ☐ d.   Senators tend to draw more visible challengers.

9. Most congressional incumbents have a strong feeling of vulnerability.
   ☐ True
   ☐ False

10. Incumbents do well in congressional elections because of
   ☐ a.   voter awareness of how members of Congress vote on important policy decisions.
   ☐ b.   presidential coattails.
   ☐ c.   favorable economic conditions.
   ☐ d.   advertising, credit-claiming, and position-taking.

11. For members of Congress, the principal goal of advertising is
   ☐ a.   raising money.
   ☐ b.   convincing other members to support their positions.
   ☐ c.   visibility.
   ☐ d.   avoiding constituents.

12. Issues play a greater role in House elections than in Senate elections.
   ☐ True
   ☐ False

13. Which of the following is NOT an incumbency advantage?
☐ a. credit-claiming
☐ b. position-taking on issues important to the constituency
☐ c. weak opponents
☐ d. scandal or a charge of corruption

14. When a state loses population, reapportionment is likely to favor the state's minority party.
☐ True
☐ False

15. It costs more to elect a Congress than to elect a president.
☐ True
☐ False

16. Which of the following statements about Political Action Committees (PACs) is FALSE?
☐ a. PACs contribute about a third of the funds raised by candidates for Congress.
☐ b. PACs sometimes make contributions after the election.
☐ c. Challengers receive more PAC money than incumbents.
☐ d. PACs make contributions to candidates because they want access to policymakers.

17. PACs will often give money to the winning candidate even if they supported his or her opponent during the election.
☐ True
☐ False

18. Money in congressional campaigns is more important to
☐ a. incumbents.
☐ b. challengers.
☐ c. members of the House.
☐ d. members from safe seats.

19. Safe seats in Congress make it more difficult for citizens to "send a message to Washington."
☐ True
☐ False

20.     A bicameral legislature is one that
- a.   uses committees.
- b.   has two houses.
- c.   is elected.
- d.   holds biannual sessions.

21.     The only state that does not have a bicameral legislature is (bonus)
- a.   California.
- b.   Texas.
- c.   Rhode Island.
- d.   Nebraska.

22.     The House of Representatives
- a.   is more centralized than the Senate.
- b.   is less hierarchical than the Senate.
- c.   is more likely to have party-line voting.
- d.   has fewer leaders than the Senate.

23.     The House Rules Committee
- a.   reviews most bills coming from a House committee.
- b.   schedules bills on the calendar.
- c.   allots time for debating bills.
- d.   all of the above.

24.     Setting the legislative agenda in the Senate is the responsibility of
- a.   the Rules Committee.
- b.   the president of the Senate.
- c.   party leaders.
- d.   the minority leader.

25.     Which of the following statements about filibusters is FALSE?
- a.   They are used in both houses.
- b.   They can tie up the legislative agenda.
- c.   They are used to talk a bill to death.
- d.   Rules adopted over the years make it easier to close off debate.

26.     Which of the following is NOT one of the roles of the Speaker of the House?
- a.   presiding over the House when it is in session
- b.   making committee assignments and appointing leaders
- c.   serving as vice president of the United States
- d.   influencing the assignment of bills to committees

27.    Which of the following is NOT among the roles of the House majority leader?
☐ a.    being the Speaker's principal party ally
☐ b.    scheduling bills in the House
☐ c.    rounding up votes along with the party whips
☐ d.    presiding over the House when it is in session

28.    Vice presidents usually ignore their senatorial chores, leaving power in the Senate up to party leaders.
☐ True
☐ False

29.    Who referred to himself as the "Majority Pleader"? (bonus)
☐ a.    President Ronald Reagan
☐ b.    Vice President Dan Quayle
☐ c.    Senator Robert Dole
☐ d.    House Speaker Tip O'Neil

30.    Members from both the House and Senate belong to
☐ a.    standing committees.
☐ b.    joint committees.
☐ c.    conference committees.
☐ d.    both b. and c.

31.    The Senate committee that looked into Watergate was a
☐ a.    standing committee.
☐ b.    joint committee.
☐ c.    conference committee.
☐ d.    select committee.

32.    Which of the following statements about committees is FALSE?
☐ a.    A committee's work is done when the marked-up bill is submitted to the full House or Senate.
☐ b.    Committee members often serve as floor managers.
☐ c.    Some standing committee members later become members of conference committees.
☐ d.    Legislative oversight keeps committee members busy monitoring bureaucratic agencies.

33. The process of monitoring the bureaucracy and its administration of policy is called
☐ a.　filibustering.
☐ b.　oversight.
☐ c.　caucus.
☐ d.　legislating.

34. Oversight does not give Congress any real power to pressure agencies to comply with their wishes.
☐ True
☐ False

35. Incentives for increasing oversight activities include
☐ a.　the increasing size and complexity of government.
☐ b.　tight budgets.
☐ c.　charges that the executive branch had become too powerful.
☐ d.　all of the above.

36. Members seek committees that will help them achieve all of the following goals EXCEPT
☐ a.　re-election.
☐ b.　influence in Congress.
☐ c.　more PAC money.
☐ d.　the opportunity to make policy in areas they think are important.

37. Committee chairs play a dominant role in
☐ a.　scheduling hearings.
☐ b.　hiring staff.
☐ c.　appointing subcommittees.
☐ d.　all of the above.

38. The seniority system is
☐ a.　based on party loyalty.
☐ b.　based on competence.
☐ c.　still the general rule for selecting committee chairs.
☐ d.　both a. and b.

39. The caucus is
☐ a.　the basis of the committee structure in Congress.
☐ b.　an informal group of members of Congress.
☐ c.　a formal group of members of Congress based strictly on party affiliation.
☐ d.　an interest group outside of Congress.

40. Personal staff help members of Congress with
   ☐ a.   constituent problems.
   ☐ b.   drafting legislation.
   ☐ c.   negotiating agreements
   ☐ d.   all of the above.

41. Bills can be formally submitted for consideration by
   ☐ a.   the president.
   ☐ b.   members of Congress.
   ☐ c.   interest groups.
   ☐ d.   all of the above.

42. Which of the following statements about presidents is FALSE?
   ☐ a.   They lobby through their congressional liaison office.
   ☐ b.   They have many resources to use in influencing Congress.
   ☐ c.   They are designated as the chief legislator by the Constitution.
   ☐ d.   They are both partners and antagonists with Congress.

43. George Edwards points out that presidential leadership of Congress is
   ☐ a.   at the margins.
   ☐ b.   insignificant.
   ☐ c.   at an all time high.
   ☐ d.   totally dominant.

44. Differences between the parties are sharpest on questions of social welfare and economic policy.
   ☐ True
   ☐ False

45. Edmund Burke favored the concept of a legislator as
   ☐ a.   instructed delegate.
   ☐ b.   constituent.
   ☐ c.   trustee.
   ☐ d.   politico.

46. The greatest way for constituents to influence members of Congress is to
   ☐ a.   answer public opinion polls.
   ☐ b.   write to them.
   ☐ c.   vote for candidates who match their positions.
   ☐ d.   join a single-issue group.

47. Which of the following statements is FALSE?
☐ a. It is difficult even for well-intentioned legislators to know what people want.
☐ b. Legislators whose votes are out-of-step with the views of their constituents are rarely re-elected.
☐ c. On obscure issues, legislators can safely ignore constituency opinion.
☐ d. On a typical issue, the prime determinant of a congressional member's vote is personal ideology.

48. Which of the following statements about lobbying is FALSE?
☐ a. Lobbyists have a dismal image.
☐ b. Lobbyists can provide members of Congress with information and campaign contributions.
☐ c. Congress has not attempted to regulate lobbyists.
☐ d. Members of Congress can ignore lobbyists.

49. John Kingdon found that no single influence was important enough to determine a congressperson's votes.
☐ True
☐ False

50. Which of the following statements about Congress is FALSE?
☐ a. Some aspects of Congress are very unrepresentative.
☐ b. Citizens have a direct role in determining leadership in Congress.
☐ c. Congress does not callously disregard people's opinions.
☐ d. Legislators find it hard to know what constituents want.

51. The congressional reforms of the 1970s particularly increased the power of
☐ a. committees.
☐ b. committee chairs.
☐ c. the full House.
☐ d. subcommittees.

52. Critics of Congress argue that the congressional reforms have created an oligarchy capable of preventing the legislature from taking comprehensive action.
☐ True
☐ False

53. Constituency service may provide members of Congress the incentive to tolerate, and even expand, big government.
☐ True
☐ False

## ESSAY QUESTIONS

1. What is the congressperson's job like? What are the characteristics of members of Congress?

2. What is the effect of incumbency in congressional elections? What other factors are associated with congressional electoral success?

3. What is the role of money in congressional campaigns? Assess the influence of interest groups and Political Action Committees (PACs) on members of Congress.

4. How do the House of Representatives and the Senate differ? How does the structure of leadership differ between the two?

5. Describe the committee system in Congress. What are the different roles of committees in the legislative process?

6. How does a bill become a law? What factors influence the legislative process and how does their influence differ?

7. Is Congress representative in its membership and its policy-making role? What structures and reforms have affected its representation function?

# Chapter 13

## THE PRESIDENCY

### CHAPTER OUTLINE

I.  The Presidents (pp. 394-398)
    A.    Great Expectations
    B.    Who They Are
    C.    How They Got There
        1.    Elections: The Normal Road to the White House
            a.    The **Twenty-second Amendment** limits presidents to two terms.
            b.    Only eleven presidents have served two or more terms.
        2.    Succession and Impeachment
            a.    **Impeachment** is the political equivalent of an indictment in criminal law.
            b.    The House Judiciary Committee voted to recommend Richard Nixon's impeachment as a result of the **Watergate** scandal.
            c.    The **Twenty-fifth Amendment** permits the vice president to become acting president if the president is disabled.

II.  Presidential Powers (pp. 398-402)
    A.    Constitutional Powers
    B.    The Expansion of Power
    C.    Perspectives on Presidential Power

III.  Running The Government: The Chief Executive (pp. 402-409)
    A.    The Vice President
    B.    The **Cabinet** consists of the heads of the executive departments.
    C.    The Executive Office
        1.    The **National Security Council (NSC)** links the president's key foreign and military policy advisors.
        2.    The **Council of Economic Advisors (CEA)** advise the president on economic policy.
        3.    The **Office of Management and Budget (OMB)** prepares the president's budget.
    D.    The White House Staff

E. The First Lady

IV. Presidential Leadership of Congress: The Politics of Shared Powers (pp. 409-417)
   A. Chief Legislator
      1. The Constitution gives the president power to **veto** congressional legislation.
      2. A **pocket veto** occurs if Congress adjourns within ten days after submitting a bill and the president fails to sign it.
   B. Party Leadership
      1. The Bonds of Party
      2. Slippage in Party Support
      3. Leading the Party
         a. **Presidential coattails** refer to voters casting their ballots for congressional candidates of the president's party because those candidates support the president.
         b. The president's party typically loses seats in midterm elections.
   C. Public Support
      1. Public Approval
      2. Mandates
   D. Legislative Skills

V. The President and National Security Policy (pp. 418-422)
   A. Chief Diplomat
      1. The president alone extends diplomatic recognition to foreign governments.
      2. The president has sole power to negotiate treaties.
      3. Presidents can negotiate *executive agreements* with heads of foreign governments.
   B. Commander In Chief
   C. War Powers
      1. The **War Powers Resolution** mandated the withdrawal of forces after sixty days unless Congress declared war or granted an extension.
      2. The use of the War Powers Resolution may constitute a **legislative veto** violating the doctrine of separation of powers.
   D. Crisis Manager
      1. A **crisis** is a sudden, unpredictable, and potentially dangerous event.
      2. Presidents can instantly monitor events almost anywhere and act quickly.
   E. Working With Congress

VI. Power from the People: The Public Presidency (pp. 422-427)
   A. Going Public
   B. Presidential Approval
   C. Policy Support
   D. Mobilizing the Public

VII. The President and the Press (pp. 427-430)
    A.    Presidents and the press tend to be in conflict.
    B.    The president's *press secretary* serves as a conduit of information from the White House to the press.
    C.    The best known direct interaction between the president and the press is the presidential press conference.
    D.    Most of the news coverage of the White House focuses on the president's personal and official activities.
    E.    News coverage of the presidency often tends to emphasize the negative.

VIII. Understanding the American Presidency (pp. 430-432)
    A.    The Presidency and Democracy
    B.    The Presidency and the Scope of Government

IX. Summary (p. 433)


## LEARNING OBJECTIVES

*After studying Chapter 13, you should be able to:*

1. Describe the American presidents—who they are, how they got there, and what they do.

2. List the constitutional powers of the president and explain how these powers have expanded.

3. Explain how the office of the presidency is organized to make policy.

4. Discuss the relationship between the president and Congress and the ways in which the president is able to lead Congress.

5. Explain the role of the president in developing national security policy.

6. Discuss the importance of public opinion to the president and his or her ability to obtain the support of the public.

7. Examine the relationship between the president and the media.

8. Understand the place of the presidency in American democracy and the effect the presidency has had on the scope of government.

*The following exercises will help you meet these objectives:*

Objective 1. Describe the American presidents—who they are, how they got there, and what they do.

1. What are the two contradictory expectations that Americans have about the presidency?

    1.

    2.

2. Make a list of whom you believe are the ten "best" presidents in history and briefly explain why.

    1.

    2.

    3.

    4.

    5.

    6.

    7.

    8.

    9.

    10.

3. Outline the procedure for removing a president from office.

Objective 2. List the constitutional powers of the president and explain how these powers have expanded.

1.      Look at Table 13.3 on page 401 and choose one constitutional power of the president from each category that you believe is the most important.

        1.

        2.

        3.

        4.

2.      Describe two ways in which the power of the president has expanded from its constitutional base.

        1.

        2.

Objective 3. Explain how the office of the presidency is organized to make policy.

1.      What is the cabinet and what does it do?

2.      List and explain the function of the three major policymaking bodies of the Executive Office.

        1.

        2.

3.

3.      What is the difference between a hierarchical organization and a wheel-and-spokes system of White House management?

Hierarchical:


Wheel-and-Spokes:


4.      Make a list of four First Ladies and how they have influenced the presidency.

1.

2.

3.

4.


Objective 4. Discuss the relationship between the president and Congress and the ways in which the president is able to lead Congress.

1.      What is the difference between a veto, a pocket veto, and a line-item veto?

Veto:


Pocket Veto:


Line-Item Veto:

2. Explain what is meant by the term "presidential coattails."

3. What are the two indicators of public support for the president?

    1.

    2.

4. What is meant by the president's "honeymoon" period?

Objective 5. Explain the role of the president in developing national security policy.

    1. What is an executive agreement and how does it differ from a treaty?

    2. What are the main provisions of the War Powers Resolution?

    3. Why is the president more equipped to handle a crisis than Congress?

    4. What are the "two presidencies"?

        1.

        2.

Objective 6. Discuss the importance of public opinion to the president and his or her ability to obtain the support of the public.

1. What is the difference between the president as head of state and head of government?

    Head of State:

    Head of Government:

2. Rank the past ten presidents in terms of their ability to garner public support.

    1.

    2.

    3.

    4.

    5.

    6.

    7.

    8.

    9.

    10.

Objective 7. Examine the relationship between the president and the media.

    1. What is the role of the president's press secretary?

    2. In what way(s) are the press biased in their coverage of the president?

Objective 8. Understand the place of the presidency in American democracy and the effect the presidency has had on the scope of government.

1.    In what way(s) is the institution of the presidency undemocratic?

2.    How does the presidency increase and decrease the scope of government?

## KEY TERMS

*Identify and Describe:*

Twenty-second Amendment

impeachment

Watergate

Twenty-fifth Amendment

cabinet

National Security Council (NSC)

Council of Economic Advisors (CEA)

Office of Management and Budget (OMB)

veto

pocket veto

presidential coattails

War Powers Resolution

legislative veto

crisis

*Compare and Contrast:*

impeachment and Watergate

Twenty-second Amendment and Twenty-fifth Amendment

National Security Council, Council of Economic Advisors, and
Office of Management and Budget


veto, pocket veto, and legislative veto


War Powers Resolution and legislative veto


*Name that Term:*

1.  It limits the president to two terms of office.

    _____

2.  Because of this scandal, the House Judiciary Committee voted to recommend the impeachment of President Nixon.

    _____

3.  Although not in the Constitution, every president has had one.

    _____

4.  It links the president's key foreign and military advisors.

    _____

5.  A two-thirds vote in each house of Congress can override it.

    _____

6.  Few congressional races are actually determined by this factor today.

    _____

7.  A sudden, unpredictable, and potentially dangerous event.

    _____

## USING YOUR UNDERSTANDING

1. Compare and contrast the Clinton presidency with the Bush presidency in terms of the principal roles the president plays. Identify particular policies in which the president is involved as head of state, commander in chief, chief legislator, and so on. You may want to collect newspaper or news magazine items that illustrate contemporary policy problems that both presidents faced. Pay special attention to presidential roles with respect to specific policy areas and national security.

2. All presidents seem to want to hold a prominent place in history. People are sometimes asked to identify the "top presidents" in our nation's history. Make a list of those presidents that you believe played prominent roles, for better or worse. You may even wish to rank them. Justify your choices by making a statement or two about each president's success or notoriety in one of the presidential roles, in policymaking achievements in domestic or foreign policy, in relations with Congress, and/or in terms of his image of power. Compare your choices with those of your colleagues. On the basis of your assessment, briefly describe what you believe to be the factors that help ensure that a president will have a prominent place in history.

## REVIEW QUESTIONS

*Check ☑ the correct answer:*

1. Powerful, strong, leader of the free world, and commander in chief describe
   - ☐ a. the intentions of the founders for the chief executive.
   - ☐ b. the presidency-as-powerhouse myth.
   - ☐ c. how the presidency has evolved in the twentieth century.
   - ☐ d. the constitutional powers of the president.

2. Richard Neustadt has emphasized that presidential power is the power to
   - ☐ a. command.
   - ☐ b. lead.
   - ☐ c. control.
   - ☐ d. persuade.

3. Which of the following statements about the presidents is FALSE?
   - ☐ a. All have been white males.
   - ☐ b. All have been Protestant.
   - ☐ c. They must be natural born citizens and at least thirty-five years old.
   - ☐ d. There has been much variety in their backgrounds.

4. Americans expect
   - [ ] a. very little out of their presidents.
   - [ ] b. presidents will be corrupt.
   - [ ] c. presidents to ensure peace, prosperity, and security.
   - [ ] d. Congress to be more powerful than the president.

5. The Twenty-second Amendment
   - [ ] a. limits presidents to two terms.
   - [ ] b. sets out procedures for presidential impeachment.
   - [ ] c. provides for succession to the presidency.
   - [ ] d. none of the above.

6. The most "accidental" president was (bonus)
   - [ ] a. Calvin Coolidge.
   - [ ] b. Harry Truman.
   - [ ] c. Lyndon Johnson.
   - [ ] d. Gerald Ford.

7. Impeachment of a president requires a
   - [ ] a. two-thirds vote in the Senate.
   - [ ] b. majority vote in the House of Representatives.
   - [ ] c. Supreme Court ruling.
   - [ ] d. popular election.

8. In 1974, the House of Representatives, as a result of the Watergate scandal, impeached President Nixon.
   - [ ] True
   - [ ] False

9. According to the Twenty-fifth Amendment, the vice president can become acting president if both he or she and the president's cabinet determine that the president is disabled.
   - [ ] True
   - [ ] False

10. After the vice president, the next person in the order of presidential succession is the
    - [ ] a. Speaker of the House.
    - [ ] b. president pro tempore of the Senate.
    - [ ] c. Secretary of State.
    - [ ] d. majority leader of the Senate.

11. The contemporary presidency closely resembles the one designed by the framers in 1787.
   ☐ True
   ☐ False

12. The founders preserved the balance of power without jeopardizing the independence of the separate branches by checking those powers that they believed to be most dangerous.
   ☐ True
   ☐ False

13. The expansion of presidential power can be attributed to
   ☐ a.  the increased prominence of the United States in the world.
   ☐ b.  technological advances.
   ☐ c.  presidential initiatives.
   ☐ d.  all of the above.

14. Which of the following is NOT a constitutional power of the president?
   ☐ a.  commander in chief of the armed forces
   ☐ b.  declare war
   ☐ c.  veto legislation
   ☐ d.  grant reprieves and pardons

15. The presidential role that receives the LEAST amount of publicity is
   ☐ a.  presiding over the administration of government.
   ☐ b.  appealing to the public for support for policy initiatives.
   ☐ c.  dealing with Congress.
   ☐ d.  negotiating with foreign powers.

16. Today, new presidents have only a very few high-level positions available for appointment.
   ☐ True
   ☐ False

17. Which vice president commented that the vice presidency was "not worth a warm bucket of spit"? (bonus)
   ☐ a.  Richard Nixon
   ☐ b.  John Nance Garner
   ☐ c.  Dan Quayle
   ☐ d.  Spiro Agnew

18. The president's cabinet
   ☐ a. was provided for by the Constitution.
   ☐ b. serves as the president's board of directors.
   ☐ c. has increased over the years with newly established executive departments approved by Congress.
   ☐ d. can veto the president on matters of executive policy.

19. Members of the president's cabinet do not need congressional approval.
   ☐ True
   ☐ False

20. Which of the following is NOT among the three main policymaking bodies in the Executive Office of the President?
   ☐ a. the National Security Council
   ☐ b. the Council of Economic Advisors
   ☐ c. the Office of Management and Budget
   ☐ d. the Attorney General

21. The Council of Economic Advisors
   ☐ a. prepares the president's budget.
   ☐ b. advises the president on economic policy.
   ☐ c. reviews legislative proposals from the cabinet.
   ☐ d. all of the above.

22. The president's clearinghouse for agency ideas is the
   ☐ a. cabinet.
   ☐ b. Office of Management and Budget.
   ☐ c. vice president.
   ☐ d. press secretary.

23. The organization of most White House staffs have been
   ☐ a. hierarchical.
   ☐ b. pluralistic.
   ☐ c. representative.
   ☐ d. disorganized.

24. In the wheel-and-spokes system of White House management,
   ☐ a. aides have very little power.
   ☐ b. aides are organized hierarchically.
   ☐ c. aides have equal status and are balanced against one another.
   ☐ d. power and responsibility are widely delegated.

25. President Reagan dispersed and delegated power widely among his advisors.
☐ True
☐ False

26. The president usually operates independently of Congress.
☐ True
☐ False

27. Which of the following is NOT mentioned in the Constitution?
☐ a. the requirement that the president give a State of the Union address to Congress
☐ b. the designation of the president as chief legislator
☐ c. the requirement that the president bring important matters to Congress' attention from time to time
☐ d. the power of the president to veto congressional legislation

28. A pocket veto
☐ a. allows a president to kill a bill without either signing or vetoing it.
☐ b. is a law sent back to Congress with the president's reasons for rejecting it.
☐ c. is a bill that automatically becomes law.
☐ d. can be overridden by a two-thirds vote in each house of Congress.

29. Which of the following statements about the president's party leadership in Congress is FALSE?
☐ a. Presidents can rely on their fellow party members to always vote on their programs.
☐ b. Party leadership in Congress provides the nucleus of coalitions supporting presidential proposals.
☐ c. Party leadership in Congress is a principle task of every president.
☐ d. Presidents are highly dependent on their party to move their programs.

30. Presidents can count on their own party members for support no more than
☐ a. one-quarter of the time.
☐ b. one-half of the time.
☐ c. one-third of the time.
☐ d. two-thirds of the time.

31. When constituency opinion and the president's proposals conflict, members of Congress are more likely to vote with their constituents.
☐ True
☐ False

32. The influence of presidential coattails
    ☐ a.  is highest in midterm elections.
    ☐ b.  has diminished in significance.
    ☐ c.  is especially important in Senate races.
    ☐ d.  creates dramatic swings in the composition of Congress.

33. Since 1953, most Republican presidents have lacked a majority in one or both houses of Congress during most of their terms.
    ☐ True
    ☐ False

34. Public approval of the president
    ☐ a.  strengthens opposition to the president's policies.
    ☐ b.  allows the president to control Congress.
    ☐ c.  gives the president leverage at the margins of coalition building.
    ☐ d.  does not affect opportunities for policy change.

35. Public approval gives the president leverage, not control.
    ☐ True
    ☐ False

36. Which of the following is NOT true of electoral mandates?
    ☐ a.  They are powerful symbols in American politics.
    ☐ b.  They give legitimacy and credibility to new presidents.
    ☐ c.  They change the premises of decisions.
    ☐ d.  They are guaranteed by large electoral majorities.

37. Which of the following is NOT among the legislative strategies of the president?
    ☐ a.  making personal appeals
    ☐ b.  avoiding bargains to build majorities
    ☐ c.  exploiting the honeymoon period
    ☐ d.  establishing priorities among legislative proposals

38. The president does not have to bargain with every member of Congress to receive support.
    ☐ True
    ☐ False

39. Which of the following statements is TRUE?
  - [ ] a. After accounting for party and public support, presidents differ greatly in terms of legislative success.
  - [ ] b. The president's legislative skills are at the core of presidential leadership of Congress.
  - [ ] c. Successful presidents exploit favorable configurations of political forces.
  - [ ] d. Most presidents have been able to change the political landscape and create opportunities for change.

40. The president must receive Senate approval prior to extending diplomatic recognition to foreign governments.
  - [ ] True
  - [ ] False

41. When the Constitution was written,
  - [ ] a. the president was not considered commander in chief.
  - [ ] b. no one expected the United States to have a permanent army.
  - [ ] c. the United States was involved in several military alliances.
  - [ ] d. the United States had a large standing army.

42. The power to declare war belongs to
  - [ ] a. the president.
  - [ ] b. Congress.
  - [ ] c. the Secretary of Defense.
  - [ ] d. the National Security Council.

43. The War Powers Resolution
  - [ ] a. strengthens presidential power during times of war.
  - [ ] b. limits congressional power during time of war.
  - [ ] c. is part of the Constitution.
  - [ ] d. provides for a legislative veto to end American involvement in overseas hostilities.

44. Since its passage in 1973, most presidents have regarded the War Powers Resolution as an unconstitutional infringement on presidential power.
  - [ ] True
  - [ ] False

45. Because of its access to information, Congress has become most prominent in handling crises.
  - [ ] True
  - [ ] False

46. When it comes to national security,
    - ☐ a. Congress has no constitutional role.
    - ☐ b. presidential leadership in policymaking is central.
    - ☐ c. members of Congress usually initiate policies.
    - ☐ d. presidents always get their way.

47. In matters of national security, the role of Congress has typically been oversight of the executive rather than initiation of policy.
    - ☐ True
    - ☐ False

48. Perhaps the greatest source of influence a president has is
    - ☐ a. public support.
    - ☐ b. party leadership.
    - ☐ c. ability to parcel out favors.
    - ☐ d. constitutional powers.

49. Which of the following statements is FALSE?
    - ☐ a. Presidents sometimes rely on persuasion.
    - ☐ b. Presidents are passive followers of public opinion.
    - ☐ c. The White House is a virtual whirlwind of public relations activity.
    - ☐ d. Most presidents make frequent public appearances.

50. Ceremonial responsibilities are not considered important by presidents and are usually given to the vice president.
    - ☐ True
    - ☐ False

51. Which of the following is NOT a key explanation of the public's support for a president?
    - ☐ a. a predisposition
    - ☐ b. party affiliation
    - ☐ c. the honeymoon period
    - ☐ d. first-hand experiences

52. Rally events have an enduring impact on presidential approval scores.
    - ☐ True
    - ☐ False

53. All presidents since Truman have had media advice from experts on lighting, makeup, stage settings, camera angles, clothing, pacing of delivery, and other facets of making speeches.
☐ True
☐ False

54. Which of the following presidents was NOT considered an effective speaker?
☐ a. Franklin D. Roosevelt
☐ b. John Kennedy
☐ c. Richard Nixon
☐ d. Ronald Reagan

55. Which of the following statements is FALSE?
☐ a. Modern presidents monitor the media closely.
☐ b. As long as their goals differ, the president and the media are likely adversaries.
☐ c. Most of what people know about the president comes through the mass media.
☐ d. White House staff members generally ignore the media.

56. The person who most often deals directly with the press is the president's press secretary.
☐ True
☐ False

57. The term "body watch" refers to the media's
☐ a. preoccupation with the president's physical health.
☐ b. analysis of the body of issues on the executive agenda.
☐ c. step-by-step account of the president's personal and official activities.
☐ d. presence at presidential press conferences.

58. Studies have shown that the media are systematically biased against the president.
☐ True
☐ False

59. Major policy change is virtually impossible under a divided government.
☐ True
☐ False

60. Most recently, the institution that has championed constraints on government and limits on spending has been
☐ a.   Congress.
☐ b.   the presidency.
☐ c.   interest groups.
☐ d.   the bureaucracy.

## ESSAY QUESTIONS

1. What are the characteristics of American presidents? How do presidents and vice presidents get into office?

2. What are the formal constitutional powers of the presidency and how have these powers expanded over the years?

3. How is the presidency organized? On whom does the president depend for advice about governmental and policy matters?

4. Explain the factors that affect presidential leadership of Congress. Why are some presidents more effective leaders than others?

5. What roles does the president play as leader of national security policy? How do these roles conflict with the role of Congress in the area of national security?

6. What factors affect presidential popularity and approval? How is popularity related to power and to policy-making?

7. Why is the press so important to the president? Give examples of the relationship between the press and the presidency.

8. How does the contemporary presidency differ from that envisioned by the Founders? Take a position on whether or not the president has become too powerful, and how this might affect democracy and the scope of government.

# Chapter 14

## THE CONGRESS, THE PRESIDENT, AND THE BUDGET: THE POLITICS OF TAXING AND SPENDING

### CHAPTER OUTLINE

I. Introduction (pp. 436-438)
   - A. Central to public policy are the questions of who bears the burdens of paying for government and who receives the benefits?
   - B. A **budget** is a policy document allocating burdens (taxes) and benefits (expenditures).
   - C. A budget deficit occurs when **expenditures** exceed **revenues** in a fiscal year.

II. Sources Of Federal Revenue (pp. 438-445)
   - A. Income Tax
     1. Individuals are required to pay the government a portion of the money they earn called an **income tax.**
     2. The **Sixteenth Amendment** permitted Congress to levy an income tax.
   - B. Social Insurance Taxes
   - C. Borrowing
     1. The **federal debt** is all of the money borrowed over the years that is still outstanding.
     2. The proposed *balanced budget amendment* would require Congress to balance peacetime federal budgets.
   - D. Taxes and Public Policy
     1. Tax loopholes consist of a tax break or tax benefit.
     2. **Tax expenditures** are revenue losses attributable to provisions of the federal tax laws.
     3. Tax reduction has frequently been called for.
     4. Tax reform has simplified taxes and made them more equitable.

III. Federal Expenditures (pp. 445-453)
   - A. Big Governments, Big Budgets
   - B. The Rise and Decline of the National Security State
   - C. The Rise of the Social Service State
     1. The **Social Security Act** intended to provide a minimal level of sustenance to older Americans.
     2. **Medicare** provides both hospital and physician coverage to the elderly.

256

D. Incrementalism
   1. **Incrementalism** means that the best predictor of this year's budget is last year's budget plus a little bit more.
   2. The budgetary process is affected by groups with interests in taxes and expenditures.
E. "Uncontrollable" Expenditures
   1. **Uncontrollable expenditures** result from policies that make some group automatically eligible for some benefit.
   2. **Entitlements** are policies in which Congress has obligated itself to pay X level of benefits to Y number of recipients each year.

IV. The Budgetary Process (pp. 453-459)
   A. Budgetary Politics
      1. Stakes and Strategies
      2. The Players
         a. The interest groups
         b. The agencies
         c. The Office of Management and Budget (OMB)
         d. The president
         e. The Tax Committees in Congress
            (1) **House Ways and Means Committee**
            (2) **Senate Finance Committee**
         f. The Budget Committees and the Congressional Budget Office
         g. The subject-matter committees
         h. The Appropriations Committees and their subcommittees
         i. The Congress as a whole
         j. The General Accounting Office (GAO)
   B. The President's Budget
   C. Congress and the Budget
      1. Reforming the Process
         a. The **Congressional Budget and Impoundment Act of 1974**
            (1) A fixed budget calendar.
            (2) A budget committee in each house.
            (3) The Congressional Budget Office (CBO).
         b. A **budget resolution** is supposed to set limits on expenditures based on revenue projections.
         c. A budget **reconciliation** revises program authorizations to achieve required savings.
         d. An **authorization bill** is an act of Congress that establishes a discretionary government program or an entitlement.
         e. An **appropriations bill** must be passed to actually fund programs established by authorization bills.

257

2. The Success of the 1974 Reforms
   a. **Continuing resolutions** are laws that allow agencies to spend at the previous year's level.
   b. The 1974 reforms have helped Congress view the entire budget early in the process.
3. More Reforms
   a. The *Gramm-Rudman-Hollings* Act mandated maximum allowable deficit levels for each year until the budget was to be balanced in 1993.
   b. In 1990 Congress switched from a focus on controlling the size of the deficit to controlling increases in spending.
   c. Republican efforts to balance the budget.

V. Understanding Budgeting (pp. 459-464)
   A. Democracy and Budgeting
   B. The Budget and the Scope of Government

VI. Summary (p. 464)

## LEARNING OBJECTIVES

*After studying Chapter 14, you should be able to:*

1. Describe the major sources of federal revenues.

2. Understand the nature of the tax system in America.

3. Explain the nature of federal expenditures and why so much of the budget is uncontrollable.

4. Discuss how the budgetary process works, who is involved, and the politics of budgetary reform.

5. Understand how budgeting affects democracy and the scope of government in America.

*The following exercises will help you meet these objectives:*

Objective 1. Describe the major sources of federal revenues.

1.      List four sources of federal revenues.

       1.

       2.

       3.

       4.

2.      How does the federal government borrow money?

3.      List two criticisms of a balanced budget amendment.

       1.

       2.

Objective 2.  Understand the nature of the tax system in America.

1.      Define tax expenditures and give three examples.

Definition:

Examples:
       1.

       2.

       3.

2.      What were the three major reforms of the Tax Reform Act of 1986?

       1.

2.

3.

Objective 3. Explain the nature of federal expenditures and why so much of the budget is uncontrollable.

1.      Name the two conditions associated with government growth in America.

     1.

     2.

2.      What is meant by the phrase "military industrial complex"?

3.      Explain how Social Security is a kind of intergenerational contract.

4.      List four features of incremental budgeting.

     1.

     2.

     3.

     4.

6.      Explain how entitlements are "uncontrollable expenditures."

Objective 4. Discuss how the budgetary process works, who is involved, and the politics of budgetary reform.

1. Beginning with the largest category, rank order the revenues and expenditures of the federal budget.

| Revenues | Expenditures |
| --- | --- |
| 1. | 1. |
| 2. | 2. |
| 3. | 3. |
| 4. | 4. |
| 5. | 5. |
| 6. | 6. |

2. List the ten main actors in the budgetary process.

1.

2.

3.

4.

5.

6.

7.

8.

9.

10.

3.    Explain the three main provisions of the Congressional Budget and Impoundment Control Act of 1974.

    1.

    2.

    3.

4.    What is meant by a budget resolution?

5.    Explain the two ways in which laws are changed to meet the budget resolution.

    1.

    2.

6.    What was the Gramm-Rudman-Hollings Act and why did it fail?

Objective 5. Understand how budgeting affects democracy and the scope of government in America.

1.    List three possible explanations as to why democracies have seen a substantial growth in government in the twentieth century.

1.

2.

3.


2.	How could the budgetary process limit government?


**KEY TERMS**

*Identify and Describe:*

budget


deficit


expenditures


revenues


income tax


Sixteenth Amendment

federal debt

tax expenditures

Social Security Act

Medicare

incrementalism

uncontrollable expenditures

entitlements

House Ways and Means Committee

Senate Finance Committee

Congressional Budget and Impoundment Control Act of 1974

Congressional Budget Office (CBO)

budget resolution

reconciliation

authorization bill

appropriations bill

continuing resolutions

*Compare and Contrast:*

budget and deficit

expenditures and revenues

income tax and Sixteenth Amendment

income tax and tax expenditures

Social Security Act and Medicare

uncontrollable expenditures and entitlements

House Ways and Means Committee and Senate Finance Committee

reconciliation and authorization bill

*Name that Term:*

1. A policy document allocating burdens and benefits.

   _____

2. All of the money borrowed over the years and still outstanding.

   _____

3. This was intended to provide a minimal level of sustenance to older Americans.

   _____

4. Revenue losses attributable to provisions of the federal tax laws that allow a special exemption, exclusion, or deduction.

   _____

5. The best predictor of this year's budget is last year's budget, plus a little bit more.

   _____

6. These result from policies that make some group automatically eligible for some benefit.

   _____

7. This agency advises Congress on the probable consequences of its budget decisions.

_____

8. This occurs in Congress every April.

_____

9. An act of Congress that actually funds programs within limits established by authorization bills.

_____

10. These allow agencies to spend at the previous year's level.

_____

## USING YOUR UNDERSTANDING

1. Take a look at a recent edition of the *United States Budget in Brief.* Identify expenditure categories that relate to specific policy arenas, such as equality, the economy, social welfare, technology, and national security. Create your own policy arenas using broad or specific categories. Briefly describe what you found in terms of the policy priorities represented by the budget. Evaluate the budget according to where you believe your tax dollars should be spent.

2. This chapter has emphasized the budget of the United States government. Locate a budget document for your state or community. These should be available in the Government Documents section of your school library, through state and local government offices, or on the Internet. Assess the sources of revenues on which this unit of government depends and the types of expenditures it makes in various policy areas. Take note of whether or not the budget represents a deficit (expenditures exceeding revenues) or a surplus (revenues exceeding expenditures) and the magnitude of the amount. Compare the major features of this budget to those of the budget of the United States. Investigate the politics of the budgetary process at the state or local level and compare what you find to the national level. Alternatively you could examine a budget of another Western democracy and compare it to that of the United States using these same guidelines.

# REVIEW QUESTIONS

*Check ☑ the correct answer:*

1. The budget deficit or surplus is equal to
   - ☐ a. expenditures/revenues.
   - ☐ b. revenues + expenditures.
   - ☐ c. revenues/expenditures.
   - ☐ d. expenditures - revenues.

2. Who said, "Taxes are what we pay for civilization"? (bonus)
   - ☐ a. Aaron Wildavsky.
   - ☐ b. Oliver Wendell Holmes, Jr.
   - ☐ c. Jean-Baptiste Colbert.
   - ☐ d. Bill Clinton.

3. The largest percentage of the government's income comes from
   - ☐ a. excise taxes.
   - ☐ b. income taxes.
   - ☐ c. social insurance taxes.
   - ☐ d. borrowing.

4. Congress was given permission to levy an income tax by the
   - ☐ a. Supreme Court case of *Pollock v. Farmer's Loan and Trust Co.*
   - ☐ b. Sixteenth Amendment.
   - ☐ c. Thirteenth Amendment.
   - ☐ d. Internal Revenue Service.

5. Corporate taxes yield more revenues than individual income taxes do.
   - ☐ True
   - ☐ False

6. Social Security taxes
   - ☐ a. come from both employers and employees.
   - ☐ b. do not go into the government's general fund.
   - ☐ c. are earmarked for a specific purpose.
   - ☐ d. all of the above.

7. The federal debt
   - ☐ a. is the amount by which expenditures exceed revenues in a given year.
   - ☐ b. has the impact of crowding out private borrowing.
   - ☐ c. finances mainly capital projects.
   - ☐ d. was never greater than under Ronald Reagan.

8.   The balanced budget amendment would require Congress to balance peacetime federal budgets.
     ☐ True
     ☐ False

9.   A tax loophole is also a
     ☐ a.   tax benefit.
     ☐ b.   tax expenditure.
     ☐ c.   tax break
     ☐ d.   all of the above.

10.  Tax loopholes cost the federal government very little.
     ☐ True
     ☐ False

11.  Which of the following is an example of a tax expenditure?
     ☐ a.   direct government support of a charity
     ☐ b.   a tax reform
     ☐ c.   mortgage interest deduction
     ☐ d.   the social security system

12.  Tax expenditures are most beneficial to poorer people.
     ☐ True
     ☐ False

13.  Ronald Reagan's 1981 tax reforms
     ☐ a.   reduced individual and corporate taxes.
     ☐ b.   provided tax incentives for personal savings and corporate investment.
     ☐ c.   indexed taxes to the cost of living.
     ☐ d.   all of the above.

14.  Ronald Reagan's 1981 tax reforms
     ☐ a.   increased social service expenditures.
     ☐ b.   did not help people at the lower end of the income ladder.
     ☐ c.   resulted in a balanced budget.
     ☐ d.   raised taxes for the rich.

15.  The Tax Reform Act of 1986
     ☐ a.   eliminated or reduced the value of many tax deductions.
     ☐ b.   increased the number of possible tax expenditures.
     ☐ c.   changed the system of fifteen tax brackets to two.
     ☐ d.   both a. and c.

16. Which of the following countries has the highest tax revenues as percentage of GDP? (bonus)
   ☐ a.   United Kingdom
   ☐ b.   Sweden
   ☐ c.   United States
   ☐ d.   Germany

17. The policies and programs the government spends money on change over time.
   ☐ True
   ☐ False

18. Total military expenditures have declined as a percentage of our GNP since the end of World War II.
   ☐ True
   ☐ False

19. The Reagan budgets brought defense back as the biggest slice of the budget pie.
   ☐ True
   ☐ False

20. Which of the following statements is TRUE?
   ☐ a.   From the mid-1960s to the early 1980s, military expenditures more than doubled.
   ☐ b.   Ronald Reagan substantially increased the defense budget during his second term.
   ☐ c.   Procurement is used to draft military personnel.
   ☐ d.   The cost of military weapons is more expensive than their predecessors.

21. Social Security checks go only to retired persons.
   ☐ True
   ☐ False

22. Which of the following statements is TRUE?
   ☐ a.   Medicare is mainly for poor persons.
   ☐ b.   Social Security was originally designed as a disability program.
   ☐ c.   As the 1980s began, the Social Security program was going broke.
   ☐ d.   Conservatives favor expansion of Social Security.

23. The Social Security system combines all social policies of the federal government.
   ☐ True
   ☐ False

270

24. Which of the following is NOT among the features of incremental budgeting?
☐ a. little attention to the budget base
☐ b. rapid growth in the federal budget
☐ c. heated debate over the proposed increment
☐ d. growth in agency budgets by only a little bit every year

25. Incrementalism
☐ a. fully describes American budgetary politics.
☐ b. facilitates budgetary reform.
☐ c. does not describe the budget process for every agency.
☐ d. makes it easy to pare the budget.

26. Uncontrollable expenditures result from
☐ a. failure to focus attention on the budgetary base.
☐ b. the increased costs of military procurement.
☐ c. incremental budgeting.
☐ d. policies that make some group automatically eligible for some benefit.

27. Policies that obligate Congress to pay X level of benefits to Y number of recipients are called
☐ a. entitlements.
☐ b. increments.
☐ c. allowances.
☐ d. tax expenditures.

28. Fully two-thirds of the federal budget is uncontrollable.
☐ True
☐ False

29. The biggest uncontrollable item in the federal budget is
☐ a. Social Security.
☐ b. welfare.
☐ c. grants-in-aid.
☐ d. defense.

30. The process of creating the national budget is confined to a few politicians in Washington, D.C.
☐ True
☐ False

31. Lobbying for a group's needs takes place
    ☐ a. in the agencies.
    ☐ b. with the president.
    ☐ c. before congressional committees.
    ☐ d. all of the above.

32. Which of the following is NOT among the congressional players in the budgetary process?
    ☐ a. Office of Management and Budget
    ☐ b. tax committees
    ☐ c. subject-matter committees
    ☐ d. Congressional Budget Office

33. The body that audits, monitors, and evaluates what agencies do with their budgets is the
    ☐ a. House Ways and Means Committee.
    ☐ b. Congressional Budget Office.
    ☐ c. General Accounting Office.
    ☐ d. Senate Finance Committee.

34. The Budget and Accounting Act of 1921
    ☐ a. created the Congressional Budget Office.
    ☐ b. mandated the reconciliation reduction.
    ☐ c. required the president to propose an executive budget to Congress.
    ☐ d. gave Congress impoundment power.

35. The Office of Management and Budget (OMB)
    ☐ a. receives budget requests from Congress.
    ☐ b. audits, monitors, and evaluates what agencies are doing with their budgets.
    ☐ c. supervises preparation of the budget and advises the president on budgetary matters.
    ☐ d. adjudicates disputes over the budget.

36. Preparation of the federal budget takes almost one year.
    ☐ True
    ☐ False

37. According to the Constitution, federal appropriations must be authorized by
    ☐ a. the Office of Management and Budget.
    ☐ b. the president.
    ☐ c. three-fifths of the states.
    ☐ d. Congress.

38. Which of the following was NOT established by the Congressional Budget and Impoundment Control Act of 1974?
□ a. a fixed budget calendar
□ b. the elimination of tax expenditures
□ c. a committee on the budget in each house
□ d. the Congressional Budget Office

39. The budget resolution requires that
□ a. the president and Congress agree on the budget.
□ b. Congress and the bureaucracy set limits on program spending.
□ c. both houses of Congress initially agree on a total expenditure level.
□ d. this year's budget roughly equals last year's budget.

40. The purpose of budget reconciliation is to
□ a. critique and analyze the president's proposed budget.
□ b. establish a discretionary government program or entitlement.
□ c. adjudicate disputes over the budget.
□ d. revise program authorizations to achieve required savings.

41. Which of the following does an authorization bill NOT provide for?
□ a. a discretionary program or an entitlement
□ b. program goals
□ c. program funds
□ d. eligibility requirements for entitlement programs

42. An appropriations bill actually funds programs, within limits established by authorizations, for the lifetime of the specific program.
□ True
□ False

43. When Congress is unable to reach agreement and pass appropriations bills, it may allow agencies to spend at the previous year's level by passing a
□ a. continuing resolution.
□ b. budget resolution.
□ c. budget reconciliation.
□ d. authorization bill.

44. The purpose of the Gramm-Rudman-Hollings Act was to
□ a. decrease the spiraling defense budget.
□ b. stabilize deficit spending at a manageable level.
□ c. introduce a constitutional amendment to balance the budget.
□ d. mandate maximum allowable deficit levels until the budget was balanced in 1993.

45. The 1990 budget law resulted in significantly reducing the deficit.
☐ True
☐ False

46. The 1990 budget law
☐ a. facilitated the ability of Congress to shift budget priorities across categories.
☐ b. shifted the focus to controlling increases in spending.
☐ c. increased the functions of the congressional budget committees.
☐ d. reduced the power of the Office of Management and Budget.

47. One reason all democracies have experienced substantial growth in government is because policymakers spend public money on things voters will like.
☐ True
☐ False

48. Allen Meltzer and Scott Richard argue that government grows in a democracy because of
☐ a. corrupt politicians.
☐ b. the equality of suffrage.
☐ c. the need for strong defense.
☐ d. an apathetic public.

49. Which of the following statements is FALSE?
☐ a. Many politicians willingly cooperate with the desire of working class voters to expand their benefits.
☐ b. Corporate elites are especially opposed to big government.
☐ c. Low-income and wealthy voters alike have voted for parties and politicians who promised them benefits.
☐ d. Government grows by responding to groups and their demands.

50. Ronald Reagan won election to the presidency twice by promising to
☐ a. raise taxes.
☐ b. spend less money.
☐ c. provide more services.
☐ d. increase the scope of government.

51. Americans have chosen to tax less and spend less on public services than almost all other democracies with developed economies.
☐ True
☐ False

52. Since 1980, policymaking in the American government could be characterized as the politics of scarcity.
   ☐ True
   ☐ False

53. The budget
   ☐ a.   is the size of government.
   ☐ b.   can be used to rein in the government.
   ☐ c.   can be used to expand the role of government.
   ☐ d.   all of the above.


## ESSAY QUESTIONS

1. Why is government so big? What are the political implications of big government, and who benefits from it?

2. What are the principal sources of revenue for the federal government? What public policy problems or issues do taxation and government borrowing raise?

3. What are the principal categories of government expenditures? What are the reasons for the increasing expenditures for Social Security?

4. What is incrementalism? How do uncontrollable expenditures contribute to incremental budget-making?

5. Who are the players in budgetary politics? What stake do they have in the budget process, and what roles do they play?

6. Compare the role of the president and the role of Congress in the budgetary process. Where does their authority in the process come from?

7. Explain how the budgetary process has been reformed. How successful have the reforms been? Why is it so difficult to reform the budgetary process?

8. How does the budgetary process affect democracy and the scope of government? How have budgetary reforms affected the scope of government and the democratic process?

# Chapter 15

## THE FEDERAL BUREAUCRACY

### CHAPTER OUTLINE

I.      The Bureaucrats (pp. 468-475)
   A.      Some Bureaucratic Myths and Realities
   1.      Americans dislike bureaucrats.
   2.      Bureaucracies are growing bigger each year.
   3.      Most federal bureaucrats work in Washington, DC
   4.      Bureaucracies are ineffective, inefficient, and always mired in red tape.
   B.      Who They Are and How They Got There
   1.      Civil Service: From Patronage to Protection
      a.      **Patronage** is a hiring and promotion system based on knowing the right people.
      b.      The **Pendleton Civil Service Act** created the federal Civil Service.
      c.      All **civil service** systems are based on merit and the desire to create a nonpartisan government service.
      d.      The **merit principle** uses entrance exams and promotion ratings to reward qualified individuals.
      e.      The **Hatch Act** prohibits civil service employees from active participation in partisan politics while on duty.
      f.      The **Office of Personnel Management (OPM)** is in charge of hiring for most federal agencies.
      g.      Each civil service job is assigned a **GS (General Schedule) rating**.
      h.      The very top of the civil service system is the **Senior Executive Service.**
   2.      The Other Route to Federal Jobs: Recruiting from the Plum Book
      a.      The plum book lists top federal jobs available for direct presidential appointment.
      b.      The most important trait of presidential appointees is their transience.

II.      What They Do: Some Theories of **Bureaucracy**  (pp. 473-475)
   A.      The Weberian Model
   B.      The Acquisitive, Monopolistic Bureaucracy
   C.      Garbage Cans and Bureaucracies

III. How Bureaucracies Are Organized (pp. 475-479)
  A. The Cabinet Departments
  B. The Regulatory Agencies
    1. Each **independent regulatory agency** has responsibility for some sector of the economy.
    2. Interest groups are closely involved with independent regulatory agencies.
  C. The **Government Corporations** provide a service that could be provided by the private sector and charge for their service.
  D. The **Independent Executive Agencies** are essentially all the rest of the government.

IV. Bureaucracies As Implementors (pp. 479-487)
  A. What Implementation Means
    1. **Policy Implementation** is the stage of policymaking between the establishment of a policy and its consequences.
    2. Implementation is the continuation of policymaking by other means.
  B. Why the Best-Laid Plans Sometimes Flunk the Implementation Test
    1. Program Design
    2. Lack of Clarity
    3. Lack of Resources
    4. Administrative Routine
      a. **Standard operating procedures** (SOPs) help bureaucrats make everyday decisions.
      b. SOPs may become "red tape" and obstacles to action.
    5. Administrators' Dispositions
      a. **Administrative discretion** is the authority of administrative actors to select among various responses to a given problem.
      b. **Street-level bureaucrats** are those bureaucrats who are in constant contact with the public and have considerable discretion.
    6. Fragmentation
  C. A Case Study: The Voting Rights Act of 1965

V. Bureaucracies As Regulators (pp. 487-492)
  A. Regulation in the Economy and in Everyday Life
    1. Government **regulation** is the use of governmental authority to control or change some practice in the private sector.
    2. A Full Day of Regulation
  B. Regulation: How It Grew, How It Works
    1. In the **command-and-control policy** the government tells business how to reach certain goals, checks that these commands are followed, and punishes offenders.
    2. An **incentive system** uses taxes and rewards to promote certain behavior.
  C. Toward **Deregulation**

VI.     Understanding Bureaucracies (pp. 492-497)
        A.      Bureaucracy and Democracy
                1.      Presidents Try to Control the Bureaucracy
                        a.      They appoint the right people to head the agency.
                        b.      They issue **executive orders.**
                        c.      They tinker with an agency's budget
                        d.      They reorganize an agency.
                2.      Congress Tries to Control the Bureaucracy
                        a.      They influence the appointment of agency heads.
                        b.      They tinker with an agency's budget.
                        c.      They hold hearings.
                        d.      They rewrite the legislation or make it more detailed.
                3.      Iron Triangles and Issue Networks
                        a.      When agencies, groups, and committees all depend on one another
                                and are in close, frequent contact, they form what are sometimes
                                called **iron triangles** or subgovernments.
                        b.      The system of subgovernments is now overlaid with an amorphous
                                system of issue networks.
        B.      Bureaucracy and the Scope of Government

VII.    Summary (pp. 498-499)


**LEARNING OBJECTIVES**

*After studying Chapter 15, you should be able to:*

        1.      Describe the bureaucrats—who they are, how they got there, and what they do.

        2.      Discuss how the federal bureaucracy is organized.

        3.      Explain how bureaucracies function as implementors of public policy.

        4.      Explain how bureaucracies function as regulators.

        5.      Evaluate the problem of controlling bureaucracies in a democratic government
                and how bureaucracies affect the scope of government.

*The following exercises will help you meet these objectives:*

Objective 1.  Describe the bureaucrats—who they are, how they got there, and what they do.

    1.      List four prevalent myths about bureaucracy

          1.

          2.

          3.

          4.

    2.      What is the difference between patronage and the merit principle?

        Patronage:

        Merit Principle:

    3.      What is the purpose of the Hatch Act?

    4.      What are some of the common characteristics of plum book appointees?

    5.      List five elements of the Weberian model of bureaucracy.

          1.

          2.

          3.

4.

5.

6. What is the difference between the acquisitive, monopolistic model of bureaucracy and the garbage can model of bureaucracy?

Acquisitive, Monopolistic Model:

Garbage Can Model:

Objective 2. Discuss how the federal bureaucracy is organized.

1. What are the four basic types of agencies in the federal executive branch?

1.

2.

3.

4.

2. Explain the relationship between interest groups and independent regulatory agencies.

3. In what two ways are government corporations like private corporations and different from other parts of the government?

1.

2.

4.      What are the three biggest independent executive agencies?

       1.

       2.

       3.


Objective 3.  Explain how bureaucracies function as implementors of public policy.

    1.      What are the three minimum elements of implementation?

       1.


       2.


       3.


    2.      List six reasons why policy implementation might fail.

       1.

       2.

       3.

       4.

       5.

       6.

3.      What are three advantages of using standard operating procedures?

      1.

      2.

      3.

4.      What is meant by administrative discretion?

Objective 4. Explain how bureaucracies function as regulators.

      1.      What was the significance of *Munn v. Illinois* (1877)?

      2.      List three elements common to all regulation.

            1.

            2.

            3.

      3.      What is the difference between command-and-control policy and incentive system?

      Command-and-Control:

      Incentive:

4.      List three criticisms of regulation.

        1.


        2.


        3.


Objective 5. Evaluate the problem of controlling bureaucracies in a democratic government and how bureaucracies affect the scope of government.

    1.      List four methods in which the president can control the bureaucracy.

            1.

            2.

            3.

            4.


    2.      List four methods in which Congress can control the bureaucracy.

            1.

            2.

            3.

            4.


    3.      Explain the difference between an iron triangle and an issue network.

            Iron Triangle:


            Issue Network:


283

4. What effect does bureaucracy have on the scope of government?

**KEY TERMS**

*Identify and Describe:*

patronage

Pendleton Civil Service Act

civil service

merit principle

Hatch Act

Office of Personnel Management (OPM)

GS (General Schedule) rating

Senior Executive Service

bureaucracy

independent regulatory agency

governmental corporations

independent executive agencies

policy implementation

standard operating procedures

administrative discretion

street-level bureaucrats

regulation

deregulation

command-and-control policy

incentive system

executive orders

iron triangles

*Compare and Contrast:*

patronage and merit principle

Pendleton Civil Service Act and civil service

civil service and merit principle

GS (General Schedule) rating and Senior Executive Service

independent regulatory agencies, government corporations, and independent executive agencies

standard operating procedures and administrative discretion

administrative discretion and street-level bureaucrats

regulation and deregulation


command-and-control policy and incentive system


*Name That Term:*

1.      This law created the federal Civil Service.

      _____

2.      This law limits the political activity of government employees.

      _____

3.      This agency is in charge of hiring for most federal agencies.

      _____

4.      The Federal Trade Commission is an example.

      _____

5.      The U.S. Postal Service is an example.

      _____

6.      This is needed because most policies are not self-executing.

      _____

7.      Examples might include a police officer or a welfare worker.

      _____

8.      Presidents sometime use these to control the bureaucracy.

      _____

9.      Also known as subgovernments.

_____

## USING YOUR UNDERSTANDING

1.      The organization of the federal government is very complex; policy
        responsibilities are delegated among many different agencies and offices.  Take a
        look at the simplified organization chart of the bureaucracy.  (See for example,
        Figure 15.3, p. 476.)  Based on what you know about the particular
        responsibilities of these many offices, try to categorize them according to different
        policy arenas such as the economy, social welfare, equality issues, environment,
        technology, or national security.  Keep in mind that these policy arenas encompass
        many different types of policies.  Take note of any agencies that fall within one or
        more of the policy groups.  Briefly describe what you found in terms of the
        relative organizational emphasis on each of the policy arenas.

2.      Regulations affect many different aspects of our everyday lives.  (See the section,
        "A Full Day of Regulation," pp. 488-490.)  Keep a record of your regulated day
        from the time you wake up to the time you go to bed, recording which aspects of
        your life are regulated and what federal agency is doing the regulation.  After your
        record is complete, make an overall assessment as to the degree to which federal
        regulation affects you.  Based on your assessment, consider whether or not the
        costs of regulation exceed the benefits it provides you.  Also consider whether or
        not any of the regulations you recorded are not necessary or could be handled to
        your satisfaction by some other method or by a private means as compared to
        governmental means.

## REVIEW QUESTIONS

*Check ☑ the correct answer:*

1.      The Constitution outlines in detail the form and rules for establishing the federal
        bureaucracy.
        ☐ True
        ☐ False

2.   Which of the following statements about bureaucracies is FALSE?
☐ a.   Americans tend to dislike bureaucrats.
☐ b.   Most federal bureaucrats work in the states.
☐ c.   As a percentage of America's work force, federal employment has been shrinking.
☐ d.   Federal bureaucrats are no more inefficient than private bureaucrats.

3.   Which of the following myths about bureaucracies is partly TRUE?
☐ a.   Americans dislike bureaucrats.
☐ b.   Most federal bureaucrats work in Washington, DC.
☐ c.   Bureaucracies are growing bigger and bigger each year.
☐ d.   Government bureaucracies are less efficient than private bureaucracies.

4.   The vast majority of tasks carried out by governments at all levels are noncontroversial.
☐ True
☐ False

5.   Which of the following agencies employ the most civilian workers?
☐ a.   the Department of Defense
☐ b.   the Department of Health and Human Services
☐ c.   the Department of Veterans Affairs
☐ d.   the U.S. Postal Service

6.   The permanent bureaucracy is less representative of the American people than legislators, judges, and presidential appointees to the executive branch.
☐ True
☐ False

7.   Patronage is a hiring and promotion system based on
☐ a.   the merit principle.
☐ b.   knowing the right people.
☐ c.   the Pendleton Act.
☐ d.   talent and skill.

8.   Who was Charles Guiteau? (bonus)
☐ a.   Chester A. Arthur's vice president
☐ b.   the first man hired under the civil service system
☐ c.   the man who shot President James A. Garfield
☐ d.   the man who coined the term "spoils system"

9. Most federal bureaucrats get their jobs through
   ☐ a.   a political contact.
   ☐ b.   presidential appointment.
   ☐ c.   the civil service system.
   ☐ d.   elections.

10. The Hatch Act prevents public employees from
    ☐ a.   being fired for partisan reasons.
    ☐ b.   being promoted for political reasons.
    ☐ c.   voting in federal elections.
    ☐ d.   active participation in partisan politics.

11. The GS (General Schedule) rating is used to
    ☐ a.   select three eligible job applicants.
    ☐ b.   assign salaries to federal employees.
    ☐ c.   nominate members of the Senior Executive Service.
    ☐ d.   evaluate federal employees prior to dismissal.

12. The plum book
    ☐ a.   lists all civil service jobs.
    ☐ b.   is published by the Office of Personnel Management.
    ☐ c.   lists top federal jobs available with presidential appointment, often with Senate confirmation.
    ☐ d.   provides rules for hiring minorities and women.

13. Who referred to the top administrative policymakers as "government of strangers"? (bonus)
    ☐ a.   President Chester A. Arthur
    ☐ b.   Charles Guiteau
    ☐ c.   President Franklin D. Roosevelt
    ☐ d.   Hugh Heclo

14. Which of the following elements is NOT part of Max Weber's model of bureaucracy?
    ☐ a.   the personal touch.
    ☐ b.   a hierarchical authority structure.
    ☐ c.   task specialization.
    ☐ d.   the merit principle and extensive rules.

15. According to the acquisitive, monopolistic model, bureaucracies try to
☐ a. reduce regulation.
☐ b. make profits from government services.
☐ c. maximize their budgets.
☐ d. curtail government growth.

16. The lack of competition in the provision of many government services is emphasized by the
☐ a. Weberian model.
☐ b. acquisitive, monopolistic model.
☐ c. garbage can model.
☐ d. hierarchical model.

17. In the "garbage can" model of bureaucracy
☐ a. technological certainty is high.
☐ b. organizations are tightly controlled.
☐ c. actions are calculating and purposive.
☐ d. the use of trial and error is typical.

18. In which model of bureaucracy do solutions look for problems?
☐ a. the Weberian model
☐ b. the acquisitive, monopolistic model
☐ c. the garbage can model
☐ d. none of the above

19. Of the fourteen cabinet departments, all are headed by a Secretary except the
☐ a. Department of Justice.
☐ b. Department of Labor.
☐ c. Department of Veterans Affairs.
☐ d. Department of State.

20. Until 1995, the largest government agency in dollars spent was the
☐ a. Department of Defense.
☐ b. Department of Health and Human Services.
☐ c. Treasury Department.
☐ d. Department of Commerce.

21. The president cannot fire regulatory commission members.
☐ True
☐ False

22. The agency that was created to regulate business practices and control monopolistic behavior is the
☐ a.   Securities and Exchange Commission.
☐ b.   Federal Trade Commission.
☐ c.   Federal Communications Commission.
☐ d.   National Labor Relations Board.

23. The idea of "capture" refers to
☐ a.   regulatory reforms pushed by groups.
☐ b.   regulation of economic monopolies.
☐ c.   control of regulators by regulatees.
☐ d.   presidential influence on regulation.

24. Government corporations
☐ a.   provide a service that the private sector could provide.
☐ b.   typically charge for the services they provide.
☐ c.   are different from other parts of the government.
☐ d.   all of the above.

25. Which of the following agencies is NOT a government corporation?
☐ a.   Tennessee Valley Authority
☐ b.   U.S. Postal Service
☐ c.   Amtrak
☐ d.   Department of Veterans Affairs

26. The General Services Administration, the National Science Foundation, and the National Aeronautics and Space Administration are
☐ a.   cabinet departments.
☐ b.   independent executive agencies.
☐ c.   regulatory commissions.
☐ d.   government corporations.

27. Most public policies are self-executing.
☐ True
☐ False

28. The policy implementation process includes all of the following activities EXCEPT
☐ a.   creation of a new agency or assignment of responsibility to an old one.
☐ b.   translation of policy goals into operation.
☐ c.   coordination of agency resources.
☐ d.   passage of a law.

29. Successful policy implementation is more likely with
   ☐ a. good program design.
   ☐ b. lack of clarity.
   ☐ c. very broad policies.
   ☐ d. limited budgets.

30. The case of assuring equal opportunity in college athletics demonstrates that bureaucracies usually resolve policy problems that Congress fails to resolve.
   ☐ True
   ☐ False

31. Bureaucratic agencies frequently lack the staff, training, funding, supplies, and equipment to carry out the tasks it has been assigned.
   ☐ True
   ☐ False

32. Administrative routine
   ☐ a. is made possible by standard operating procedures.
   ☐ b. is not essential to bureaucracy.
   ☐ c. make it impossible to exchange personnel.
   ☐ d. prevent policies from being applied uniformly.

33. Standard operating procedures
   ☐ a. save time.
   ☐ b. bring uniformity to complex organizations.
   ☐ c. make personnel interchangeable.
   ☐ d. all of the above.

34. A paradox of bureaucracy is the coexistence of
   ☐ a. routines and discretion.
   ☐ b. equity and efficiency.
   ☐ c. rules and regulations.
   ☐ d. red tape and detail.

35. Administrative discretion is greatest when rules do not fit.
   ☐ True
   ☐ False

36. An example of a street-level bureaucrat is a
   ☐ a. Supreme Court justice.
   ☐ b. member of Congress.
   ☐ c. welfare worker.
   ☐ d. presidential appointee.

37. It is not easy to control the exercise of administrative discretion because
☐ a. it is not easy to fire bureaucrats in the civil service.
☐ b. removing appointed officials may be politically embarrassing to the president.
☐ c. special bonuses are rare in the public sector.
☐ d. all of the above.

38. Policies within the areas of human services and drug enforcement are
☐ a. well-coordinated.
☐ b. highly fragmented.
☐ c. handled by a single agency.
☐ d. uniform.

39. Government reorganization to reduce fragmentation is difficult because
☐ a. congressional committees would gain jurisdiction over too many agencies.
☐ b. too many agencies want to remain within a broader bureaucratic unit.
☐ c. interest groups do not want to give up the close relationships they have with their agencies.
☐ d. all of the above.

40. Which of the following statements about regulation is FALSE?
☐ a. Regulation pervades the everyday lives of Americans.
☐ b. Regulation is the least controversial bureaucratic role.
☐ c. The idea of a free enterprise economy is out of date.
☐ d. Almost all bureaucratic agencies are regulators.

41. In the case of *Munn v. Illinois* (1877), the Supreme Court
☐ a. upheld the right of government to regulate business.
☐ b. struck down the authority of the states to regulate.
☐ c. held that government regulation was unconstitutional.
☐ d. upheld the creation of the Interstate Commerce Commission.

42. Government agencies are not permitted to go to court to enforce their rules and guidelines.
☐ True
☐ False

43. Which of the following is NOT among the key elements of all government regulation?
☐ a. a grant of power and set of directions from Congress
☐ b. a set of rules and guidelines by the regulatory agency
☐ c. permits and licenses for regulated industries
☐ d. some means of enforcing compliance with congressional goals and agency regulations

44. Proponents of deregulation argue that regulation
☐ a. keeps prices low.
☐ b. enhances competition abroad.
☐ c. is reasonably effective.
☐ d. distorts market forces.

45. Critics of regulation claim that it
☐ a. raises prices.
☐ b. hurts America's competitive position abroad.
☐ c. doesn't work.
☐ d. all of the above.

46. Advocates of deregulation include conservatives and liberals.
☐ True
☐ False

47. Bureaucracies are America's only unelected policymaking institution.
☐ True
☐ False

48. Which of the following is NOT among the key methods used by presidents to control the bureaucracy?
☐ a. pay raises
☐ b. appointments
☐ c. budgets
☐ d. executive orders

49. Congress finds a big bureaucracy congenial because it can provide services to constituents.
☐ True
☐ False

50. Congress can oversee the bureaucracy by
    ☐ a. influencing the appointment of agency heads.
    ☐ b. holding hearings.
    ☐ c. rewriting the legislation.
    ☐ d. all of the above.

51. Which of the following would NOT be part of an iron triangle?
    ☐ a. a congressional committee
    ☐ b. a government agency
    ☐ c. a political party
    ☐ d. an interest group

52. Subgovernments or iron triangles can foster
    ☐ a. democracy.
    ☐ b. centralization.
    ☐ c. fragmentation.
    ☐ d. policy cooperation.

53. Issue networks have
    ☐ a. created new iron triangles.
    ☐ b. challenged formerly closed subgovernments.
    ☐ c. replaced the system of subgovernments.
    ☐ d. decreased participation in bureaucratic policymaking.

54. Which of the following statements regarding the scope of the bureaucracy is FALSE?
    ☐ a. The federal bureaucracy has not grown over the past two generations.
    ☐ b. Originally the bureaucracy had a modest role in promoting the economy.
    ☐ c. The bureaucracy has been able to prevent much of the deregulation attempted by Congress and the president.
    ☐ d. Today, the bureaucracy is expected to play an active role in dealing with social and economic problems.

## ESSAY QUESTIONS

1. How does one become a bureaucrat? What myths surround the bureaucracy in the United States?

2. Compare and contrast the different theories of bureaucracy. Which one do you believe best reflects reality?

3.  How is the United States bureaucracy organized? What policymaking roles do the different federal executive agencies play?

4.  What is policy implementation and what are its main features? What factors facilitate and what factors hinder successful implementation of a public policy? Use specific examples of implementation to illustrate your points.

5.  What is needed for an agency to perform its regulatory role? What are the pros and cons of deregulation?

6.  How does politics permeate bureaucracies? What factors make it difficult to control bureaucracies? What methods are available to the president and Congress to control bureaucracies?

7.  What is the role of bureaucracies in the federal system? Is the federal bureaucracy too big? What are the pros and cons of a large bureaucracy?

# Chapter 16

# THE FEDERAL COURTS

## CHAPTER OUTLINE

I. The Nature Of The Judicial System (pp. 504-507)
- A. Introduction
  1. In criminal law cases, an individual is charged by the government with violating a specific law.
  2. Civil law involves no charge of criminality, but concerns a dispute between two parties.
- B. Participants in the Judicial System
  1. Litigants
     - a. Every case is a dispute between a plaintiff and a defendant.
     - b. **Standing to sue** means that litigants must have serious interest in a case.
     - c. **Class action suits** permit a small number of people to sue on behalf of all other people similarly situated.
     - d. **Justiciable disputes** are issues that are capable of being settled by legal methods.
  2. Groups sometimes try to influence courts by using ***amicus curiae* briefs.**
  3. Attorneys

II. The Structure Of The Federal Judicial System (pp. 507-512)
- A. Introduction
  1. Congress has created constitutional courts and legislative courts.
  2. Courts with **original jurisdiction** are those in which a case is heard first, usually in a trial.
  3. Courts with **appellate jurisdiction** hear cases brought to them on appeal from a lower court.
- B. District Courts
  1. The entry point for most litigation in the federal courts is one of the ninety-one **district courts.**
  2. Most of the cases handled in the district courts are routine.
- C. Courts of Appeal
  1. The U.S. **courts of appeal** are appellate courts empowered to review all final decisions of district courts.
  2. The courts of appeal focus on correcting errors of procedure and law that occurred in the original proceedings of legal cases.

D. The Supreme Court
1. The pinnacle of the American judicial system is the U.S. **Supreme Court.**
2. Almost all of the business of the Court comes from the appellate process.

III. The Politics Of Judicial Selection (pp. 512-516)
A. The Lower Courts
1. According to **senatorial courtesy**, nominations for lower court positions are not confirmed when opposed by a senator of the president's party from the state in which the nominee is to serve.
2. The president usually has more influence in the selection of judges to the federal courts of appeal than to the federal district courts.
B. The Supreme Court
1. Nominations to the Court may be a president's most important legacy to the nation.
2. The president operates under fewer constraints in nominating members to the Supreme Court.

IV. The Background Of Judges And Justices (pp. 516-520)
A. Judges serving on the federal district and circuit courts are all lawyers and overwhelmingly white males.
B. Supreme Court justices are an elite group.

V. The Courts As Policymakers (pp. 520-526)
A. Accepting Cases
1. The most common way for the Court to put a case on its docket is by issuing to a lower federal or state court a *writ of certiorari,* a formal document that calls up a case.
2. The **solicitor general** is in charge of the appellate court litigation of the federal government.
B. Making Decisions
1. *Amicus curiae* ("friend of the court") **briefs** are briefs from parties who are interested in the outcome of the case but are not formal litigants.
2. An **opinion** is a statement of the legal reasoning behind the decision.
3. The vast majority of cases reaching the courts are settled on the principle of *stare decisis*, meaning that an earlier decision should hold for the case being considered.
4. All courts rely heavily upon **precedent**, the way similar cases were handled in the past, as a guide to current decisions.
5. **Original intent** holds that judges and justices should determine the intent of the framers of the Constitution regarding a particular matter and decide cases in line with that intent.

C.   Implementing Court Decisions
1.   **Judicial implementation** refers to how and whether court decisions are translated into actual policy, affecting the behavior of others.
2.   Implementation of court decisions involves an interpreting, implementing, and consumer population.

VI.   The Courts And The Policy Agenda (pp. 526-530)
A.   A Historical Review
1.   John Marshall and the Growth of Judicial Review
In ***Marbury v. Madison*** (1803), Chief Justice Marshall established the power of **judicial review,** the power of the courts to hold acts of Congress, and by implication the executive, in violation of the Constitution.
2.   The "Nine Old Men"
3.   The Warren Court
4.   The Burger Court
a.   The Burger Court was more conservative than the liberal Warren Court.
b.   In ***United States v. Nixon*** (1974), the Burger Court ordered President Nixon to turn over White House tapes to the courts.
5.   The Rehnquist Court

VII.   Understanding The Courts (pp. 530-536)
A.   The Courts and Democracy
B.   What Courts Should Do: The Scope of Judicial Power
1.   **Judicial restraint** is when judges adhere closely to precedent and play minimal policymaking roles.
2.   **Judicial activism** is when judges make bolder policy decisions, even charting new constitutional ground.
3.   The doctrine of **political questions** is a means to avoid deciding some cases, principally those regarding conflicts between the president and Congress.
4.   If an issue is one of **statutory construction,** in which a court interprets an act of Congress, the legislature routinely passes legislation that clarifies existing laws.

VIII.   Summary (p. 536)


## LEARNING OBJECTIVES

*After studying Chapter 16, you should be able to:*

1.   Understand the nature of the judicial system.

2. Explain how courts in the United States are organized and the nature of their jurisdiction.

3. Describe the role of judges in the judicial process, including their backgrounds and how they were selected.

4. Discuss Supreme Court policymaking and judicial implementation.

5. Explain the role of the courts in shaping the policy agenda in America.

6. Evaluate how the courts operate in a democratic system and how their activities affect the scope of government.

*The following exercises will help you meet these objectives:*

Objective 1. Understand the nature of the judicial system.

1. Explain the difference between criminal law and civil law.

Criminal Law:

Civil Law:

2. List three regular participants in the judicial system other than judges.

1.

2.

3.

3.      What is meant by "justiciable disputes"?

Objective 2. Explain how courts in the United States are organized and the nature of their jurisdiction.

1.      What are the differences between constitutional courts and legislative courts?

Constitutional Courts:

Legislative Courts:

2.      Complete the following table on the structure of the federal judicial system.

| Court | Number of Courts | Number of Judges | Jurisdiction | Policy Implications |
|---|---|---|---|---|
| District Court | | | | |
| Court of Appeal | | | | |
| Supreme Court | | | | |

3.      What is the role of an U.S. attorney?

Objective 3. Describe the role of judges in the judicial process, including their backgrounds and how they were selected.

1.       Explain the practice of "senatorial courtesy."

2.       Name three conditions in which nominations to the Supreme Court are more likely to run into trouble.

      1.

      2.

      3.

3.       Present a demographic profile of the "typical" federal judge.

4.       List six criteria that have been important in choosing Supreme Court justices over the years.

      1.

      2.

      3.

      4.

      5.

      6.

Objective 4. Discuss Supreme Court policymaking and judicial implementation.

1.      What are the four key functions of the solicitor general?

        1.

        2.

        3.

        4.


2.      What are the functions of *amicus curiae* briefs?


3.      What is the difference between a majority opinion, a dissenting opinion, and a concurring opinion?

        Majority Opinion:


        Dissenting Opinion:


        Concurring Opinion:


4.      What is the difference between *stare decisis* and precedent?

        *Stare Decisis:*



        Precedent:



5.      List and explain the three elements of judicial implementation according to Charles Johnson and Bradley Canon.

1.

2.

3.

tive 5. Explain the role of the courts in shaping the policy agenda in America.

1.      Explain the principle of judicial review.

2.      Complete the following table on public policy and the Supreme Court.

| Court | Basic Ideology | Judicial Restraint or Judicial Activism | Key Cases |
|---|---|---|---|
| Warren Court | | | |
| Burger Court | | | |
| Rehnquist Court | | | |

tive 6. Evaluate how the courts operate in a democratic system and how their activities the scope of government.

1.      In what ways might it be said that courts are not a very democratic institution?

2.      Explain the difference between judicial activism and judicial restraint.

Judicial Activism:


Judicial Restraint:


3.  Define the terms "political question" and "statutory construction" as they apply to the Supreme Court and give an example of each.

| Term | Definition | Example |
|---|---|---|
| Political Question | | |
| Statutory Construction | | |


## KEY TERMS

*Identify and Describe:*

standing to sue


class action suits


justiciable disputes

original intent

judicial implementation

*Marbury v. Madison*

judicial review

*United States v. Nixon*

judicial restraint

judicial activism

political questions

statutory construction

*Compare and Contrast:*

standing to sue and class action suits

al jurisdiction and appellate jurisdiction

ct courts, courts of appeal, and Supreme Court

decisis and precedent

ury v. *Madison* and judicial review

al restraint and judicial activism

al questions and statutory construction

*That Term:*

1.  Capable of being settled by legal methods.

    _____

2.  The way of disposing of state-level federal judicial nominations.

    _____

3.  This office represents the government before the Supreme Court.

    _____

4.  Interested parties who are not litigants submit these.

    _____

5.  A statement of the legal reasoning behind a Supreme Court decision.

    _____

6.  How and whether court decisions are translated into policy.

    _____

7.  This is sometimes referred to as strict constructionism.

    _____

8.  This Supreme Court case hastened the resignation of a president.

    _____

9.  The doctrine used to avoid deciding some cases.

    _____

## USING YOUR UNDERSTANDING

1.  Investigate the composition of the current Supreme Court in terms of the different types of individuals that are found there. Find out who appointed them, their political party affiliation, their age, their ethnicity, their religion, their home state, their previous occupation, and other such defining characteristics. Then see if you can find out how the different justices voted on some recent court cases having to do with public policy issues. Try to develop a profile of the Supreme Court in which you relate the characteristics of its members to their voting behavior. Briefly discuss the implications of a justice's background for the way he or she behaves on the bench.

2.  Conduct a study of judicial selection by comparing two recent Supreme Court nominations such as David H. Souter, Clarence Thomas, Ruth Bader Ginsburg, or Stephen G. Breyer. How do the two individuals differ? How did the two nominations differ? What were the most important factors influencing the

presidents' choices?  Who else was considered as potential nominees by each president, and why were the successful candidates chosen instead of any of the others?  How did the public react to the nominations?  How did the Senate react to the nominations?  Compare the confirmation hearings of the two nominees.  How did they differ and how were they similar?  Evaluate the judicial selection process for Supreme Court justices in light of these two cases.  Is the process fair?  How might the process be improved?

## REVIEW QUESTIONS

*Check* ☑ *the correct answer:*

1.  The Supreme Court makes the majority of American judicial policy.
    ☐ True
    ☐ False

2.  Federal judges
    ☐ a.   actively initiate cases.
    ☐ b.   issue advisory opinions on hypothetical cases.
    ☐ c.   cannot resolve justiciable disputes.
    ☐ d.   are impartial arbiters between two contending views.

3.  Which of the following is NOT associated with civil law?
    ☐ a.   a plaintiff and a defendant
    ☐ b.   a charge that a law has been violated
    ☐ c.   statutes and common law
    ☐ d.   a dispute between two parties

4.  Most civil and criminal cases begin and end in the state courts.
    ☐ True
    ☐ False

5.  Every judicial case involves
    ☐ a.   a plaintiff and defendant.
    ☐ b.   a jury.
    ☐ c.   a federal judge.
    ☐ d.   criminal law.

6.  Litigants must have
    ☐ a.  a jury trial.
    ☐ b.  standing to sue.
    ☐ c.  original jurisdiction.
    ☐ d.  a civil dispute.

7.  The concept of standing to sue has been broadened by the use of
    ☐ a.  class action suits.
    ☐ b.  appellate jurisdiction.
    ☐ c.  common law.
    ☐ d.  justiciable disputes.

8.  Which of the following is NOT a justiciable dispute?
    ☐ a.  a divorce proceeding
    ☐ b.  a dispute over an insurance claim
    ☐ c.  a suit calling for the abolishment of a federal program
    ☐ d.  a murder trial

9.  Interest groups ignore the judicial process because of its limited impact on public policy.
    ☐ True
    ☐ False

10. The federal government provides legal assistance to the poor through the
    ☐ a.  National Association for the Advancement of Colored People.
    ☐ b.  American Civil Liberties Union.
    ☐ c.  Legal Services Corporation.
    ☐ d.  all of the above.

11. The Constitution specifically created the
    ☐ a.  Supreme Court.
    ☐ b.  federal district courts.
    ☐ c.  federal courts of appeal.
    ☐ d.  all of the above.

12. Courts with appellate jurisdiction
    ☐ a.  review the factual record of cases.
    ☐ b.  hear the majority of court cases in the United States.
    ☐ c.  review the legal issues involved in cases.
    ☐ d.  are all federal courts.

13.    The Court of Military Appeals and the Tax Court are
☐ a.    constitutional courts.
☐ b.    legislative courts.
☐ c.    state courts.
☐ d.    local courts.

14.    Each state has at least one federal district court.
☐ True
☐ False

15.    Cases in the federal district courts
☐ a.    are usually presided over by one judge.
☐ b.    cannot involve litigants from different states.
☐ c.    are heard on appeal from state courts.
☐ d.    involving civil law are rarely settled.

16.    Duties of the federal magistrates include all of the following EXCEPT
☐ a.    issuing warrants for arrest.
☐ b.    hearing motions subject to review by the district judge.
☐ c.    representing the U.S. government in civil cases.
☐ d.    presiding over some trials.

17.    Most of the cases handled in the district courts
☐ a.    are settled by a jury.
☐ b.    are routine.
☐ c.    result in policy innovations.
☐ d.    are published by the U.S. government.

18.    Cases in the federal courts of appeal
☐ a.    involve trials and testimony
☐ b.    focus on the correction of errors in procedure and law
☐ c.    rarely come from the federal district courts
☐ d.    must be decided by a unanimous vote

19.    Which of the following is NOT among the functions of the Supreme Court?
☐ a.    maintaining national supremacy in the law.
☐ b.    ensuring uniformity in interpretations of national laws.
☐ c.    enforcing the orders of federal regulatory agencies.
☐ d.    resolving conflicts among the states.

20. Few cases arise under the Supreme Court's original jurisdiction.
   ☐ True
   ☐ False

21. Cases appealed to the Supreme Court from state courts must involve
   ☐ a.   a crime.
   ☐ b.   at least $50,000 in a civil case.
   ☐ c.   a substantial federal question.
   ☐ d.   all of the above.

22. Federal judges and justices
   ☐ a.   serve for life.
   ☐ b.   cannot be impeached.
   ☐ c.   can be removed for political reasons.
   ☐ d.   are elected to office.

23. The only Supreme Court Justice who was tried but not convicted by the Senate was (bonus)
   ☐ a.   Robert Bork.
   ☐ b.   Samuel Chase.
   ☐ c.   John Marshall.
   ☐ d.   William Rehnquist.

24. Senatorial courtesy allows any Senator to prevent the confirmation of a federal judiciary nominee.
   ☐ True
   ☐ False

25. Nominees for the federal judiciary are evaluated by
   ☐ a.   the Department of Justice.
   ☐ b.   the Federal Bureau of Investigation.
   ☐ c.   sitting judges.
   ☐ d.   all of the above.

26. The president's appointments to the Supreme Court may be his or her most important legacy.
   ☐ True
   ☐ False

27. Which of the following does the president rely on most to identify and screen candidates for the Supreme Court?
☐ a. the Senate Judiciary Committee
☐ b. the attorney general and the Department of Justice
☐ c. sitting justices
☐ d. the American Bar Association

28. Candidates for the Supreme Court usually aggressively pursue the position, especially by politicking the Senate Judiciary Committee.
☐ True
☐ False

29. Which of the following works to the advantage of a Supreme Court nominee?
☐ a. a reputation for judicial activism
☐ b. nomination by a president at the end of his term
☐ c. nomination by a president whose party is in the minority in the Senate
☐ d. ethics, competence, and a low profile

30. Which of the following statements is TRUE?
☐ a. Federal judges are highly representative of the American people.
☐ b. The Constitution does not require federal judges to be lawyers.
☐ c. Most federal judges have never been involved in politics.
☐ d. The Reagan administration ignored ideology in making judicial appointments.

31. The race and gender of nominees for Supreme Court justice have become less salient in recent years.
☐ True
☐ False

32. Many Supreme Court Justices, including some of the most distinguished ones, have not had previous judicial experience.
☐ True
☐ False

33. An important influence on the selection of judges and justices is
☐ a. partisanship.
☐ b. ideology.
☐ c. politics.
☐ d. all of the above.

34.  Which of the following statements is FALSE?
☐ a.  Partisan politics affects judicial appointments.
☐ b.  Presidents usually nominate judges and justices who share their ideological beliefs.
☐ c.  Members of the federal bench may time their retirement so that the president can choose compatible successors.
☐ d.  Presidents can always rely on their judicial appointees to vote the way the president wants them to vote.

35.  Which of the following statements is FALSE?
☐ a.  Republican judges are somewhat more conservative than Democratic judges are.
☐ b.  Judges who are former prosecutors are somewhat less sympathetic toward defendant rights.
☐ c.  Judges' ethnicity and gender strongly influences their judicial behavior.
☐ d.  The influence of background on judicial decision making is generally limited.

36.  A *writ of certiorari* is a formal document that
☐ a.  calls up a case for review by the Supreme Court.
☐ b.  is used to sentence convicted criminals.
☐ c.  initiates a civil law suit.
☐ d.  requires a witness to testify in federal court.

37.  The solicitor general of the United States
☐ a.  represents the United States before the Supreme Court.
☐ b.  is a presidential appointee.
☐ c.  typically has the confidence of the Supreme Court.
☐ d.  all of the above.

38.  A Supreme Court decision without explanation is known as
☐ a.  a *writ of certiorari.*
☐ b.  a *writ of mandamus.*
☐ c.  a *per curiam* decision.
☐ d.  an *amicus curiae* brief.

39.  Which of the following is NOT a characteristic of *amicus curiae* briefs?
☐ a.  Parties who are formal litigants file them.
☐ b.  They are intended to influence court decisions.
☐ c.  Some are filed by the solicitor general on behalf of the government.
☐ d.  They raise additional points of view and information.

40. The written opinion in a Supreme Court case
   ☐ a.   is irrelevant compared to the decision itself.
   ☐ b.   is a statement of the legal reasoning behind a decision.
   ☐ c.   is always prepared by the chief justice.
   ☐ d.   always represents the views of all nine justices.

41. Opinions written not only to support a majority decision but also to stress a different constitutional or legal basis are called
   ☐ a.   majority opinions.
   ☐ b.   dissenting opinions.
   ☐ c.   opposing opinions.
   ☐ d.   concurring opinions.

42. The vast majority of cases reaching the courts are settled on the principle of *stare decisis.*
   ☐ True
   ☐ False

43. When judicial precedents are clear, the Supreme Court tends to be divided in ideological terms.
   ☐ True
   ☐ False

44. The idea of original intent refers to
   ☐ a.   original jurisdiction.
   ☐ b.   the intent of the Constitution's framers.
   ☐ c.   the ideological positions of justices.
   ☐ d.   the views of a popular majority.

45. How and whether court decisions are translated into actual policy is called
   ☐ a.   judicial activism.
   ☐ b.   judicial precedents.
   ☐ c.   judicial implementation.
   ☐ d.   judicial policymaking.

46. Which of the following is NOT among the key elements of judicial implementation according to Charles Johnson and Bradley Canon?
   ☐ a.   interpreting population
   ☐ b.   implementing population
   ☐ c.   consumer population
   ☐ d.   general population

47. From 1938 to the present the Supreme Court has enlarged the scope of personal freedom and civil rights.
☐ True
☐ False

48. The case of *Marbury v. Madison* (1803) established the Supreme Court's
☐ a. power of judicial review.
☐ b. use of writs of *certiorari*.
☐ c. application of the principle of *stare decisis*.
☐ d. power to expand its original jurisdiction.

49. During the New Deal era, President Roosevelt sought to create a more sympathetic Supreme Court by
☐ a. getting Congress to expand the court's size.
☐ b. changing the chief justice.
☐ c. removing unsympathetic justices.
☐ d. directly influencing court decisions.

50. In the shift from the Warren Court to the Burger Court, the Supreme Court became more
☐ a. conservative.
☐ b. liberal.
☐ c. activist.
☐ d. none of the above.

51. Who said "It seems to me that there's nothing more antithetical to the idea of what a good judge should be than to think it has something to do with representative democracy"?  (bonus)
☐ a. Justice Potter Stewart
☐ b. Chief Justice William Rehnquist
☐ c. Justice Thurgood Marshall
☐ d. Alexander Hamilton

52. It may be said that the courts are not a very democratic institution because
☐ a. federal judges are not elected.
☐ b. it is almost impossible to remove judges.
☐ c. the courts are dominated by elites.
☐ d. all of the above.

53. The Supreme Court is generally insulated from the normal forms of politics.
☐ True
☐ False

54. Which of the following statements is FALSE?
☐ a. In some ways, courts are very undemocratic.
☐ b. Supreme Court decisions are often in line with public opinion.
☐ c. Few major policy decisions actually end up in court.
☐ d. Agencies and businesses commonly find themselves ordered by different courts to do opposite things.

55. Which of the following is NOT a general characteristic of judicial restraint?
☐ a. deference to Congress
☐ b. deference to state legislatures
☐ c. a minimum policymaking role
☐ d. achieving political ends through judicial means

56. The policy in which judges make bold policy decisions, even charting new constitutional ground, is called
☐ a. judicial restraint.
☐ b. judicial activism.
☐ c. judicial liberalism.
☐ d. judicial conservatism.

57. Liberal members of the Supreme Court tend toward judicial activism whereas conservatives tend toward judicial restraint.
☐ True
☐ False

58. The federal courts use the doctrine of "political questions"
☐ a. to settle disputes regarding the political parties.
☐ b. to make bold policy decisions.
☐ c. when the federal government is one of the litigants.
☐ d. as a means to avoid deciding some cases.

59. Congress can influence the Supreme Court and its decisions by
☐ a. beginning the process of amending the Constitution.
☐ b. altering the structure of the courts.
☐ c. passing legislation that clarifies existing laws and, in effect, overturns the courts.
☐ d. all of the above.

**ESSAY QUESTIONS**

1. How do the courts work? Who are the key participants in the American judicial system and what do they do?

2. Explain the structure of the American judicial system. What are the differences between the federal district courts, courts of appeal, and the Supreme Court?

3. What is the process by which members of the Supreme Court are chosen? How does the appointment process for other federal courts differ?

4. What are the typical characteristics of American judges and justices? How do their background and personal characteristics affect their judicial behavior?

5. How do courts shape public policy in their decisions and in the opinions by judges used to justify decisions? What effect have the courts had on the policy agenda? Use historical examples in your answer.

6. How do court decisions become public policy? What is involved in judicial implementation? Use examples to illustrate the potential problems of implementing court decisions.

7. What is the role of courts in a democracy? What are the major criticisms of the court system in the United States today? In what ways might the courts be considered too strong or weak?

# Chapter 17

## ECONOMIC POLICYMAKING

**CHAPTER OUTLINE**

I.  Government and the Economy (pp. 542-545)
    A.    Introduction
        1.    **Capitalism** is an economic system in which individuals and corporations own the principal means of production.
        2.    A **mixed economy** is a system in which the government, while not commanding the economy, is still deeply involved in economic decisions.
    B.    Unemployment and Inflation
        1.    The **unemployment rate** has a direct affect on government and politics.
        2.    The **Consumer Price Index (CPI)** measures **inflation**.
    C.    Elections and the Economy
    D.    Political Parties and the Economy

II.  Instruments for Controlling the Economy (pp. 545-549)
    A.    **Laissez-faire** is the principle that government should not meddle with the economy.
    B.    Monetary Policy and the Fed
        1.    **Monetary policy** is the manipulation of the supply of money and credit in private hands.
        2.    **Monetarism** holds that the supply of money is the key to the nation's economic health.
        3.    The main agency for making monetary policy is the Board of Governors of the **Federal Reserve System.**
    C.    Fiscal Policy: Keynesian versus Supply-Side Economics
        1.    **Fiscal policy** describes the impact of the federal budget on the economy.
        2.    **Keynesian economic theory** holds that government spending can help the economy weather its normal ups and downs.
        3.    **Supply-side economics** argues that the key task for government economic policy is to stimulate the supply of goods, not their demand.

III.  Obstacles To Controlling The Economy (pp. 549-550)
    A.    Instruments for controlling the economy are difficult to use.
    B.    Economic policies take a long time to implement.

C. The private sector dominates the economy.

D. Most of the budget expenditures are uncontrollable.

IV. Arenas of Economic Policymaking (pp. 550-556)

    A. Business and Public Policy: Subsidies Amidst Regulations

        1. Some **transnational corporations,** businesses with vast holdings in many countries, are bigger than most governments.

        2. The Changing Face of Corporate Capitalism

        3. Regulating Business

            a. **Antitrust policy** ensures competition and prevents monopoly.

            b. Antitrust suits are more often threatened than carried out.

        4. Benefiting Business

    B. Consumer Policy: The Rise of the Consumer Lobby

        1. The **Food and Drug Administration (FDA)** has broad regulatory powers over the manufacturing, contents, marketing, and labeling of food and drugs.

        2. The **Federal Trade Commission (FTC)** has become a defender of consumer interests in truth in advertising.

    C. Labor and Government

        1. The **National Labor Relations Act** guarantees workers the right of **collective bargaining,** the right to have labor union representatives negotiate with management to determine working conditions.

        2. The **Taft-Hartley Act** continued to guarantee collective bargaining, but prohibited unfair practices by unions as well.

        3. Section 14B of Taft-Hartley permitted **right-to-work laws** that forbid labor contracts from requiring workers to join unions to hold their jobs.

    D. New Economy, New policy Arenas

V. Understanding Economic Policymaking (pp. 556-558)

    A. Democracy and Economic Policymaking

    B. Economic Policymaking and the Scope of Government

VI. Summary (pp. 558-559)

## LEARNING OBJECTIVES

*After studying Chapter 17, you should be able to:*

1. Understand the relationship between politics and the economy.

2. Describe the instruments and programs that policymakers use to affect the state of the economy.

3. Explain the obstacles to controlling the economy.

4. Discuss the major issues and policy directions that have been pursued in the areas of business, consumer, and labor policy.

5. Understand the relationship between democracy, the scope of government, and economic policymaking in the United States.

*The following exercises will help you meet these objectives:*

Objective 1. Understand the relationship between politics and the economy.

1. Briefly explain how the unemployment rate is measured.



2. What is meant by the Consumer Price Index (CPI) and why is it important?



3. Explain the basic difference between the Republican Party and the Democratic Party in terms of their approach to economic policies.

Republicans:



Democrats:



Objective 2. Describe the instruments and programs that policymakers use to affect the state of the economy.

1.	What are the three basic instruments available to the Federal Reserve System for controlling the money supply?

   1.


   2.


   3.



2.	What is meant by fiscal policy?



3.	Explain the basic differences between Keynesian economic theory and supply-side economics.

   Keynesian Theory:



   Supply-Side Economics:



Objective 3.  Explain the obstacles to controlling the economy.

   1.	List three reasons why it is difficult to precisely control unemployment and inflation.

      1.


      2.


      3.

2.     Explain how the American capitalist system imposes restraints on controlling the economy.

Objective 4.  Discuss the major issues and policy directions that have been pursued in the areas of business, consumer, and labor policy.

1.     Complete the following table listing one major congressional act and one major governmental policy for each of the arenas of economic policymaking discussed in the text.

| Arena | Major Congressional Act | Major Government Policy |
|---|---|---|
| Business | | |
| Consumers | | |
| Labor | | |

2.     List four ways in which the government benefits business.

       1.

       2.

       3.

       4.

3.     How does the Food and Drug Administration (FDA) and the Federal Trade Commission (FTC) benefit consumers?

FDA:


FTC:


4.    What were the main provisions of the National Labor Relations Act and the Taft-Hartley Act?

National Labor Relations Act:


Taft-Hartley Act:


Objective 5.  Understand the relationship between democracy, the scope of government, and economic policymaking in the United States.

1.    What are some of the main flaws of a command economy such as was found in the former Soviet Union?


2.    What is the main difference between the liberal and conservative view of the scope of government in economic policymaking?

Liberals:


Conservatives:

**KEY TERMS**

*Identify and Describe:*

capitalism

mixed economy

unemployment rate

inflation

Consumer Price Index (CPI)

laissez-faire

monetary policy

monetarism

Federal Reserve System

fiscal policy

Keynesian economic theory

supply-side economics

transnational corporations

antitrust policy

Food and Drug Administration (FDA)

Federal Trade Commission (FTC)

National Labor Relations Act

collective bargaining

Taft-Hartley Act

right-to-work laws

*Compare and Contrast:*

capitalism and mixed economy

inflation and consumer price index (CPI)

laissez-faire, monetarism, and Keynesian economic theory

monetary policy and fiscal policy

Keynesian economic theory and supply-side economics

Food and Drug Administration and Federal Trade Commission

National Labor Relations Act and collective bargaining

Taft Hartley Act and right-to-work laws

*Name That Term:*

1.  The percentage of Americans actively seeking employment but unable to find work.

    _____

2.      It regulates the lending practices of banks.

_____

3.      An economic theory popularized by President Reagan.

_____

4.      Some of these have annual budgets exceeding that of foreign countries.

_____

5.      This is used to ensure competition and prevent monopoly.

_____

6.      These laws forbid labor contracts from requiring workers to join unions to hold their jobs.

_____

## USING YOUR UNDERSTANDING

1.      Find copies of the government's objective indicators of economic conditions—the unemployment and inflation rates—for some recent years. The government documents section of your school library would be a good place to start. Try your hand at plotting these indicators on a graph. Then try to locate an indicator of the importance of these issues on the public agenda, as measured by public opinion about the seriousness of these economic problems. Plot this indicator along with the objective indicators you found. If a national election occurred during the time frame you are considering, draw a line representing when the election occurred. Briefly describe what you found in terms of the relationship between the government's measurement of economic problems and their place on the public's agenda. If applicable, describe the apparent impact of the election on the indicators you plotted.

2.      Using newspapers and/or newsmagazines collect some current examples of economic policymaking in the United States. Try to find items that illustrate the different tools that policymakers use to try to control the economy and the

different sectors of the economy that they seek to control. Consider the impact of the political party in power on current economic policymaking and whether or not it is consistent with what would be expected. Describe what you found in terms of the direction and impact of contemporary policies in the economic arena.

## REVIEW QUESTIONS

*Check ☑ the correct answer:*

1. James Madison and Karl Marx had in common a belief in
   ☐ a.   communism.
   ☐ b.   capitalism.
   ☐ c.   economic conflict as the root of politics.
   ☐ d.   Keynesian economic philosophy.

2. The Bureau of Labor Statistics measures the unemployment rate as the total number of adults without jobs.
   ☐ True
   ☐ False

3. Our key measure of inflation is called the
   ☐ a.   Consumer Price Index (CPI).
   ☐ b.   Gross National Product (GNP).
   ☐ c.   Laffer Curve.
   ☐ d.   National Inflation Index (NII).

4. According to a study by Robert Kiewiet, people who felt that unemployment was a serious national problem
   ☐ a.   leaned toward the Democratic party.
   ☐ b.   leaned toward the Republican party.
   ☐ c.   were unaffected by party politics.
   ☐ d.   tended not to vote.

5. Which of the following statements is FALSE?
   ☐ a.   Voters pay attention to economic trends when making up their minds.
   ☐ b.   Voters concerned with unemployment are more likely to vote Democratic.
   ☐ c.   The parties pay close attention to economic conditions when selecting their policies.
   ☐ d.   Inflation influences how people vote more than any other economic factor.

6. The coalition behind the Republican Party is most likely to be concerned with
   - ☐ a. inflation.
   - ☐ b. inflation and unemployment.
   - ☐ c. unemployment.
   - ☐ d. expanding government's role.

7. Laissez-faire was an economic philosophy embraced by
   - ☐ a. Herbert Hoover.
   - ☐ b. Franklin D. Roosevelt.
   - ☐ c. Lyndon Johnson.
   - ☐ d. Jimmy Carter.

8. Monetarists seek to keep the money supply in line with the
   - ☐ a. Consumer Price Index.
   - ☐ b. gross domestic product.
   - ☐ c. unemployment rate.
   - ☐ d. amount of available credit.

9. According to monetarists, too much money and credit leads to
   - ☐ a. recession.
   - ☐ b. unemployment.
   - ☐ c. inflation.
   - ☐ d. a budget surplus.

10. The Board of Governors of the Federal Reserve System
    - ☐ a. consists of twelve members.
    - ☐ b. belong to the president's party.
    - ☐ c. regulates the lending practices of banks.
    - ☐ d. is formally controlled by Congress and the president.

11. Which of the following is NOT among the instruments used by the Federal Reserve System to affect the money supply?
    - ☐ a. determining tax rates
    - ☐ b. buying and selling government securities
    - ☐ c. setting discount rates
    - ☐ d. setting reserve requirements

12. The financial dealings of the Federal Reserve Board directly or indirectly affect
    - ☐ a. interest rates.
    - ☐ b. inflation.
    - ☐ c. availability of jobs.
    - ☐ d. all of the above.

13. The president has ultimate influence over the policies of the Federal Reserve System.
    ☐ True
    ☐ False

14. The impact of the federal budget—taxes, spending, and borrowing—on the economy describes
    ☐ a.   laissez-faire policy.
    ☐ b.   monetary policy.
    ☐ c.   fiscal policy.
    ☐ d.   economic policy.

15. Fiscal policy is almost entirely determined by
    ☐ a.   Congress and the president.
    ☐ b.   the Federal Reserve System.
    ☐ c.   the Internal Revenue Service.
    ☐ d.   the Office of Management and Budget.

16. Our dominant economic philosophy since World War II has been
    ☐ a.   laissez-faire.
    ☐ b.   monetarism.
    ☐ c.   Keynesianism.
    ☐ d.   supply-side economics.

17. An example of a Keynesian economic policy is
    ☐ a.   borrowing funds to cover the federal deficit.
    ☐ b.   allowing the free market to determine economic health.
    ☐ c.   deregulating commerce and industry.
    ☐ d.   creating government jobs to ease unemployment.

18. Which of the following statements is TRUE?
    ☐ a.   Fiscal policy uses the Federal Reserve System.
    ☐ b.   Supply-side economics holds that tax cuts will stimulate the economy.
    ☐ c.   Conservative politicians have long favored Keynesian economic theory.
    ☐ d.   The Laffer curve shows the relationship between inflation and unemployment.

19. Who, according to legend, wrote his economic theory on the back of a cocktail napkin? (bonus)
☐ a. Karl Marx
☐ b. John Maynard Keynes
☐ c. Arthur Laffer
☐ d. Adam Smith

20. A study by Edward Tufte discovered that
☐ a. economic ups and downs were largely unsynchronized with elections.
☐ b. real disposable income tends to increase at election time more than at other times.
☐ c. transfer payments tend to decrease after elections.
☐ d. inflation tends to decrease just prior to election time.

21. Economists have shown that decisions to artificially influence the economy at election time have been made on a regular basis.
☐ True
☐ False

22. The instruments for controlling the economy are relatively easy to use.
☐ True
☐ False

23. Our capitalist system presents a restraint on controlling the economy because
☐ a. the private sector dominates the economy.
☐ b. big business dominates economic policymaking.
☐ c. no one can predict American consumer behavior.
☐ d. none of the above.

24. Unlike most policymaking in the United States, the power to make economic policy is highly centralized.
☐ True
☐ False

25. Liberals tend to favor
☐ a. government involvement in the economy.
☐ b. minimal regulation.
☐ c. supply-side economics.
☐ d. laissez-faire.

26. Most interest groups seek government
    ☐ a. benefits.
    ☐ b. protection from unemployment.
    ☐ c. safeguards against harmful business practices.
    ☐ d. all of the above.

27. At the center of the American economy has long stood the
    ☐ a. corporation.
    ☐ b. family farm.
    ☐ c. consumer.
    ☐ d. labor union.

28. Some American corporations control assets larger than the governmental budgets of most of the world's nations.
    ☐ True
    ☐ False

29. In the 1980s, corporate capitalism was characterized by
    ☐ a. hard times.
    ☐ b. increased regulation.
    ☐ c. increased number of mergers.
    ☐ d. nationalism.

30. One of the best examples of the "new economy" is
    ☐ a. publishing companies.
    ☐ b. airlines.
    ☐ c. Internet companies.
    ☐ d. agriculture.

31. Government policy has tried to control excess power in the corporate world in both the old and new economy.
    ☐ True
    ☐ False

32. Antitrust policy is implemented by the
    ☐ a. Justice Department.
    ☐ b. General Service Administration.
    ☐ c. Small Business Administration.
    ☐ d. Patent Office.

33.  One of the most recent antitrust suits resulted in the breakup of
     ☐ a.  International Business Machines (IBM).
     ☐ b.  General Motors.
     ☐ c.  American Telephone & Telegraph (AT&T).
     ☐ d.  Exxon.

34.  Antitrust policy is the only way in which the government is able to regulate business.
     ☐ True
     ☐ False

35.  The government aids American business by
     ☐ a.  collecting data on products and markets.
     ☐ b.  issuing and protecting patents.
     ☐ c.  providing research and development funds.
     ☐ d.  all of the above.

36.  Who said, "the business of America is business"? (bonus)
     ☐ a.  John Maynard Keynes
     ☐ b.  Calvin Coolidge
     ☐ c.  Herbert Hoover
     ☐ d.  Ronald Reagan

37.  The first major consumer protection policy was the
     ☐ a.  Food and Drug Act.
     ☐ b.  Consumer Product Safety Act.
     ☐ c.  Consumer Credit Protection Act.
     ☐ d.  Wagner Act.

38.  The agency that became a zealous defender of consumer interests in truth in advertising in the 1960s and 1970s was the
     ☐ a.  Small Business Administration.
     ☐ b.  Food and Drug Administration.
     ☐ c.  Consumer Product Safety Commission.
     ☐ d.  Federal Trade Commission.

39.  Perhaps the biggest change in economic policymaking over the past century has been the virtual 180-degree turn in public policy toward
     ☐ a.  consumers.
     ☐ b.  business.
     ☐ c.  labor unions.
     ☐ d.  farmers.

40. The National Labor Relations Act
☐ a. provided for a right-to-work law.
☐ b. enforced "yellow dog contracts."
☐ c. exempted unions from antitrust laws.
☐ d. guaranteed the right of collective bargaining.

41. The Taft-Hartley Act
☐ a. continued to guarantee unions the right of collective bargaining.
☐ b. gave the president a means to halt major strikes.
☐ c. permitted states to adopt right-to-work laws.
☐ d. all of the above.

42. Right-to-work laws allow workers to enjoy the benefits of union negotiations without contributing dues to support the union.
☐ True
☐ False

43. The new economy involves issues of
☐ a. income inequality.
☐ b. information inequality.
☐ c. gender inequality.
☐ d. product inequality.

44. In America, solutions to many of the problems of a free enterprise economy have been achieved through
☐ a. violence.
☐ b. the democratic process.
☐ c. business initiatives.
☐ d. economic upheavals.

45. Democracy regularly facilitates an economic policy that looks after general rather than specific interests.
☐ True
☐ False

46. In general, liberals would favor letting business and the free market create new jobs and prepare people for them.
☐ True
☐ False

## ESSAY QUESTIONS

1. How are politics and economics related? Why do politicians and policymakers try to control the economy?

2. What are the principle instruments available to policymakers for controlling the economy? Compare monetarism, Keynesian economic theory, and supply-side economics.

3. What obstacles does the government face in attempting to control the economy?

4. What policies has government used to try to control American business? Has the government been successful?

5. When and why did the consumer movement emerge? What are some of the major developments in consumer policy?

6. How has government policy toward labor changed in the last century? What public policies have emerged to protect workers?

7. How closely does economic policymaking in the United States conform to democratic theory?

# Chapter 18

## SOCIAL WELFARE POLICYMAKING

## CHAPTER OUTLINE

I.  Introduction (pp. 562-564)
    A.  The social welfare system has become politically controversial.
    B.  **Social welfare policies** attempt to provide assistance and support to specific groups in society.

II. The Social Welfare Debate (pp. 564-565)
    A.  **Entitlement programs** consist of government benefits that certain qualified individuals are entitled to by law, regardless of need.
    B.  **Means-tested programs** are benefits provided only to people with specific needs.

III. Income, Poverty, and Public Policy (pp. 565-571)
    A.  Who's Getting What?
        1.  **Income distribution** describes the share of national income earned by various groups in the United States.
        2.  **Income** is the amount of money collected between any two points in time.
        3.  **Wealth** is the amount already owned.
    B.  Who's Poor in America?
        1.  The **poverty line** takes into account what a family would need to spend to maintain an "austere" standard of living.
        2.  Poverty may be more extensive than the poverty line suggests.
        3.  Because of the high incidence of poverty among unmarried mothers and their children, experts on poverty often describe the problem today as the **feminization of poverty.**
    C.  What Part Does Government Play?
        1.  Taxation
            a.  A **progressive tax** takes a bigger bite from the incomes of the rich than the poor.
            b.  A **proportional tax** takes the same percentage from everyone.
            c.  A **regressive tax** takes a higher percentage from the lower income levels than from the rich.
            d.  Through the **Earned Income Tax Credit (EITC)**, the poorest of the poor receive a check from Washington instead of sending one.
            e.  The net effect of taxes on people's incomes (**tax incidence**) in the United States is proportional.

2. Government Expenditures
   a. **Transfer payments** transfer money from the general treasury to those in specific need.
   b. Transfer payments have done little to redistribute income in America.

IV. The Evolution of America's Social Welfare Programs (pp. 571-577)
   A. The New Deal and the Elderly. The Social Security Act brought government into the equation of one generation's obligations to another.
   B. President Johnson's Great Society expanded welfare programs.
   C. President Reagan and Limits to the Great Society. President Reagan limited social welfare spending.
   D. Welfare Reform in the 1990s

V. The Future of Social Welfare Policy (pp. 577-580)
   A. The Entitlement Programs: Living on Borrowed Time?
   B. The Means-Tested Programs: Do They Work?
   C. Social Welfare Policy Elsewhere

VI. Understanding Social Welfare Policy (pp. 580-583)
   A. Democracy and Social Welfare
   B. Social Welfare Policy and the Scope of Government

VII. Summary (p. 583)

## LEARNING OBJECTIVES

*After studying Chapter 18, you should be able to:*

1. Understand the debate over social welfare policy in the United States.

2. Discuss the nature of wealth and poverty and how public policy affects income in the United States.

3. Explain the evolution of social welfare programs in the United States.

4. Understand the debate concerning the future of social welfare policy.

5. Understand the place for social welfare policies in a democracy and how they contribute to the scope of government.

*The following exercises will help you meet these objectives:*

Objective 1.  Understand the debate over social welfare policy in the United States.

    1.      Define "social welfare policies."


    2.      What is the difference between entitlement programs and means-tested programs?

          Entitlement Programs:


          Means-Tested Programs:


Objective 2.  Discuss the nature of wealth and poverty and how public policy affects income in the United States.

    1.      What is the difference between income and wealth?

          Income:


          Wealth:


    3.      How does the U.S. Bureau of the Census define poverty?


    4.      What are the three types of taxes and how can each affect citizens' incomes?

          1.

2.


3.


5.     What is meant by a transfer payment?  Give an example.


6.     Make a list of three entitlement programs and three means-tested programs.

| Entitlement Programs | Means-Tested Programs |
|---|---|
|  |  |
|  |  |
|  |  |

Objective 3.     Explain the evolution of social welfare programs in the United States.

1.     Complete the following table by briefly summarizing the major emphasis of social welfare and listing a major social welfare act during the New Deal (Roosevelt), Great Society (Johnson), and Reagan eras.

| Era | Social Welfare Emphasis | Social Welfare Act |
|---|---|---|
| New Deal |  |  |
| Great Society |  |  |
| Reagan |  |  |

2.     List the three major provisions of the 1996 Welfare Reform Bill.

1.

2.

3.

Objective 4.  Understand the debate concerning the future of social welfare policy.

1.    Briefly explain the major problem facing entitlement programs today.

2.    Summarize Charles Murray's arguments concerning the social programs of the Great Society.

3.    List three ways in which social welfare in the United States differs from most Western European countries.

1.

2.

3.

Objective 5.  Understand the place for social welfare policies in a democracy and how they contribute to the scope of government.

1.    What is the difference between the poor and the elderly in terms of their ability to influence social welfare policy?

Poor:


Elderly:


2.      In what ways has social welfare policy increased the scope of government?


**KEY TERMS**

*Identify and Describe:*

social welfare policies


entitlement programs


means-tested programs


income distribution


income


wealth

poverty line

feminization of poverty

progressive tax

proportional tax

regressive tax

tax incidence

Earned Income Tax Credit

transfer payments

Temporary Assistance to Needy Families

*Compare and Contrast:*

social welfare policies and transfer payments

entitlement programs and means-tested programs

income and wealth

progressive tax, proportional tax, and regressive tax

*Name That Term:*

1. The share of national income earned by various groups in the United States.

   _____

2. A measure that takes into account what a family would need to spend to maintain an "austere" standard of living.

   _____

3. The increasing concentration of poverty among women.

   _____

4. An example is when the rich pay 5 percent of their income in taxes while the poor pay 50 percent of theirs.

   _____

5. A negative income tax.

   _____

6. The proportion of income a particular group pays in taxes.

   _____

7. Benefits that are paid either in cash or in-kind.

   _____

8.      The new name for public assistance to needy families.

      _____

## USING YOUR UNDERSTANDING

1.      Look for various ways in which income is distributed in the United States. For example, you may want to find out how income differs between various regions, states, cities, age groups, races, and genders. Illustrate differences between groups using bar or pie charts. You may also want to examine how income has changed over time in the categories you use. Try to explain why incomes are higher for one group and not another. Identify public policies, such as taxes, that affect the incomes of the different groups.

2.      Develop a comparison of a social welfare policy in the United States with that of another western democracy. For example, Medicare and Medicaid could be compared with the National Health Service in Great Britain. Briefly describe the history of each policy. Examine the issues or controversies associated with the policy today. Find out how much the policy costs and what benefits are bestowed, in their entirety and on a per capita basis. Find out how the policy is paid for through taxes. Who are the primary recipients of the benefits? Consider whether one system has any advantages over the other.

## REVIEW QUESTIONS

*Check ☑ the correct answer:*

1..     The largest and most expensive social welfare programs in America are
      ☐ a.   public assistance programs.
      ☐ b.   entitlements.
      ☐ c.   poverty programs.
      ☐ d.   means-tested programs.

2.      Government programs available only to persons below a poverty line are called
      ☐ a.   social welfare policies.
      ☐ b.   entitlement programs.
      ☐ c.   means-tested programs.
      ☐ d.   income distribution policies.

3. Americans have the highest per capita income in the world.
☐ True
☐ False

4. Who responded to the remark that "The rich are different from you and me" with "Yes, they have more money"? (bonus)
☐ a. Ernest Hemingway
☐ b. F. Scott Fitzgerald
☐ c. Thomas B. Edsall
☐ d. Dan Quayle

5. The idea that the "rich get richer and the poor get poorer" was particularly applicable during the
☐ a. 1950s.
☐ b. 1960s.
☐ c. 1970s.
☐ d. 1980s.

6. Which of the following is NOT considered wealth?
☐ a. stocks and bonds
☐ b. cars and houses
☐ c. bank deposits
☐ d. the amount earned between two points in time

7. The percentage of wealth possessed by the top one percent of wealth-holders in the United States is about
☐ a. 1 percent.
☐ b. 17 percent.
☐ c. 37 percent.
☐ d. 57 percent.

8. A decade-long study of five thousand families showed that
☐ a. the poverty line is an accurate portrayal of poverty in America.
☐ b. almost one-third of the families were below the poverty level at least once during the decade.
☐ c. poverty is not as extensive as the poverty line suggests.
☐ d. a culture of poverty exists in the United States.

9. Poverty is particularly common among
☐ a. African Americans.
☐ b. Hispanics.
☐ c. young people.
☐ d. all of the above.

10. Poverty is particularly a problem among
   □ a. unmarried women and children.
   □ b. the elderly.
   □ c. single men.
   □ d. urban dwellers.

11. Government can directly affect people's income through
   □ a. taxation.
   □ b. expenditure policies.
   □ c. regulation.
   □ d. both a. and b.

12. Who said, "Nothing is certain in life but death and taxes"? (bonus)
   □ a. George Bush
   □ b. Abraham Lincoln
   □ c. Benjamin Franklin
   □ d. the Supreme Court

13. Taxes that take a bigger share of a rich family's income than a poor family's income are known as
   □ a. progressive taxes.
   □ b. proportional taxes.
   □ c. regressive taxes.
   □ d. none of the above.

14. Many taxes are purposively regressive.
   □ True
   □ False

15. State sales taxes tend to be
   □ a. progressive.
   □ b. proportional.
   □ c. regressive.
   □ d. neutral.

16. Earned Income Tax Credit benefits
   □ a. the wealthiest individuals who overpay taxes.
   □ b. the poorest of the poor.
   □ c. college students.
   □ d. the working class.

17. The evidence suggests that the overall effect of taxes in America is
    ☐ a. progressive.
    ☐ b. proportional.
    ☐ c. regressive.
    ☐ d. none of the above.

18. Transfer payments can be either cash or in-kind payments.
    ☐ True
    ☐ False

19. An example of an in-kind transfer payment is
    ☐ a. a social security check.
    ☐ b. a federal pension.
    ☐ c. unemployment compensation.
    ☐ d. food stamps.

20. Transfer payments to the elderly have gone a long way in turning the elderly from one of our poorest groups to a group whose income is above average.
    ☐ True
    ☐ False

21. After the Great Depression, many Americans began to think that governments must do more to protect their citizens against the vicissitudes of economic downturns.
    ☐ True
    ☐ False

22. The act which first brought government into the equation of one generation's obligations to another was the
    ☐ a. Medicare Act.
    ☐ b. Medicaid Act.
    ☐ c. Social Security Act.
    ☐ d. Omnibus Budget Reconciliation Act.

23. Lyndon Johnson's social policy programs were known as
    ☐ a. the New Deal.
    ☐ b. the Great Society.
    ☐ c. the New Frontier.
    ☐ d. a More Kind and Gentle America.

24. Advocates for greater spending for poverty programs had a difficult time because
    ☐ a. poverty was closely tied to race issues.
    ☐ b. poor people were less organized and powerful.
    ☐ c. poor people had lower voter turnout rates.
    ☐ d. all of the above.

25. The most important element for the success of social welfare programs has been
    ☐ a. congressional initiatives.
    ☐ b. interest group activity.
    ☐ c. strong presidential leadership.
    ☐ d. judicial decisions.

26. Republican Richard Nixon dismantled most of the social policy programs put into place by Lyndon Johnson.
    ☐ True
    ☐ False

27. As one major way to cut government spending, Ronald Reagan chose to target
    ☐ a. entitlements.
    ☐ b. poverty programs.
    ☐ c. military spending.
    ☐ d. all of the above.

28. President Reagan
    ☐ a. reduced the growth rates of many social welfare programs.
    ☐ b. shifted the burden of social welfare programs to the states.
    ☐ c. removed many previously eligible social welfare recipients from the rolls.
    ☐ d. all of the above.

29. The 1996 Welfare Reform Bill
    ☐ a. gave each state a fixed amount of money to run its own welfare programs.
    ☐ b. required people on welfare to find work within two years or lose all their benefits.
    ☐ c. placed a lifetime maximum of 5 years on welfare.
    ☐ d. all of the above.

30. The 1996 Welfare Reform Bill failed to reduce the number of people on welfare.
    ☐ True
    ☐ False

31. At some point in the near future Social Security payouts will exceed income.
    ☐ True
    ☐ False

32. Morgan Reynolds and Eugene Smolensky demonstrated that government spending between 1950 and 1970
    ☐ a. caused incomes to become more equal.
    ☐ b. had no effect on income equality.
    ☐ c. lowered income levels.
    ☐ d. reduced the number of people below the poverty line.

33. Charles Murray contends that social policies
    ☐ a. shield the poor from shocks to the system.
    ☐ b. actually make the poverty situation worse.
    ☐ c. encourage the poor to escape poverty.
    ☐ d. are unprofitable to the poor and victimized.

34. According to David Ellwood and Lawrence Summers, much of the movement into and out of poverty during the post-1965 period was due to
    ☐ a. economic growth and recessions.
    ☐ b. a culture of poverty.
    ☐ c. Lyndon Johnson's social programs.
    ☐ d. a rising crime rate.

35. The United States is one of the skimpiest providers of social welfare policies among Western democracies.
    ☐ True
    ☐ False

36. France provides
    ☐ a. far more social welfare policies than the U.S.
    ☐ b. far less social welfare policies than the U.S.
    ☐ c. about the same social welfare policies than the U.S.
    ☐ d. no social welfare policy benefits.

37. Compared to Americans, Europeans
    ☐ a. tend to support greater governmental responsibility for social welfare problems.
    ☐ b. have more positive attitudes toward government.
    ☐ c. pay higher taxes to support social welfare programs.
    ☐ d. all of the above.

38. Government benefits are
    ☐ a. difficult to obtain.
    ☐ b. difficult to withdraw.
    ☐ c. rapidly decreasing.
    ☐ d. both a. and b.

39. Social welfare policies have created a huge social welfare bureaucracy at all levels of government, federal, state, and local.
    ☐ True
    ☐ False

## ESSAY QUESTIONS

1. Explain the nature of the distribution of income and wealth in the United States. What are the characteristics of poverty and poor people in the United States?

2. How does public policy affect the distribution of income in the United States?

3. What are the different types of social welfare programs in the United States and how do they compare to social welfare programs in other countries?

4. How have social welfare programs evolved in the United States? In particular, compare the New Deal legislation and Great Society legislation with President Reagan's policies.

5. What are the major problems facing social welfare programs today? Speculate on the future of social welfare in the United States.

6. Describe the debate concerning the causes of poverty and whether social welfare policies really work in our democracy. Take sides on the debate and defend your position.

# Chapter 19

## POLICYMAKING FOR HEALTH CARE AND THE ENVIRONMENT

### CHAPTER OUTLINE

I.      Health Care Policy (pp. 588-595)
      A.     The Health of Americans
      B.     The Cost of Health Care
      C.     Access to Health Care
            1.     Health Insurance
            2.     Managed Care (**health maintenance organizations, HMOs**)
      D.     The Role of Government in Health Care
             1.     Much medical research is financed through the National Institutes of Health (NIH).
             2.     **National health insurance** is a proposal for a compulsory insurance program to finance all Americans' medical care.
             3.     **Medicare** is part of the Social Security system and covers more than 38 million people.
             4.     **Medicaid** is a program designed to provide health care for the poor.
      E.     Policymaking for Health Care
             1.     Traditionally there has been no single institution paying medical bills in the United States.
             2.     Many interests are involved in health care policies.
                  a.     The elderly
                  b.     Workers in low paying jobs
                  c.     Business
                  d.     Insurance companies
             3.     The Clinton Health Care Reform Plan
             4.     The Health Policy Issues Ahead

II.     Environmental Policy (pp. 598-609)
      A.     Economic Growth and the Environment
      B.     Environmental Policies in America
             1.     The **Environmental Protection Agency (EPA)** is the nation's largest federal regulatory agency.
             2.     Environmental Impacts. The **National Environmental Policy Act (NEPA)** requires both government and private agencies to complete **environmental impact statements (EIS).**

3. Clean Air. The **Clean Air Act of 1970** charges the Department of Transportation with the responsibility of reducing automobile emissions.
4. Clean Water. The **Water Pollution Control Act of 1972** is designed to control pollution in the nation's lakes and rivers.
5. Wilderness Preservation.
6. Endangered Species. The **Endangered Species Act of 1973** created an endangered species protection program in the U.S. Fish and Wildlife Service.

C. Energy, the Environment, and Global Warming
1. Energy issues present thorny problems for policymakers.
2. Global Warming.
D. Toxic Wastes
1. The **Superfund** was created to clean up toxic wastes by taxing chemical products.
2. Cleaning up toxic wastes has become more expensive and difficult than hoped.
E. Making Environmental Policy

III. Understanding Health Care and Environmental Policy (pp. 610-611)
A. Democracy and Health Care and Environmental Policy
B. The Scope of Government and Health Care and Environmental Policy

IV. Summary (pp. 611-614)

## LEARNING OBJECTIVES

*After studying Chapter 19, you should be able to:*

1. Explain the nature of health care and health care policy in the United States.

2. Discuss the issues surrounding the environment and the programs and policies to deal with them.

3. Understand the relationship between health and environmental policy and democracy and the scope of government.

*The following exercises will help you meet these objectives:*

Objective 1. Explain the nature of health care and health care policy in the United States.

1.  How do life expectancy and infant mortality rates in the United States compare with other nations?

    Life Expectancy:


    Infant Mortality:



2.  What is meant by "defensive medicine"?




3.  In what ways is access to health insurance unequal in the United States?




4.  What are some of the advantages and disadvantages of managed care?





5.  What is the difference between Medicare and Medicaid?

    Medicare:


    Medicaid:


6.  List and explain the involvement of four interest groups in health care policy.

    1.


    2.

3.


4.


7.      What were the main provisions of President Clinton's health care reform plan?




Objective 2.  Discuss the issues surrounding the environment and the programs and policies to deal with them.

1.      What is meant by the "nondegradation" standard?


2.      What is an environmental impact statement?


3.      List the main provisions of the Clean Air Act of 1970, the Water Pollution Control Act of 1972, and the Endangered Species Act of 1973.

        Clean Air Act:


        Water Pollution Control Act:


        Endangered Species Act:


4.      What are the four most important sources of energy in the United States?

        1.

        2.

        3.

4.

5.     What are the main problems for each of the following energy sources?

Coal:

Petroleum:

Nuclear:

6.     What are the main arguments against the 1997 treaty on global warming?

7.     Explain how the Superfund works.

5.     What has been the primary argument of opponents of strict environmental laws?

Objective 3. Understand the relationship between health and environmental policy and democracy and the scope of government.

1.     Why are individual citizens rarely involved in policymaking for technological issues?

2.     How have technological issues affected the scope of government?

## KEY TERMS

*Identify and Describe:*

health maintenance organizations (HMOs)


national health insurance


Medicare


Medicaid


Environmental Protection Agency (EPA)


National Environmental Policy Act (NEPA)


environmental impact statement (EIS)


Clean Air Act of 1970


Water Pollution Control Act of 1972


Endangered Species Act of 1973

Superfund

*Compare and Contrast:*

national health insurance and Medicare

Medicare and Medicaid

National Environmental Policy Act (NEPA) and environmental impact statement (EIS)

Clean Air Act of 1970 and Water Pollution Control Act of 1972

*Name that Term:*

1.   A popular managed care system designed to keep health care costs down.

_____

2.   Our largest federal regulatory agency.

_____

3.   The law that requires the government to actively protect each of hundreds of species listed as endangered.

_____

4.   It is funded through taxes on chemical products.

_____

## USING YOUR UNDERSTANDING

1.      Drawing from newspapers and newsmagazines, find some current examples of cases where public policy may be affected in the areas of health, energy, and/or the environment. High-tech medicine and medical research may evoke ethical, policy, or legal questions concerning life itself. The need for cheap and abundant energy may pose a threat to the environment. Make a list of the issues involved in each case and how it was resolved. Identify the tradeoffs involved and who would benefit and suffer from the different policy options available. Who are the individuals and groups, in and out of government, most involved in the issue and how much influence do they have on policy decisions? Consider how your examples reflect the current agenda in each policy area.

2.      Analyze an environmental impact statement and report on its contents. It may be particularly useful to examine an EIS on an energy project, such as a power plant. Pay particular attention to the numerous types of environmental impacts predicted by the statement. Compare the amount of attention paid to physiographic, biological, social, and economic impacts and evaluate the sophistication of the analysis. Analyze the comment section of the statement and determine who commented on the proposal, what they said, and whether their views were incorporated into the body of the report. Identify the groups in favor of the project and those who opposed it. Find out whether the proposed project or policy was actually implemented.

## REVIEW QUESTIONS

*Check ☑ the correct answer:*

1.      Infant mortality rates in the United States are the lowest in the world.
☐ True
☐ False

2.      What percentage of the gross national product goes to the health industry?
☐ a.    one-seventh
☐ b.    one-fifth
☐ c.    one-third
☐ d.    one-half

3. Which of the following countries has the highest life expectancy rate? (bonus)
   - ☐ a. Canada
   - ☐ b. United States
   - ☐ c. Japan
   - ☐ d. Britain

4. Health care costs are increasing rapidly in the United States because
   - ☐ a. health providers have overbuilt medical care facilities.
   - ☐ b. doctors and hospitals have few incentives to be more efficient.
   - ☐ c. insurance companies pay for most health care expenses.
   - ☐ d. all of the above.

5. "Defensive medicine" refers to
   - ☐ a. the increase in the use of prescription drugs.
   - ☐ b. the emphasis on diet and environment to prevent disease.
   - ☐ c. doctors ordering extra tests to ensure that they are not sued.
   - ☐ d. public policies designed to alleviate crime and poverty.

6. Access to medical care in the United States is not universal.
   - ☐ True
   - ☐ False

7. Which of the following groups is most likely to have good access to medical care in the United States?
   - ☐ a. African Americans
   - ☐ b. employed persons
   - ☐ c. Hispanics.
   - ☐ d. uninsured persons

8. African-American infant mortality is over twice as high as that for whites.
   - ☐ True
   - ☐ False

9. Health maintenance organizations
   - ☐ a. restrict physician lists for the provision of care.
   - ☐ b. negotiate with physician groups and hospitals on fees and costs.
   - ☐ c. try to monitor most aspects of care to control unnecessary use.
   - ☐ d. all of the above.

10. What percentage of America's total health bill is paid for by government sources?
- [ ] a. 16 percent.
- [ ] b. 26 percent.
- [ ] c. 46 percent.
- [ ] d. 66 percent.

11. The National Institutes of Health
- [ ] a. is a government-run hospital in Washington, D.C. for federal employees.
- [ ] b. finances much of the medical research in the United States.
- [ ] c. is the name of the federally funded national health insurance program.
- [ ] d. none of the above.

12. National health insurance
- [ ] a. is supported by the American Medical Association.
- [ ] b. was first proposed in the 1980s.
- [ ] c. would provide compulsory insurance for all Americans.
- [ ] d. is a voluntary system of health care.

13. Medicare is
- [ ] a. the name of America's national health insurance.
- [ ] b. entirely voluntary.
- [ ] c. entirely compulsory.
- [ ] d. part of the social security system.

14. Medicaid provides health care assistance for
- [ ] a. poor Americans.
- [ ] b. workers.
- [ ] c. elderly people.
- [ ] d. states.

15. The highest percentage of medical costs in the United States are paid by
- [ ] a. Medicaid and other public assistance.
- [ ] b. cash payments.
- [ ] c. Medicare.
- [ ] d. private insurance.

16. Health care in the United States focuses on
- [ ] a. equality of care.
- [ ] b. cost containment.
- [ ] c. technological advance.
- [ ] d. all of the above.

17. Americans have high-tech, expensive, and unequal care.
☐ True
☐ False

18. Which of the following groups would be LEAST likely to support any kind of national health insurance?
☐ a. the elderly
☐ b. workers in low-paying service jobs
☐ c. business groups
☐ d. insurance companies

19. President Clinton's health care reform plan failed because
☐ a. it was considered too bureaucratic and complicated.
☐ b. it was the target of an aggressive advertising campaign mounted by opponents.
☐ c. the middle class felt its' health care threatened.
☐ d. all of the above.

20. Public opinion polls show that support for pollution control is
☐ a. overwhelming.
☐ b. nonexistent.
☐ c. limited.
☐ d. dependent on party affiliation.

21. Business leaders support stringent pollution control because they believe it helps attract new industries and businesses.
☐ True
☐ False

22. Many believe that pollution control represents a trade-off between
☐ a. clean water and clean air.
☐ b. environment and economic development.
☐ c. politics and economics.
☐ d. the Sunbelt and the Frostbelt.

23. The 1977 amendments to the Clean Air Act
☐ a. relaxed air pollution requirements.
☐ b. established strict ozone controls to curb global warming.
☐ c. established the nondegredation standard.
☐ d. established the policy of emissions trading.

24. Probably the most powerful influence on politicians regarding environmental policy is
   ☐ a.  scientific evidence showing the effects of pollution.
   ☐ b.  states' interest in attracting business through lax environmental laws.
   ☐ c.  the need to stimulate the economy through economic development.
   ☐ d.  strong public support for environmental protection.

25. Although Americans support pollution control, they are not willing to see the government spend money to clean up the environment.
   ☐ True
   ☐ False

26. The Environmental Protection Agency is the largest federal regulatory agency.
   ☐ True
   ☐ False

27. The centerpiece of federal environmental policy is the
   ☐ a.  National Environmental Policy Act.
   ☐ b.  Clean Air Act.
   ☐ c.  Water Pollution Control Act.
   ☐ d.  Superfund legislation.

28. Environmental impact statements
   ☐ a.  must be filed for every government policy that may disrupt the environment.
   ☐ b.  are in theory only a procedural requirement.
   ☐ c.  alert environmentalists to proposed projects.
   ☐ d.  all of the above.

29. Responsibility for implementing the Clean Air Act of 1970 rests with
   ☐ a.  the Environmental Protection Agency.
   ☐ b.  the Department of Transportation.
   ☐ c.  Congress.
   ☐ d.  the president.

30. Ever since 1916, the United States has been a world leader in wilderness preservation.
   ☐ True
   ☐ False

31. What percent of the United States is designated as wilderness?
- a. 4 percent
- b. 14 percent
- c. 24 percent
- d. 40 percent

32. The "God Squad" is another name for the
- a. Environmental Protection Agency.
- b. cabinet-level committee empowered to make exceptions to the endangered species list.
- c. EPA office which decides how Superfund money will be spent.
- d. congressional subcommittee on the environment.

33. America's most abundant, but dirtiest, fuel is
- a. coal.
- b. oil.
- c. natural gas.
- d. hydroelectric power.

34. Nonrenewable resources are not replaced by nature once consumed.
- True
- False

35. The nuclear power industry was devastated because of
- a. accidents.
- b. cost overruns.
- c. the environmental movement.
- d. all of the above.

36. The United States has not initiated any new nuclear power plants since 1978.
- True
- False

37. The 1992 energy bill
- a. encourages the development of renewable energy sources.
- b. mandates efficiency standards for buildings and home appliances.
- c. encourages state utilities to reward conservation.
- d. all of the above.

38. Opponents of the 1997 global warming treaty argue that
   ☐ a. it is unfair that the developed nations should bear the burden of cutting greenhouse emissions.
   ☐ b. cutting greenhouse emissions will cost too much
   ☐ c. there is no proof that global warming is a serious threat.
   ☐ d. all of the above.

39. Superfund was created to
   ☐ a. clean up toxic waste sites.
   ☐ b. fund the Environmental Protection Agency.
   ☐ c. help agencies file environmental impact statements.
   ☐ d. provide money for environmental research.

40. Money for restoring lands spoiled by chemical and radioactive wastes is the fastest growing segment of the nation's environmental budget.
   ☐ True
   ☐ False

41. Environmental concerns often conflict with concerns about
   ☐ a. foreign trade.
   ☐ b. economic growth.
   ☐ c. jobs.
   ☐ d. all of the above.

42. Environmental interest groups
   ☐ a. have little impact on politicians.
   ☐ b. grew rapidly in the 1960s and 1970s.
   ☐ c. are usually not well informed on technical matters.
   ☐ d. all of the above.

43. "NIMBY" refers to (bonus)
   ☐ a. National Industrial, Mining, and Business Year.
   ☐ b. National Innovative Movement for Better Byproducts.
   ☐ c. Not In My Back Yard.
   ☐ d. New International Management of Business Youth.

44. Policymaking for technological issues seems to rely heavily on
   ☐ a. individual citizens.
   ☐ b. political parties.
   ☐ c. group representation.
   ☐ d. presidential leadership.

45. Most Americans believe that high-technology issues should be a private matter and not involve government interference.
☐ True
☐ False

## ESSAY QUESTIONS

1. Describe the nature of American health. How does the health of the American public compare with that of other nations?

2. How has the American government been involved in the public's health? What factors tend to influence policymaking for health care?

3. Describe and evaluate American environmental policy. What are the biggest obstacles to a clean environment?

4. Describe the American energy profile. What resources do we have? What resources do we use? What political and policy issues are involved with each energy resource?

5. How do democracies handle technological issues? What is the impact of technological issues on the scope of American government?

# Chapter 20

## FOREIGN AND DEFENSE POLICYMAKING

### CHAPTER OUTLINE

I.  American Foreign Policy: Instruments, Actors, and Policymakers (pp. 618-626)
    A.    **Foreign policy** involves making choices about relations with the rest of the world.
    B.    Instruments of Foreign Policy
    C.    Actors on the World Stage
        1.    International organizations like the **United Nations (UN)** play an increasingly important role on the world stage.
        2.    Regional organizations have proliferated in the post-World War II era.
            a.    The **North Atlantic Treaty Organization (NATO)** is a military alliance between the United States, Canada, and most of Western Europe.
            b.    The **European Union (EU)** is an economic alliance of the major Western European nations.
        3.    Multinational corporations are sometimes more powerful than the governments under which they operate.
        4.    Nongovernmental organizations are important actors on the global stage.
        5.    Individuals are also actors on the global stage.
    D.    The Policymakers
        1.    The President
        2.    The Diplomats
            a.    The **secretary of state** has traditionally been the key advisor to the president on foreign policy matters.
            b.    Some recent presidents have established more personal systems for receiving foreign policy advice.
        3.    The National Security Establishment
            a.    The **secretary of defense** is the president's main civilian advisor on national defense matters.
            b.    The commanding officers of each of the services, plus a chair, constitute the **Joint Chiefs of Staff.**
            c.    The National Security Council (NSC) was formed to coordinate foreign and military policies.
            d.    The **Central Intelligence Agency (CIA)** coordinates American information and data-gathering intelligence activities abroad.
        4.    Congress

II. American Foreign Policy: An Overview (pp. 626-632)
    A. **Isolationism** was the foreign policy course followed throughout most of American history.
    B. The Cold War
        1. Containment Abroad and Anti-Communism at Home
            a. The **containment doctrine** called for the United States to isolate the Soviet Union, contain its advances, and resist its encroachments.
            b. At the height of the **Cold War** the United States and the Soviet Union were often on the brink of war.
            c. **McCarthyism** assumed that international communism was conspiratorial and infiltrating American institutions.
        2. The Swelling of the Pentagon
            a. The military industrial complex refers to the interests shared by the armed services and defense contractors.
            b. In the 1950s, the Soviet Union and the United States engaged in an **arms race.**
        3. The Vietnam War
    C. The Era of Détente
        1. **Détente** represented a slow transformation from conflict thinking to cooperative thinking in foreign policy strategy.
        2. One major initiative emerging from détente was the Strategic Arms Limitation Talks (SALT).
    D. The Reagan Rearmament
        1. President Reagan proposed the largest peacetime defense spending increase in American history.
        2. The **Strategic Defense Initiative (SDI)** was a plan for defense against missiles through a global umbrella in space.
    E. The Final Thaw in the Cold War

III. The Politics Of Defense Policy (pp. 632-637)
    A. Defense Spending
    B. Personnel
    C. Weapons

IV. The New Global Agenda (pp. 637-648)
    A. The Decreasing Role Of Military Power
        1. Military power is losing much of its utility.
        2. Economic Sanctions.
    B. Nuclear Proliferation
    C. Terrorism
    D. The International Economy

1.      Today's international economy is characterized by **interdependency.**

2.      International Trade

    a.     The **tariff** is a special tax added to the cost of imported goods.

    b.     The North American Free Trade Agreement would eliminate most tariffs among North American countries.

    c.     The General Agreement on Tariffs and Trade is the mechanism by which most of the world's nations negotiate trade agreements.

3.      Balance of Trade

    a.     **Balance of trade** is the ratio of what a country pays for imports to what it earns from exports.

    b.     Year after year, the American balance of trade has been negative.

E.      International Inequality and Foreign Aid

F.      The Global Connection, Energy, and the Environment

    1.      Growing Energy Dependency (**Organization of Petroleum Exporting Countries, OPEC**)

    2.      Environment and the World Commons

V.     Understanding Foreign And Defense Policymaking (pp. 648-650)

    A.     Foreign and Defense Policymaking and Democracy

    B.     Foreign and Defense Policymaking and the Scope of Government

VI.    Summary (p. 650)

## LEARNING OBJECTIVES

*After studying Chapter 20, you should be able to:*

1.      Identify the many actors involved in making and shaping American foreign policy and discuss the roles they play.

2.      Describe how American foreign policy has changed since the end of World War II.

3.      Discuss the politics of defense policy.

4.      Examine the new issues on the global agenda, particularly those concerning the world economy, energy, and environment.

5.      Understand the role of foreign and defense policymaking in a democracy and how foreign and defense policy affects the scope of government.

*The following exercises will help you meet these goals:*

Objective 1. Identify the many actors involved in making and shaping American foreign policy and discuss the roles they play.

    1.      What are the three types of tools that foreign policies ultimately depend on?

            1.

            2.

            3.

    2.      List five types of actors on the world scene and give an example of each.

            1.

            2.

            3.

            4.

            5.

    3.      List some of the primary foreign policy functions of the president.

    4.      What is the purpose of the National Security Council?

5.   Complete the following table on the major national security agencies.  In the last column, comment on the agency's inclinations toward involvement in foreign ventures, giving an example when relevant.

| Agency | Composition | Purpose | Comments |
|---|---|---|---|
| Joint Chiefs of Staff | | | |
| National Security Council | | | |
| Central Intelligence Agency | | | |

Objective 2.  Describe how American foreign policy has changed since the end of World War II.

1.   Complete the following timeline on the cold war by indicating the event or events that occurred during the year or years listed.

1946:

1948-1949:

1949:

1950-1953:

1964:

1972:

1973:

1975:

1979:

1983:

1989:

2.       What types of foreign policies were followed during the era of détente?

3.       What was the purpose of the Strategic Defense Initiative (SDI)?

Objective 3. Discuss the politics of defense policy.

1.       What is meant by the "peace dividend"?

2.       What is the triad of nuclear weapons that the United States relies on for national defense?

        1.

        2.

        3.

Objective 4. Examine the new issues on the global agenda, particularly those concerning the world economy, energy, and environment.

1.       Why isn't military power as important in foreign policy as it used to be?

2.   Define the term "interdependency" as it relates to the international economy.

3.   What are the four major provisions of the General Agreement on Tariffs and Trade?

   1.

   2.

   3.

   4.

4.   What is the Organization of Petroleum Exporting Countries and why is it an important international actor?

5.   List three consequences of a balance of trade deficit.

   1.

   2.

   3.

6.   List four events that illustrate the importance of energy and the environment to the global connection.

   1.

2.

3.

4.


Objective 5.  Understand the role of foreign and defense policymaking in a democracy and how foreign and defense policy affects the scope of government.

    1.       How might one argue that American foreign policymaking is a democratic process?




    2.       How has foreign and defense policymaking contributed to the scope of government?




**KEY TERMS**

*Identify and Describe:*

foreign policy


United Nations (UN)


North Atlantic Treaty Organization (NATO)


European Union (EU)

secretary of state

secretary of defense

Joint Chiefs of Staff

Central Intelligence Agency (CIA)

isolationism

containment doctrine

Cold War

McCarthyism

arms race

détente

Strategic Defense Initiative (SDI)

interdependency

tariff

balance of trade

Organization of Petroleum Exporting Countries (OPEC)

*Compare and Contrast:*

foreign policy and isolationism

United Nations (UN), North Atlantic Treaty Organization (NATO), and European Union (EU)

secretary of state and secretary of defense

isolationism and interdependency

containment doctrine and McCarthyism

Cold War and détente

Organization of Petroleum Exporting Countries (OPEC) and interdependency

tariff and balance of trade

*Name That Term:*

1.    A regional organization involving the U.S. and most of Western Europe.

      _____

2.    A major regional organization based on an economic alliance.

      _____

3.    The commanding officers of each of the armed services.

      _____

4.    They have often been involved in other nations' internal affairs.

      _____

5.    This eventually resulted in a situation of mutual assured destruction.

      _____

6.    A change from conflict to cooperative thinking in foreign policy.

      _____

7.    Also known as "Star Wars."

      _____

## USING YOUR UNDERSTANDING

1.  Organize your colleagues to try to simulate a military or foreign policy decision-making situation. The situation may be a political or economic crisis, such as the threat of war, an oil embargo, or some other crisis. Alternatively, it may be an ongoing policy problem, such as global inequalities in human rights, inequalities in the distribution of the world's wealth, or the continued over-consumption of the world commons and pollution of the global environment. Different students should represent each of the key international actors concerned with the situation and the policymaking actors responsible for addressing it. Representatives from nations other than the United States may also be present. Try to identify the major issues involved in the situation and the tradeoffs involved, keeping in mind that each of the actors on the stage has a different interest to protect. Collectively, try to come to agreement on a United States foreign policy that would contribute to a resolution of the situation.

2.  Given the end of the cold war, international relations and the global agenda are changing dramatically. Find examples, using newspapers and/or newsmagazines that illustrate the changing global agenda. Include examples that stem from the decline of communism as well as the more traditional concerns about defense and military spending and the emerging agenda issues centering on the economy, equality, energy, and environment. Identify those issues that seem to take a prominent position on the contemporary global agenda. At the same time, identify those issues that you see as important global concerns but that are not being given much attention. Assess the global agenda in terms of the relative importance of defense issues as compared to other policy issues and whether or not the agenda seems to be changing.

## REVIEW QUESTIONS

*Check ☑ the correct answer:*

1.  The end of the cold war has lessened the importance of national security policy.
    ☐ True
    ☐ False

2.  Foreign policy is like domestic policy because
   - [ ] a. the president is the dominant actor.
   - [ ] b. Congress sets the agenda.
   - [ ] c. public opinion has very little impact.
   - [ ] d. it involves choice-taking.

3.  The instruments of foreign policy are basically the same as those of domestic policy.
   - [ ] True
   - [ ] False

4.  The quietest of the principal foreign policy instruments is
   - [ ] a. the threat of war.
   - [ ] b. economic policy.
   - [ ] c. diplomacy.
   - [ ] d. war.

5.  The real seat of power in the United Nations is the
   - [ ] a. General Assembly.
   - [ ] b. Secretary General.
   - [ ] c. Security Council.
   - [ ] d. Secretariat.

6.  The North Atlantic Treaty Organization is
   - [ ] a. a regional military organization.
   - [ ] b. an economic federation.
   - [ ] c. a multinational corporation.
   - [ ] d. a branch of the United Nations.

7.  The European Union is
   - [ ] a. a regional military organization.
   - [ ] b. an economic federation.
   - [ ] c. a multinational corporation.
   - [ ] d. a foreign policymaking agency of the United States.

8.  Which of the following statements about multinational corporations (MNCs) is FALSE?
   - [ ] a. They account for more than one-fifth of the global economy.
   - [ ] b. Most try not to become involved in internal politics.
   - [ ] c. Some are wealthier than the governments under which they operate.
   - [ ] d. Some have linked forces with the CIA to overturn governments.

9. The president's foreign policy duties include
   - ☐ a. making treaties.
   - ☐ b. acting as commander in chief of the armed forces.
   - ☐ c. deploying troops abroad.
   - ☐ d. all of the above.

10. Which of the following presidents relied more on their special assistant for national security affairs than on their secretary of state?
   - ☐ a. Richard Nixon
   - ☐ b. Ronald Reagan
   - ☐ c. George Bush
   - ☐ d. Bill Clinton

11. The Secretary of Defense manages a budget larger than that of most nations.
   - ☐ True
   - ☐ False

12. The governmental body responsible for coordinating foreign and military policy is the
   - ☐ a. National Security Council.
   - ☐ b. Department of State.
   - ☐ c. Joint Chiefs of Staff.
   - ☐ d. Central Intelligence Agency.

13. The activities of the Central Intelligence Agency have included
   - ☐ a. nurturing coups.
   - ☐ b. training and supporting foreign armies.
   - ☐ c. infiltrating American interest groups.
   - ☐ d. all of the above.

14. Which of the following is NOT among the foreign policy functions of the U.S. Congress?
   - ☐ a. declaring war
   - ☐ b. initiating treaties
   - ☐ c. confirming ambassadorial appointments
   - ☐ d. appropriating funds

15. Isolationism was reaffirmed by
   - ☐ a. World War II.
   - ☐ b. the Marshall Plan.
   - ☐ c. the League of Nations.
   - ☐ d. the Monroe Doctrine.

16. The containment doctrine proposed the containment of
    - ☐ a. Germany during World War II.
    - ☐ b. the Soviet Union after World War II.
    - ☐ c. McCarthyism in the 1950s.
    - ☐ d. nuclear arms in the 1980s.

17. The American policy of helping other nations oppose communism was enunciated in the
    - ☐ a. Monroe Doctrine.
    - ☐ b. Marshall Plan.
    - ☐ c. Truman Doctrine.
    - ☐ d. Isolationist doctrine.

18. During the cold war, the policy of "brinkmanship" meant that the United States
    - ☐ a. was prepared to use nuclear weapons in order to influence the actions of the Soviet Union and China.
    - ☐ b. would isolate the Soviet Union and contain its advances at all costs.
    - ☐ c. would stay out of other nations' conflicts.
    - ☐ d. was prepared to fight communist infiltration at home as well as abroad.

19. The term "military-industrial complex" was coined by (bonus)
    - ☐ a. John F. Kennedy.
    - ☐ b. Richard Nixon.
    - ☐ c. Dwight Eisenhower.
    - ☐ d. Joseph McCarthy.

20. The Vietnam War finally came to an end due to the superior firepower of the United States.
    - ☐ True
    - ☐ False

21. Which of the following does the Vietnam War NOT illustrate?
    - ☐ a. a presidential campaign issue
    - ☐ b. how war abroad can result in protest at home
    - ☐ c. the ability of the government to lie to its citizens
    - ☐ d. the superiority of United States military might

22. Détente refers to
  □ a. the irrevocable differences between the United States and the Soviet Union.
  □ b. the threat of nuclear war.
  □ c. a transformation from conflict thinking to cooperative thinking.
  □ d. Ronald Reagan's foreign policy.

23. The United States Senate approved the SALT II treaty in 1979.
  □ True
  □ False

24. The first president to extend formal diplomatic recognition to the People's Republic of China was
  □ a. Richard Nixon.
  □ b. Gerald Ford.
  □ c. Jimmy Carter.
  □ d. Ronald Reagan.

25. From the middle of the 1950s to 1981, the defense budget had generally been declining as a percentage of the total federal budget and gross national product.
  □ True
  □ False

26. The first president in recent history who committed more of the national budget to social services than to military services was
  □ a. Lyndon Johnson.
  □ b. Richard Nixon.
  □ c. Gerald Ford.
  □ d. Jimmy Carter.

27. Defense spending came to a standstill during the second term of Ronald Reagan's presidency.
  □ True
  □ False

28. The Strategic Defense Initiative (SDI) refers to
  □ a. Ronald Reagan's initiation of arms control talks.
  □ b. a defense system using high-tech devices to destroy invading missiles.
  □ c. an international organization bent on eliminating nuclear weapons.
  □ d. an arm of the Pentagon that prepares the country for defending against a nuclear attack.

29. The end of the cold war was characterized by the
☐ a. fall of the Berlin Wall.
☐ b. unification of East and West Germany.
☐ c. split of the Soviet Union into 15 separate nations.
☐ d. all of the above.

30. China took a major step toward democratization as a result of the 1989 protests at Tiananmen Square.
☐ True
☐ False

31. What percentage of the federal budget is devoted to defense?
☐ a. about one-sixth
☐ b. about one-fourth
☐ c. about one-third
☐ d. about one-half

32. Conservatives
☐ a. believe the Pentagon wastes money.
☐ b. insist that America needs to retain its readiness at a high level.
☐ c. argue that a strong economy is the best defense.
☐ d. believe the U.S. should invest in human capital.

33. Liberals credit the collapse of communism to
☐ a. the American military buildup.
☐ b. the ideological defects of communism.
☐ c. defects at the core of the Soviet economy.
☐ d. the Soviet Communist Party.

34. Both liberal and conservative members of Congress tend to fight hard to help constituencies win and keep defense contracts.
☐ True
☐ False

35. America's nuclear arsenal has relied primarily on
☐ a. ground-based intercontinental ballistic missiles.
☐ b. submarine-launched ballistic missiles.
☐ c. strategic bombers.
☐ d. all of the above.

36. The first president to sign a treaty to reduce current levels of nuclear weapons was
☐ a.   Richard Nixon.
☐ b.   Gerald Ford.
☐ c.   Jimmy Carter.
☐ d.   Ronald Reagan.

37. The first accord mandating the elimination of strategic nuclear weaponry was
☐ a.   SALT I.
☐ b.   SALT II.
☐ c.   the Intermediate-Range Nuclear Forces Pact.
☐ d.   the Strategic Arms Reduction Treaty.

38. How long did it take to win the Gulf War? (bonus)
☐ a.   1 hour
☐ b.   1 day
☐ c.   100 hours
☐ d.   100 days

39. Americans are more likely to perceive threats to their security in economic competition from allies than from military rivalry with potential adversaries.
☐ True
☐ False

40. Economic sanctions
☐ a.   are a recent tool of diplomacy.
☐ b.   are often a first resort in times of crises.
☐ c.   have never accomplished their goals.
☐ d.   tend to receive wide support.

41. The key word that describes today's international economy is
☐ a.   isolationism.
☐ b.   tariffs.
☐ c.   interdependency.
☐ d.   deficits.

42. Since the end of World War II,
☐ a.   trade among nations has declined.
☐ b.   a globalization of finances has taken place.
☐ c.   tariffs have become the main instrument of international economic policy.
☐ d.   interdependency has declined.

43. Nontariff barriers include
□ a.  quotas.
□ b.  subsidies.
□ c.  quality specifications.
□ d.  all of the above.

44. The ratio of what we pay for imports to what we earn from exports is called
□ a.  interdependency.
□ b.  the balance of trade.
□ c.  a tariff.
□ d.  foreign aid.

45. Which of the following statements is FALSE?
□ a.  A decline in the dollar makes American products cheaper abroad.
□ b.  A poor balance of payments exacerbates unemployment.
□ c.  In recent years, America has had a balance of trade surplus.
□ d.  Trade deficits decrease the dollar's buying power.

46. The income gap between rich, industrialized nations, and poor, underdeveloped ones has been narrowing in recent years.
□ True
□ False

47. Less developed countries have usually responded to their poverty by
□ a.  borrowing money.
□ b.  adopting socialist policies.
□ c.  raising tariffs.
□ d.  all of the above.

48. Which of the following is TRUE?
□ a.  The poorer the nation, the wider the gap between rich and poor.
□ b.  Washington has supported resolutions to redistribute the world's wealth.
□ c.  The United States devotes a larger share of its GNP to foreign economic development than any other developed nation.
□ d.  It is becoming easier for the United States to ignore global equality issues.

49. American policy initiatives directed at the problem of world poverty include
□ a.  foreign-aid programs.
□ b.  Food for Peace programs.
□ c.  Peace Corps volunteers.
□ d.  all of the above.

50. Foreign aid is very popular with Americans.
   ☐ True
   ☐ False

51. The United States is less dependent on imported oil than most nations.
   ☐ True
   ☐ False

52. Underdeveloped countries tend to pay little attention to environmental problems because
   ☐ a. environmental despoliation is not yet a problem in the third world.
   ☐ b. most governments in the third world are run by military despots.
   ☐ c. the need for economic development for salvation is a more immediate concern.
   ☐ d. all of the above.

53. Which of the following statements is FALSE?
   ☐ a. Americans are usually more interested in domestic policy than foreign policy.
   ☐ b. When the American people hold strong opinions regarding international relations, they find policymakers responsive to them.
   ☐ c. The system of separation of powers plays a crucial role in foreign policy.
   ☐ d. Elitism is pervasive in the arena of international economic policy.

54. The decline of the United States as a world superpower has and will continue to reduce the scope of American government in foreign and defense policy.
   ☐ True
   ☐ False

## ESSAY QUESTIONS

1. Who are the actors on the world's foreign policy stage? Who makes foreign policy in the United States?

2. What was the Cold War, and why did it emerge from isolationism? What were its consequences at home and abroad?

3. Compare the politics and policy of the Cold War to the politics and policy of détente. Be sure to include a discussion of the containment doctrine and the arms talks in your answer.

4. How did the Cold War end? What consequences does the end of the cold war have on American foreign and defense policymaking?

5. What is the politics of military spending? How do liberals and conservatives differ in regard to their view of defense spending?

6. Why does the United States often have troubles in their foreign policy initiatives?

7. Describe the changing global agenda in terms of the policy arenas of the economy, equality, energy, and environment. What is the importance of issues within each arena on the contemporary global agenda of the United States?

8. Critique the statement "democracy has very little to do with the international relations of the United States." In what ways is American foreign and defense policymaking a democratic process and in what ways is it not?

# Chapter 21

## THE NEW FACE OF STATE AND LOCAL GOVERNMENT

### CHAPTER OUTLINE

I.  State Constitutions  (pp. 657-659)
    A.    Introduction (**sub-national governments** are state and local governments)
    B.    Amending State Constitutions

II.  State Elections (pp. 659-666)
    A.    Gubernatorial Elections
    B.    State Legislative Elections
    C.    Partisan Competition, Legislative Turnover, and Term Limits
    D.    The Changing Face of State-Elected Officials

III.  Governors and The Executive Branch (pp. 666-670)
    A.    The Job of Governor
        1.    Governors perform many roles
        2.    The **line-item veto** allows governors to veto only certain parts of a bill while allowing the rest of it to pass into law.
    B.    Other Executive Officers
        1.    **Lieutenant governors** preside over the state senate and are first in succession for governor.
        2.    Other state executives may include attorney general, treasurer, secretary of state, auditor, comptroller, and various commissioners.

IV.  State Legislatures (pp. 670-672)
    A.    Legislative professionalism reforms have improved the effectiveness of state legislatures.
    B.    Some states have seen the beginning of a "de-professionalizing" trend.

V.  State Court Systems  (pp. 672-675)
    A.    State Court Organization
    B.    Selecting Judges
        1.    In many states, voters elect judges for various courts.

2.	Many states follow a form of the **Merit Plan** that attempts to make appointments to the courts based upon merit.

VI.	**Direct Democracy** (pp. 675-678)
A.	Under the legislative **initiative**, the people directly author and vote on legislation.
B.	Under the **referendum**, the people can approve or reject measures submitted to them by the legislature.
C.	Under the **recall**, voters can gather enough signatures to call an election to decide whether a representative should continue in office.

VII.	State and Local Government Relations (pp. 678-679)
A.	According to **Dillon's Rule**, local governments have only those powers that are explicitly given to them by the states.
B.	A **local charter** is the organizational statement and grant of authority from the state to a local government often used to give **home rule** to local governments.

VIII.	Local Governments (pp. 679-686)
A.	Types of Local Government
1.	Counties
2.	Townships
3.	Municipalities
a.	Originally, many local communities operated under a form of direct democracy called the **town meeting.**
b.	Mayor-council government.
c.	Council-manager government. An appointed **city manager** carries out policy with the city bureaucracy.
d.	Commission government.
4.	School Districts
5.	Special Districts
B.	Fragmentation, Cooperation, and Competition
1.	Each governing body in a fragmented metropolis tends to look at problems from its own narrow, partial perspective.
2.	A **council of governments** (COG) consists of officials from various localities who meet to discuss mutual problems and plan joint action.

IX.	State and Local Finance Policy (pp. 686-688)

X.	Understanding State and Local Governments (pp. 688-691)
A.	Democracy at the Subnational Level
B.	The Scope of Subnational Governments

XI.	Summary (pp. 691-693)

## LEARNING OBJECTIVES

*After studying Chapter 21, you should be able to:*

1. Describe the nature of state constitutions and how they differ from the U.S. Constitution.

2. Discuss the different types of state elections and how they differ from national elections.

3. Explain the function of state governors and the executive branch.

4. Understand the nature and function of state legislatures and how legislatures make policy.

5. Describe the structure of the state court systems.

6. Explain how direct democracy is used in the states.

7. Discuss the relationship between state and local governments.

8. Compare and contrast the different types of local government in the United States in terms of organization, functions, and policy roles.

9. Discuss the fiscal and budgetary policies of state and local governments.

10. Evaluate state and local government in the United States in terms of their contributions to democracy and the scope of government.

*The following exercises will help you meet these objectives:*

Objective 1. Describe the nature of state constitutions and how they differ from the U.S. Constitution.

1. What is the key difference between the federal and state constitutions?

2. Explain three methods used by states to amend their constitutions.

1.

2.

3.

Objective 2. Discuss the different types of state elections and how they differ from national elections.

1.       Explain what is meant by the "presidentialization" of gubernatorial elections.

2.       Explain what is meant by the "congressionalization" of state legislative elections.

3.       What are the major consequences of divided government in the states?

4.       List and explain three things that tend to increase legislative partisanship and polarize legislative deliberations in the states.

       1.

       2.

       3.

Objective 3. Explain the function of state governors and the executive branch.

    1.     Explain the two most important formal powers that governors have for controlling state government.

        1.

        2.

    2.     What is the role played by most lieutenant governors?

    3.     List four major executive positions elected in some states and explain their primary duties.

        1.

        2.

        3.

        4.

Objective 4. Understand the nature and function of state legislatures and how legislatures make policy.

    1.     List four functions performed by all state legislatures.

        1.

394

2.

3.

4.

2. Explain the three legislative professionalism reforms.

1.

2.

3.

3. Explain what is meant by the "de-professionalizing" trend in some state legislatures.

Objective 5. Describe the structure of the state court systems.

1. Complete the following table on the nature of state courts.

| Court | Geographic Jurisdiction | Number of Presiding Judges | Types of Cases | Use of Jury |
|---|---|---|---|---|
| Trial Courts | | | | |
| Intermediate Courts of Appeals | | | | |
| Court of Last Resort | | | | |

2.     What is the "Merit Plan"?

Objective 6. Explain how direct democracy is used in the states.

    1.     List and explain three procedures for direct democracy used in the states.

        1.

        2.

        3.

    2.     Give three examples of how initiatives have been used in the states.

        1.

        2.

3.

Objective 7. Discuss the relationship between state and local governments.

    1.      Explain what is meant by Dillion's Rule.

    2.      What are three ways which local governments can influence their own destiny?

        1.

        2.

        3.

Objective 8. Compare and contrast the different types of local government in the United States in terms of organization, functions, and policy roles.

    1.      What are the common functions of most counties?

    2.      List the three modern forms of municipal government and complete the following table explaining where executive and legislative power lies and naming at least one city as an example.

| Government Form | Executive | Legislature | Example |
|---|---|---|---|
|  |  |  |  |
|  |  |  |  |
|  |  |  |  |

3.      Explain why regional cooperation at the local level is so difficult to achieve.

4.      What does a "council of government" mean and what purpose does it serve?

Objective 9. Discuss the fiscal and budgetary policies of state and local governments.

    1.      List the three main sources of state revenues.

        1.

        2.

        3.

    2.      List four main areas of state expenditures.

        1.

        2.

        3.

        4.


3.      List the three main sources of local revenues.

        1.

        2.

        3.


4.      List the three main areas of local expenditures.

        1.

        2.

        3.


Objective 10.  Evaluate state and local government in the United States in terms of their contributions to democracy and the scope of government.

    1.      Explain four reasons why state and local politics may fall short of the democratic ideal.

        1.

        2.

        3.

        4.

    2.      Explain two ways in which state and local governments have attempted to control spending, taxing, and employment growth.

1.

2.

**KEY TERMS**

*Identify and Describe:*

subnational governments

term limits

item veto

lieutenant governor

Merit Plan

direct democracy

initiative

referendum

recall

Dillon's Rule

local charter

home rule

town meeting

city manager

council of governments

*Compare and Contrast:*

direct democracy, initiative, referendum, and recall

Dillon's Rule and local charter

local charter and home rule

*Name That Term:*

1. Also known as state and local governments.

   _____

2. An attempt to diminish the power of career-oriented state legislators.

   _____

3. A governor's power to veto part of a bill while leaving the rest intact.

   _____

4. The second-highest state executive officer.

   _____

5. Under this system, state judges are appointed from a list of persons recommended by the state bar or a committee of officials.

   _____

6. Under this system, all voting-age adults in a community gathers once a year to make public policy.

   _____

7. The local government administrator who implements and administers council-manager government.

   _____

8. An organization of officials from various localities created to discuss mutual problems and plan cooperative action.

   _____

# USING YOUR UNDERSTANDING

1. Choose a state of interest to you, such as your home state or the state in which your college or university is situated. Compare the government of this state to the federal government on a number of dimensions including, but not necessarily limited to, constitutional arrangements, the structure and organization of government, the powers of the policymaking bodies, particularly the legislature and executive bodies, the judicial structure and the role of the courts, the budgetary process including how revenues are collected and spent, and the nature and extent of regulation, and bureaucratic involvement. You may wish to either write a comprehensive outline or use this exercise as the basis of a term paper.

2. Explore the issue of federalism by choosing a federal policy that is implemented by the states. Examples include various environmental regulations or social welfare policies. How do states implement these policies? Which state bureaucracies are involved and how? Does the state legislature get involved in the act? Are any local governments involved and, if so, how? What individuals have the most impact on implementing the policy and how? What are the financial arrangements? Who controls how the money is spent? Evaluate the implementation of the policy on the basis of the policy's intention. This exercise may be a case study of one state or a comparison of different states.

# REVIEW QUESTIONS

*Check ☑ the correct answer:*

1. Sub-national governments have gained in importance in recent years.
   ☐ True
   ☐ False

2. Two important characteristics of sub-national governments today are
   ☐ a. conservatism and unity.
   ☐ b. revitalization and diversity.
   ☐ c. innovation and dominance.
   ☐ d. stagnation and indifference.

3. State constitutions are subordinate to
   ☐ a.   the U.S. Constitution.
   ☐ b.   laws of the United States.
   ☐ c.   state laws.
   ☐ d.   both a and b.

4. Most state constitutions are shorter than the U.S. Constitution.
   ☐ True
   ☐ False

5. Typical of all state constitutions are provisions for
   ☐ a.   separation of powers.
   ☐ b.   taxation and finance.
   ☐ c.   local governments.
   ☐ d.   all of the above.

6. The most common method used by states to amend their constitution is the
   ☐ a.   legislative proposal.
   ☐ b.   constitutional convention.
   ☐ c.   popular initiative.
   ☐ d.   federal directive.

7. Most governors are elected during presidential years.
   ☐ True
   ☐ False

8. In recent years, gubernatorial elections have become
   ☐ a.   less important.
   ☐ b.   linked to presidential elections.
   ☐ c.   more personalized.
   ☐ d.   less dependent on money.

9. The result of the personalization of gubernatorial elections has been
   ☐ a.   less predictability in the outcomes.
   ☐ b.   more divided government in the states.
   ☐ c.   better-known candidates.
   ☐ d.   all of the above.

10. Campaign costs for state legislative campaigns have skyrocketed.
    ☐ True
    ☐ False

11. Divided government in the states has facilitated coherent policy action.
☐ True
☐ False

12. In recent years, state legislatures have been characterized by
☐ a. increased party competition.
☐ b. divided government.
☐ c. majority party switching.
☐ d. all of the above.

13. State governments have traditionally been characterized by less-than-representative percentages of women and ethnic minorities in elected officials.
☐ True
☐ False

14. Modernization in state governments has
☐ a. resulted in enhanced powers for governors.
☐ b. resolved the fragmentation of executive power.
☐ c. spread power more evenly in state government.
☐ d. resulted in more efficient and smaller government.

15. Which of the following states has the strongest governor? (bonus)
☐ a. California
☐ b. Rhode Island
☐ c. Maryland
☐ d. Vermont

16. The primary initiator of public policy in the states is
☐ a. interest groups.
☐ b. the speaker of the assembly.
☐ c. legislative committee heads.
☐ d. the governor.

17. Most governors have the power of the line-item veto.
☐ True
☐ False

18. The individual who is next in line to succeed the governor is called the
☐ a. vice governor.
☐ b. lieutenant governor.
☐ c. secretary of state.
☐ d. state commissioner.

19. State legislatures
☐ a. make almost all of the basic laws of the state.
☐ b. appropriate the money that is needed for state government to function.
☐ c. oversee the activities of the executive branch.
☐ d. all of the above.

20. Legislative professionalism reform has included
☐ a. lengthening legislative sessions.
☐ b. increasing legislators' salaries.
☐ c. increasing the staff available to help legislators.
☐ d. all of the above.

21. All state legislatures have become full-time professional bodies.
☐ True
☐ False

22. The state courts that have taken on many of the functions of specialized courts are
☐ a. court of appeals.
☐ b. court of last resort.
☐ c. trial courts.
☐ d. circuit courts.

23. The state courts that have the responsibility for administering and regulating the justice system in the state are the
☐ a. trial courts.
☐ b. court of appeals.
☐ c. court of last resort.
☐ d. circuit courts.

24. In the Merit Plan, judges are selected on the basis of
☐ a. competitive partisan election.
☐ b. recommendation by the state bar or other officials.
☐ c. competitive nonpartisan election.
☐ d. patronage.

25. The purest form of direct democracy would be the
☐ a. legislative proposal.
☐ b. constitutional convention.
☐ c. popular initiative.
☐ d. federal directive.

26. A form of direct democracy in which the legislature sends a bill to the voters instead of the governor for approval is called a
☐ a. legislative initiative.
☐ b. recall.
☐ c. referendum.
☐ d. popular initiative.

27. A form of direct democracy in which voters can decide whether a representative should continue in office is called a
☐ a. legislative initiative.
☐ b. recall.
☐ c. referendum.
☐ d. popular initiative.

28. The idea that local governments have only those powers that are explicitly given to them by the states is called
☐ a. Dillon's Rule.
☐ b. Merit Plan.
☐ c. Local Rule.
☐ d. State Rule.

29. The organizational statement and grant of authority from the state to a local government is called a
☐ a. constitution.
☐ b. local charter.
☐ c. council of government.
☐ d. intergovernmental agreement.

30. Which of the following states has the most number of local governments? (bonus)
☐ a. New York
☐ b. California
☐ c. Illinois
☐ d. Texas

31. Public policy is usually made in county governments by
☐ a. a county commission.
☐ b. row officers.
☐ c. a county administrator.
☐ d. the state.

32. The type of local government that usually has the least amount of power is the
☐ a.   county.
☐ b.   municipality.
☐ c.   township.
☐ d.   special district.

33. Most basic local programs and services are provided by
☐ a.   municipalities.
☐ b.   townships.
☐ c.   school districts.
☐ d.   special districts.

34. At one time, most towns in the United States operated through direct democracy.
☐ True
☐ False

35. Today, municipal governments take the form of
☐ a.   mayor-council government.
☐ b.   council-manager government.
☐ c.   commission government.
☐ d.   all of the above.

36. Traditionally, city council members
☐ a.   represented the city at-large.
☐ b.   were elected on a nonpartisan ballot.
☐ c.   represented a district or ward.
☐ d.   were appointed by the mayor.

37. An unintended consequence of at-large representation in city councils is that
☐ a.   the mayor's power has increased dramatically.
☐ b.   the number of committees in the council has grown.
☐ c.   minority group members have had difficulty gaining election.
☐ d.   the role of the city council has diminished.

38. Most school systems in the United States are run as independent local governments.
☐ True
☐ False

39. Supreme Court decisions have put an end to discrimination in schools, but have not solved the financial problem.
☐ True
☐ False

40. The fastest-growing form of local government is the
☐ a. county.
☐ b. municipality.
☐ c. township.
☐ d. special district.

41. Which of the following statements is TRUE?
☐ a. There is no limit on the number of special districts.
☐ b. Local governments in different parts of the same metropolitan area will sometimes offer different services to their citizens.
☐ c. Local governments rarely need to compete with each other for economic development.
☐ d. Regional coordination has become the norm in state government.

42. Most metropolitan areas have created regional bodies to surmount the problems of metropolitan fragmentation and local parochialism.
☐ True
☐ False

43. Councils of governments
☐ a. are usually well-funded.
☐ b. lack any real legislative power.
☐ c. have large staffs.
☐ d. are found in most metropolitan areas.

44. States receive the largest share of their revenue from
☐ a. federal aid.
☐ b. taxes.
☐ c. state insurance programs.
☐ d. charges for services.

45. The largest percentage of state money goes to
☐ a. aid local governments.
☐ b. education.
☐ c. operate state programs.
☐ d. finance loans.

46. Local governments receive their revenues from
☐ a. taxes.
☐ b. user charges.
☐ c. intergovernmental aid.
☐ d. all of the above.

47. The highest percentage of the local governments' monies is allocated to public education.
☐ True
☐ False

48. Democracy at the state and local levels may suffer because
☐ a. politics at the state level is poorly covered by the media.
☐ b. term limits may constrain voter choice.
☐ c. business interests have substantial leverage in state and city affairs.
☐ d. all of the above.

49. For most of this century, growth in state and local government has
☐ a. been slowing down.
☐ b. been overshadowed by growth in the federal government.
☐ c. proceeded at a pace exceeding that of the federal government.
☐ d. remained unchanged.

50. Reforms and professionalization in sub-national governments have all had the affect of reducing the scope of government.
☐ True
☐ False

51. Sunset legislation is used to
☐ a. increase democratic participation in state governments.
☐ b. appropriate money for state budgets.
☐ c. control the growth of state governments.
☐ d. create new programs and agencies in the states.

## ESSAY QUESTIONS

1. Why are state and local governments important to the American political system and how has this importance increased in recent years?

2. What are the typical provisions found in state constitutions and how are these different from or similar to the provisions found in the U.S. Constitution?

3. What are the primary characteristics of state elections?

4. Compare the job of governor to the job of president of the United States. How are they different and how are they similar?

5. What is the role of state legislatures and how have they changed in recent years?

6. Write an outline of a state court system that includes how the courts are organized, their jurisdiction, and their role in policymaking.

7. Explain the relationship between state governments and their local governments.

8. List the different types of local governments in the United States, along with their organizational structure and responsibilities.

9. Where do state and local governments get their money and how do they spend it?

# ANSWERS TO REVIEW QUESTIONS

## Chapter 1

### INTRODUCTION

1.  a (p. 4)
2.  b (p. 6)
3.  b (p. 7)
4.  a (p. 7)
5.  a (p. 7)
6.  T (p. 7)
7.  a (p. 8)
8.  a (p. 9)
9.  F (p. 9)
10. d (p. 9)
11. T (p. 11)
12. a (p. 11)
13. d (p. 11)
14. c (p. 11)
15. F (p. 11)
16. b (p. 11)
17. d (p. 11)
18. d (p. 12)
19. c (p. 12)
20. a (p. 13)
21. d (p. 14)

22. c (p. 14)
23. c (p. 15)
24. a (p. 15)
25. T (p. 15)
26. b (p. 15)
27. a (p. 16)
28. c (p. 16)
29. F (p. 17)
30. d (p. 17)
31. b (p. 17)
32. F (p. 17)
33. c (p. 18)
34. T (p. 18)
35. c (p. 18)
36. c (p. 20)
37. d (p. 20)
38. b (p. 20)
39. d (p. 21)
40. T (p. 21)
41. c (p. 22)

## Chapter 2

### THE CONSTITUTION

1. d (p. 28)
2. b (p. 28)
3. c (p. 29)
4. b (p. 30)
5. d (p. 31)
6. c (p. 31)
7. F (p. 31)
8. T (p. 33)
9. a (p. 33)
10. d (p. 33)
11. a (p. 34)
12. d (p. 35)
13. b (p. 35)
14. c (p. 37)
15. F (p. 38)
16. c (p. 39)
17. b (p. 39)
18. a (p. 40)
19. d (p. 41)
20. T (p. 41)
21. d (p. 42)
22. c (p. 43)
23. T (p. 44)
24. a (p. 44)
25. T (p. 46)
26. d (p. 46)
27. b (p. 46)
28. a (p. 46)
29. c (p. 47)
30. F (p. 48)
31. b (p. 48)
32. d (p. 49)
33. F (p. 50)
34. c (p. 50)
35. a (p. 52)
36. a (p. 52)
37. T (p. 53)
38. a (p. 53)
39. T (p. 54)
40. d (p. 56)
41. a (p. 56)
42. b (p. 56)
43. T (p. 57)
44. c (p. 57)
45. T (p. 58)
46. c (p. 59)
47. c (p. 59)
48. d (p. 60)

# Chapter 3

## FEDERALISM

| | | | |
|---|---|---|---|
| 1. | c (p. 66) | 26. | c (p. 76) |
| 2. | F (p. 66) | 27. | F (p. 76) |
| 3. | d (p. 66) | 28. | c (p. 77) |
| 4. | T (p. 66) | 29. | b (p. 77) |
| 5. | F (p. 67) | 30. | b (p. 78) |
| 6. | d (p. 67) | 31. | a (p. 78) |
| 7. | F (p. 68) | 32. | b (p. 80) |
| 8. | T (p. 69) | 33. | F (p. 80) |
| 9. | c (p. 69) | 34. | a (p. 81) |
| 10. | F (p. 70) | 35. | b (p. 82) |
| 11. | b (p. 71) | 36. | c (p. 82) |
| 12. | d (p. 71) | 37. | a (p. 82) |
| 13. | a (p. 71) | 38. | b (p. 82) |
| 14. | d (p. 71) | 39. | T (p. 83) |
| 15. | c (p. 71) | 40. | T (p. 83) |
| 16. | d (p. 72) | 41. | F (p. 83) |
| 17. | c (p. 73) | 42. | a (p. 84) |
| 18. | a (p. 73) | 43. | d (p. 85) |
| 19. | T (p. 73) | 44. | F (p. 86) |
| 20. | b (p. 73) | 45. | b (p. 86) |
| 21. | a (p. 73) | 46. | c (p. 88) |
| 22. | b (p. 74) | 47. | c (p. 88) |
| 23. | a (p. 74) | 48. | F (p. 88) |
| 24. | d (p. 75) | 49. | a (p. 89) |
| 25. | b (p. 76) | | |

# Chapter 4

## Civil Liberties and Public Policy

| | | | |
|---|---|---|---|
| 1. | b (p. 96) | 26. | T (p. 112) |
| 2. | a (p. 96) | 27. | d (p. 113) |
| 3. | F (p. 96) | 28. | T (p. 114) |
| 4. | c (p. 97) | 29. | c (p. 114) |
| 5. | b (p. 97) | 30. | T (p. 114) |
| 6. | T (p. 97) | 31. | d (p. 115) |
| 7. | c (p. 98) | 32. | F (p. 115) |
| 8. | c (p. 98) | 33. | F (p. 116) |
| 9. | c (p. 99) | 34. | T (p. 117) |
| 10. | b (p. 99) | 35. | a (p. 117) |
| 11. | F (p. 100) | 36. | b (p. 119) |
| 12. | b (p. 101) | 37. | a (p. 119) |
| 13. | T (p. 102) | 38. | c (p. 120) |
| 14. | a (p. 104) | 39. | d (p. 120) |
| 15. | c (p. 104) | 40. | b (p. 122) |
| 16. | d (p. 105) | 41. | T (p. 122) |
| 17. | b (p. 106) | 42. | b (p. 123) |
| 18. | T (p. 108) | 43. | a (p. 123) |
| 19. | c (p. 109) | 44. | a (p. 124) |
| 20. | T (p. 109) | 45. | F (p. 126) |
| 21. | a (p. 110) | 46. | d (p. 127) |
| 22. | d (p. 110) | 47. | c (p. 127) |
| 23. | b (p. 110) | 48. | T (p. 129) |
| 24. | T (p. 112) | 49. | b (p. 130) |
| 25. | b (p. 112) | | |

# Chapter 5

## CIVIL RIGHTS AND PUBLIC POLICY

| | | | |
|---|---|---|---|
| 1. | a (p. 138) | 27. | b (p. 148) |
| 2. | c (p. 138) | 28. | d (p. 149) |
| 3. | a (p. 138) | 29. | T (p. 150) |
| 4. | c (p. 138) | 30. | c (p. 151) |
| 5. | T (p. 139) | 31. | F (p. 152) |
| 6. | c (p. 139) | 32. | c (p. 152) |
| 7. | c (p. 139) | 33. | F (p. 152) |
| 8. | T (p. 140) | 34. | a (p. 152) |
| 9. | a (p. 141) | 35. | T (p. 153) |
| 10. | c (p. 141) | 36. | a (p. 153) |
| 11. | T (p. 142) | 37. | d (p. 154) |
| 12. | d (p. 142) | 38. | T (p. 155) |
| 13. | b (p. 143) | 39. | c (p. 155) |
| 14. | F (p. 144) | 40. | b (p. 156) |
| 15. | d (p. 144) | 41. | b (p. 156) |
| 16. | c (p. 144) | 42. | T (p. 156) |
| 17. | a (p. 145) | 43. | F (p. 158) |
| 18. | c (p. 145) | 44. | F (p. 159) |
| 19. | d (p. 145) | 45. | d (p. 161) |
| 20. | b (p. 146) | 46. | d (p. 162) |
| 21. | T (p. 147) | 47. | T (p. 162) |
| 22. | b (p. 147) | 48. | c (p. 163) |
| 23. | a (p. 147) | 49. | F (p. 163) |
| 24. | F (p. 147) | 50. | c (p. 164) |
| 25. | d (p. 148) | 51. | c (p. 165) |
| 26. | d (p. 148) | 52. | d (p. 167) |

# Chapter 6

## PUBLIC OPINION AND POLITICAL ACTION

| | | | |
|---|---|---|---|
| 1. | T (p. 174) | 27. | d (p. 186) |
| 2. | c (p. 174) | 28. | a (p. 187) |
| 3. | c (p. 174) | 29. | F (p. 187) |
| 4. | b (p. 174) | 30. | T (p. 188) |
| 5. | F (p. 175) | 31. | c (p. 188) |
| 6. | d (p. 176) | 32. | c (p. 189) |
| 7. | d (p. 176) | 33. | c (p. 189) |
| 8. | b (p. 177) | 34. | b (p. 189) |
| 9. | T (p. 177) | 35. | d (p. 190) |
| 10. | b (p. 177) | 36. | a (p. 191) |
| 11. | c (p. 178) | 37. | F (p. 192) |
| 12. | c (p. 180) | 38. | a (p. 192) |
| 13. | b (p. 180) | 39. | d (p. 192) |
| 14. | a (p. 180) | 40. | F (p. 194) |
| 15. | a (p. 180) | 41. | b (p. 194) |
| 16. | F (p. 180) | 42. | c (p. 194) |
| 17. | T (p. 180) | 43. | F (p. 195) |
| 18. | b (p. 182) | 44. | d (p. 195) |
| 19. | F (p. 182) | 45. | a (p. 196) |
| 20. | d (p. 182) | 46. | c (p. 197) |
| 21. | a (p. 182) | 47. | F (p. 197) |
| 22. | b (p. 183) | 48. | b (p. 198) |
| 23. | b (p. 184) | 49. | T (p. 199) |
| 24. | c (p. 185) | 50. | b (p. 200) |
| 25. | a (p. 185) | 51. | a (p. 201) |
| 26. | b (p. 186) | 52. | T (p. 202) |

# Chapter 7

## THE MASS MEDIA AND THE POLITICAL AGENDA

| | | | |
|---|---|---|---|
| 1. | T (p. 208) | 24. | T (p. 217) |
| 2. | c (p. 208) | 25. | c (p. 217) |
| 3. | F (p. 208) | 26. | d (p. 220) |
| 4. | F (p. 208) | 27. | b (p. 221) |
| 5. | b (p. 208) | 28. | c (p. 222) |
| 6. | d (p. 210) | 29. | d (p. 222) |
| 7. | T (p. 210) | 30. | a (p. 223) |
| 8. | a (p. 211) | 31. | T (p. 223) |
| 9. | b (p. 211) | 32. | b (p. 224) |
| 10. | F (p. 212) | 33. | c (p. 224) |
| 11. | d (p. 212) | 34. | T (p. 224) |
| 12. | d (p. 213) | 35. | F (p. 224) |
| 13. | c (p. 213) | 36. | b (p. 225) |
| 14. | d (p. 213) | 37. | F (p. 225) |
| 15. | b (p. 213) | 38. | c (p. 225) |
| 16. | T (p. 214) | 39. | d (p. 225) |
| 17. | T (p. 215) | 40. | T (p. 227) |
| 18. | a (p. 215) | 41. | b (p. 227) |
| 19. | F (p. 215) | 42. | F (p. 227) |
| 20. | d (p. 215) | 43. | F (p. 228) |
| 21. | b (p. 215) | 44. | d (p. 229) |
| 22. | c (p. 217) | 45. | T (p. 230) |
| 23. | F (p. 217) | | |

# Chapter 8

## POLITICAL PARTIES

 1.  F (p. 235)
 2.  b (p. 236)
 3.  a (p. 236)
 4.  b (p. 236)
 5.  d (p. 237)
 6.  d (p. 237)
 7.  c (p. 238)
 8.  F (p. 238)
 9.  c (p. 238)
10.  T (p. 240)
11.  c (p. 240)
12.  a (p. 241)
13.  b (p. 241)
14.  c (p. 241)
15.  F (p. 241)
16.  d (p. 242)
17.  T (p. 242)
18.  F (p. 244)
19.  b (p. 244)
20.  a (p. 244)
21.  c (p. 244)
22.  d (p. 245)
23.  T (p. 245)
24.  c (p. 247)
25.  c (p. 247)
26.  T (p. 247)
27.  a (p. 247)
28.  F (p. 247)
29.  c (p. 248)
30.  b (p. 248)
31.  d (p. 249)
32.  a (p. 250)
33.  c (p. 250)
34.  d (p. 250)
35.  b (p. 250)
36.  a (p. 252)
37.  F (p. 252)
38.  d (p. 252)
39.  d (p. 254)
40.  c (p. 254)
41.  b (p. 255)
42.  a (p. 256)
43.  T (p. 256)
44.  b (p. 256)
45.  c (p. 257)
46.  b (p. 257)
47.  b (p. 258)
48.  c (p. 259)
49.  T (p. 259)
50.  b (p. 260)

# Chapter 9

## NOMINATIONS AND CAMPAIGNS

1. d (p. 266)
2. c (p. 266)
3. c (p. 266)
4. b (p. 266)
5. a (p. 266)
6. b (p. 267)
7. d (p. 267)
8. T (p. 267)
9. a (p. 267)
10. d (p. 268)
11. c (p. 269)
12. b (p. 270)
13. F (p. 270)
14. F (p. 271)
15. b (p. 272)
16. d (p. 272)
17. T (p. 272)
18. b (p. 272)
19. F (p. 273)
20. F (p. 273)
21. c (p. 273)
22. F (p. 273)
23. T (p. 274)
24. d (p. 278)
25. b (p. 278)
26. c (p. 279)
27. F (p. 279)
28. F (p. 280)
29. d (p. 282)
30. b (p. 282)
31. F (p. 284)
32. b (p. 285)
33. c (p. 286)
34. T (p. 286)
35. a (p. 287)
36. c (p. 289)
37. d (p. 289)
38. T (p. 289)
39. c (p. 290)

# Chapter 10

## ELECTIONS AND VOTING BEHAVIOR

1. d (p. 296)
2. d (p. 296)
3. a (p. 296)
4. T (p. 296)
5. c (p. 297)
6. b (p. 299)
7. d (p. 299)
8. d (p. 299)
9. c (p. 300)
10. T (p. 301)
11. d (p. 302)
12. T (p. 302)
13. a (p. 303)
14. T (p. 304)
15. b (p. 304)
16. a (p. 304)
17. c (p. 304)
18. T (p. 304)
19. b (p. 305)
20. T (p. 305)
21. F (p. 309)
22. a (p. 310)
23. c (p. 311)
24. c (p. 312)
25. d (p. 312)
26. c (p. 312)
27. T (p. 313)
28. d (p. 314)
29. a (p. 314)
30. F (p. 314)
31. d (p. 314)
32. c (p. 314)
33. T (p. 314)
34. T (p. 315)
35. a (p. 315)
36. b (p. 315)
37. b (p. 315)
38. c (p. 316)
39. T (p. 317)

# Chapter 11

## INTEREST GROUPS

| | | | |
|---|---|---|---|
| 1. | F (p. 322) | 27. | T (p. 332) |
| 2. | F (p. 322) | 28. | d (p. 333) |
| 3. | b (p. 323) | 29. | a (p. 333) |
| 4. | T (p. 323) | 30. | b (p. 334) |
| 5. | a (p. 325) | 31. | T (p. 335) |
| 6. | c (p. 325) | 32. | d (p. 335) |
| 7. | a (p. 325) | 33. | c (p. 336) |
| 8. | T (p. 325) | 34. | F (p. 336) |
| 9. | d (p. 325) | 35. | b (p. 336) |
| 10. | b (p. 326) | 36. | d (p. 337) |
| 11. | T (p. 326) | 37. | b (p. 338) |
| 12. | b (p. 326) | 38. | F (p. 338) |
| 13. | c (p. 327) | 39. | d (p. 339) |
| 14. | d (p. 328) | 40. | a (p. 340) |
| 15. | c (p. 328) | 41. | T (p. 340) |
| 16. | F (p. 328) | 42. | F (p. 340) |
| 17. | a (p. 328) | 43. | b (p. 341) |
| 18. | d (p. 329) | 44. | d (p. 341) |
| 19. | d (p. 329) | 45. | a (p. 342) |
| 20. | d (p. 329) | 46. | a (p. 342) |
| 21. | c (p. 330) | 47. | T (p. 344) |
| 22. | b (p. 330) | 48. | b (p. 344) |
| 23. | a (p. 330) | 49. | b (p. 344) |
| 24. | T (p. 330) | 50. | c (p. 344) |
| 25. | F (p. 331) | 51. | a (p. 346) |
| 26. | b (p. 332) | 52. | T (p. 347) |

# Chapter 12

## CONGRESS

1. T (p. 353)
2. a (p. 354)
3. c (p. 354)
4. c (p. 355)
5. c (p. 356)
6. F (p. 357)
7. b (p. 358)
8. c (p. 358)
9. T (p. 359)
10. d (p. 360)
11. c (p. 360)
12. F (p. 362)
13. d (p. 362)
14. F (p. 362)
15. T (p. 363)
16. c (p. 363)
17. T (p. 364)
18. b (p. 364)
19. T (p. 364)
20. b (p. 365)
21. d (p. 365)
22. a (p. 365)
23. a (p. 365)
24. c (p. 366)
25. a (p. 366)
26. c (p. 367)
27. d (p. 368)
28. T (p. 368)
29. c (p. 369)
30. d (p. 369)
31. d (p. 369)
32. a (p. 370)
33. b (p. 370)
34. F (p. 370)
35. d (p. 371)
36. c (p. 372)
37. d (p. 372)
38. c (p. 372)
39. b (p. 373)
40. d (p. 374)
41. b (p. 375)
42. c (p. 377)
43. a (p. 378)
44. T (p. 379)
45. c (p. 380)
46. c (p. 380)
47. b (p. 380)
48. c (p. 382)
49. T (p. 383)
50. b (p. 383)
51. d (p. 385)
52. T (p. 386)
53. T (p. 387)

# Chapter 13

## THE PRESIDENCY

1. b (p. 393)
2. d (p. 394)
3. b (p. 394)
4. c (p. 394)
5. a (p. 395)
6. d (p. 397)
7. b (p. 397)
8. F (p. 398)
9. T (p. 398)
10. a (p. 398)
11. F (p. 398)
12. T (p. 400)
13. d (p. 401)
14. b (p. 401)
15. a (p. 402)
16. F (p. 402)
17. b (p. 403)
18. c (p. 403)
19. F (p. 404)
20. d (p. 405)
21. b (p. 405)
22. b (p. 406)
23. a (p. 407)
24. c (p. 407)
25. T (p. 408)
26. F (p. 409)
27. b (p. 409)
28. a (p. 409)
29. a (p. 410)
30. d (p. 411)
31. T (p. 411)
32. b (p. 412)
33. T (p. 413)
34. c (p. 414)
35. T (p. 414)
36. d (p. 414)
37. b (p. 415)
38. T (p. 415)
39. c (p. 417)
40. F (p. 418)
41. b (p. 419)
42. b (p. 420)
43. d (p. 420)
44. T (p. 420)
45. F (p. 421)
46. b (p. 421)
47. T (p. 421)
48. a (p. 422)
49. b (p. 422)
50. F (p. 423)
51. d (p. 423)
52. F (p. 425)
53. T (p. 426)
54. c (p. 426)
55. d (p. 428)
56. T (p. 428)
57. c (p. 428)
58. F (p. 428)
59. F (p. 431)
60. b (p. 432)

424

# Chapter 14

## THE CONGRESS, THE PRESIDENT, AND THE BUDGET: THE POLITICS OF TAXING AND SPENDING

| | | | |
|---|---|---|---|
| 1. | b (p. 438) | 28. | T (p. 452) |
| 2. | b (p. 438) | 29. | a (p. 453) |
| 3. | b (p. 438) | 30. | F (p. 453) |
| 4. | b (p. 438) | 31. | d (p. 454) |
| 5. | F (p. 439) | 32. | a (p. 454) |
| 6. | d (p. 439) | 33. | c (p. 454) |
| 7. | b (p. 440) | 34. | c (p. 455) |
| 8. | T (p. 441) | 35. | c (p. 455) |
| 9. | d (p. 442) | 36. | T (p. 455) |
| 10. | T (p. 442) | 37. | d (p. 456) |
| 11. | c (p. 442) | 38. | b (p. 456) |
| 12. | F (p. 443) | 39. | c (p. 456) |
| 13. | d (p. 444) | 40. | d (p. 457) |
| 14. | b (p. 444) | 41. | c (p. 457) |
| 15. | d (p. 444) | 42. | F (p. 457) |
| 16. | b (p. 445) | 43. | a (p. 458) |
| 17. | T (p. 445) | 44. | d (p. 459) |
| 18. | T (p. 448) | 45. | F (p. 459) |
| 19. | F (p. 448) | 46. | b (p. 459) |
| 20. | d (p. 448) | 47. | T (p. 460) |
| 21. | F (p. 450) | 48. | b (p. 461) |
| 22. | c (p. 450) | 49. | b (p. 461) |
| 23. | F (p. 451) | 50. | b (p. 462) |
| 24. | b (p. 452) | 51. | T (p. 462) |
| 25. | c (p. 452) | 52. | T (p. 462) |
| 26. | d (p. 452) | 53. | d (p. 462) |
| 27. | a (p. 452) | | |

# Chapter 15

## THE FEDERAL BUREAUCRACY

1. F (p. 467)
2. a (p. 468)
3. c (p. 468)
4. T (p. 469)
5. a (p. 469)
6. F (p. 470)
7. b (p. 471)
8. c (p. 471)
9. c (p. 472)
10. d (p. 472)
11. b (p. 472)
12. c (p. 472)
13. d (p. 472)
14. a (p. 473)
15. c (p. 474)
16. b (p. 474)
17. d (p. 474)
18. c (p. 474)
19. a (p. 475)
20. b (p. 475)
21. T (p. 477)
22. b (p. 477)
23. c (p. 478)
24. d (p. 478)
25. d (p. 478)
26. b (p. 479)
27. F (p. 480)

28. d (p. 480)
29. a (p. 480)
30. F (p. 480)
31. T (p. 482)
32. a (p. 483)
33. d (p. 483)
34. a (p. 483)
35. T (p. 483)
36. c (p. 484)
37. d (p. 485)
38. b (p. 486)
39. c (p. 486)
40. b (p. 487)
41. a (p. 490)
42. F (p. 490)
43. c (p. 491)
44. c (p. 492)
45. d (p. 492)
46. T (p. 492)
47. F (p. 492)
48. a (p. 493)
49. T (p. 494)
50. d (p. 494)
51. c (p. 495)
52. c (p. 495)
53. b (p. 495)
54. c (p. 497)

# Chapter 16

## THE FEDERAL COURTS

1. F (p. 504)
2. d (p. 504)
3. b (p. 504)
4. T (p. 504)
5. a (p. 505)
6. b (p. 505)
7. a (p. 505)
8. c (p. 506)
9. F (p. 506)
10. c (p. 506)
11. a (p. 507)
12. c (p. 508)
13. b (p. 508)
14. T (p. 508)
15. a (p. 509)
16. c (p. 509)
17. b (p. 509)
18. b (p. 510)
19. c (p. 510)
20. T (p. 511)
21. c (p. 512)
22. a (p. 512)
23. b (p. 512)
24. F (p. 512)
25. d (p. 512)
26. T (p. 513)
27. b (p. 513)
28. F (p. 514)
29. d (p. 514)
30. b (p. 516)
31. F (p. 516)
32. T (p. 516)
33. d (p. 518)
34. d (p. 519)
35. c (p. 519)
36. a (p. 521)
37. d (p. 521)
38. c (p. 521)
39. a (p. 522)
40. b (p. 522)
41. d (p. 523)
42. T (p. 523)
43. T (p. 523)
44. b (p. 524)
45. c (p. 525)
46. d (p. 525)
47. T (p. 526)
48. a (p. 527)
49. a (p. 529)
50. a (p. 529)
51. a (p. 530)
52. d (p. 530)
53. F (p. 531)
54. c (p. 532)
55. d (p. 533)
56. b (p. 533)
57. F (p. 533)
58. d (p. 534)
59. d (p. 534)

# Chapter 17

## Economic Policymaking

| | | | |
|---|---|---|---|
| 1. | c (p. 542) | 24. | F (p. 550) |
| 2. | F (p. 543) | 25. | a (p. 550) |
| 3. | a (p. 544) | 26. | d (p. 551) |
| 4. | a (p. 545) | 27. | a (p. 551) |
| 5. | d (p. 545) | 28. | T (p. 551) |
| 6. | a (p. 545) | 29. | c (p. 551) |
| 7. | a (p. 545) | 30. | c (p. 551) |
| 8. | b (p. 546) | 31. | T (p. 551) |
| 9. | c (p. 546) | 32. | a (p. 552) |
| 10. | c (p. 546) | 33. | c (p. 552) |
| 11. | a (p. 546) | 34. | F (p. 552) |
| 12. | d (p. 546) | 35. | d (p. 552) |
| 13. | F (p. 546) | 36. | b (p. 552) |
| 14. | c (p. 546) | 37. | a (p. 553) |
| 15. | a (p. 546) | 38. | c (p. 553) |
| 16. | c (p. 546) | 39. | c (p. 554) |
| 17. | d (p. 548) | 40. | d (p. 554) |
| 18. | b (p. 548) | 41. | d (p. 554) |
| 19. | c (p. 548) | 42. | T (p. 555) |
| 20. | b (p. 549) | 43. | b (p. 555) |
| 21. | F (p. 549) | 44. | b (p. 557) |
| 22. | F (p. 549) | 45. | T (p. 558) |
| 23. | a (p. 550) | 46. | F (p. 558) |

# Chapter 18

## SOCIAL WELFARE POLICYMAKING

| | | | |
|---|---|---|---|
| 1. | b (p. 564) | 21. | T (p. 573) |
| 2. | c (p. 564) | 22. | c (p. 573) |
| 3. | F (p. 565) | 23. | b (p. 574) |
| 4. | a (p. 565) | 24. | d (p. 574) |
| 5. | d (p. 565) | 25. | c (p. 574) |
| 6. | d (p. 566) | 26. | F (p. 574) |
| 7. | c (p. 566) | 27. | b (p. 574) |
| 8. | b (p. 568) | 28. | d (p. 574) |
| 9. | d (p. 568) | 29. | d (p. 576) |
| 10. | a (p. 570) | 30. | F (p. 576) |
| 11. | d (p. 570) | 31. | T (p. 577) |
| 12. | c (p. 570) | 32. | b (p. 578) |
| 13. | a (p. 570) | 33. | b (p. 578) |
| 14. | F (p. 570) | 34. | a (p. 579) |
| 15. | c (p. 570) | 35. | T (p. 579) |
| 16. | b (p. 570) | 36. | a (p. 580) |
| 17. | b (p. 571) | 37. | d (p. 580) |
| 18. | T (p. 571) | 38. | d (p. 581) |
| 19. | d (p. 571) | 39. | T (p. 583) |
| 20. | T (p. 571) | | |

# Chapter 19

## POLICYMAKING FOR HEALTH CARE AND THE ENVIRONMENT

1. F (p. 588)
2. a (p. 588)
3. c (p. 589)
4. d (p. 589)
5. c (p. 590)
6. T (p. 590)
7. b (p. 590)
8. T (p. 591)
9. d (p. 592)
10. c (p. 593)
11. b (p. 593)
12. c (p. 594)
13. d (p. 594)
14. a (p. 594)
15. d (p. 594)
16. c (p. 595)
17. T (p. 595)
18. d (p. 597)
19. d (p. 597)
20. a (p. 598)
21. F (p. 599)
22. b (p. 599)
23. c (p. 599)
24. d (p. 600)
25. F (p. 600)
26. T (p. 600)
27. a (p. 600)
28. d (p. 600)
29. b (p. 601)
30. T (p. 601)
31. a (p. 601)
32. b (p. 602)
33. a (p. 603)
34. T (p. 603)
35. d (p. 604)
36. T (p. 604)
37. d (p. 604)
38. d (p. 605)
39. a (p. 606)
40. T (p. 606)
41. d (p. 607)
42. b (p. 608)
43. c (p. 609)
44. c (p. 610)
45. F (p. 611)

# Chapter 20

## FOREIGN AND DEFENSE POLICYMAKING

| | | | |
|---|---|---|---|
| 1. | F (p. 617) | 28. | b (p. 631) |
| 2. | d (p. 618) | 29. | d (p. 632) |
| 3. | F (p. 618) | 30. | F (p. 632) |
| 4. | c (p. 619) | 31. | a (p. 633) |
| 5. | c (p. 619) | 32. | b (p. 633) |
| 6. | a (p. 620) | 33. | c (p. 634) |
| 7. | b (p. 620) | 34. | T (p. 634) |
| 8. | b (p. 620) | 35. | d (p. 635) |
| 9. | d (p. 622) | 36. | d (p. 636) |
| 10. | a (p. 623) | 37. | d (p. 636) |
| 11. | T (p. 624) | 38. | c (p. 637) |
| 12. | a (p. 625) | 39. | T (p. 637) |
| 13. | d (p. 625) | 40. | b (p. 638) |
| 14. | b (p. 626) | 41. | c (p. 640) |
| 15. | d (p. 627) | 42. | b (p. 642) |
| 16. | b (p. 627) | 43. | d (p. 642) |
| 17. | c (p. 627) | 44. | b (p. 643) |
| 18. | a (p. 628) | 45. | c (p. 643) |
| 19. | c (p. 628) | 46. | F (p. 644) |
| 20. | F (p. 629) | 47. | a (p. 644) |
| 21. | d (p. 629) | 48. | a (p. 645) |
| 22. | c (p. 630) | 49. | d (p. 645) |
| 23. | F (p.630) | 50. | F (p. 645) |
| 24. | c (p. 630) | 51. | T (p. 646) |
| 25. | T (p. 631) | 52. | c (p. 647) |
| 26. | b (p. 631) | 53. | d (p. 648) |
| 27. | T (p. 631) | 54. | F (p. 650) |

# Chapter 21

## THE NEW FACE OF STATE AND LOCAL GOVERNMENT

1. T (p. 656)
2. b (p. 656)
3. d (p. 657)
4. F (p. 657)
5. d (p. 657)
6. a (p. 659)
7. F (p. 659)
8. c (p. 659)
9. d (p. 660)
10. T (p. 661)
11. F (p. 662)
12. d (p. 662)
13. T (p. 664)
14. a (p. 667)
15. c (p. 667)
16. d (p. 668)
17. T (p. 668)
18. b (p. 669)
19. d (p. 670)
20. d (p. 671)
21. F (p. 672)
22. c (p. 673)
23. c (p. 673)
24. b (p. 675)
25. c (p. 675)
26. c (p. 677)
27. b (p. 677)
28. a (p. 678)
29. b (p. 679)
30. c (p. 679)
31. a (p. 680)
32. c (p. 680)
33. a (p. 680)
34. T (p. 681)
35. d (p. 681)
36. c (p. 682)
37. c (p. 682)
38. T (p. 683)
39. T (p. 683)
40. d (p. 683)
41. d (p. 684)
42. F (p. 685)
43. d (p. 685)
44. b (p. 687)
45. c (p. 687)
46. d (p. 688)
47. T (p. 688)
48. d (p. 690)
49. c (p. 690)
50. F (p. 691)
51. c (p. 691)